Trial and Triumph

TRIAL AND TRIUMPH

STORIES FROM CHURCH HISTORY

RICHARD M. HANNULA

Canon Press

MOSCOW, IDAHO

Special thanks to my wife, Kathy, for her support and patience; to Linus Breul, whose much needed advice improved the stories substantially; to Bob Rogland, Doug Bond, and Peggy King Anderson for their helpful comments; and to Rob Rayburn for encouragement given and books lent.

Richard M. Hannula
Trial and Triumph: Stories from Church History

© 1999 by Richard M. Hannula
Published by Canon Press, P.O. Box 8741, Moscow, ID 83843
800-488-2034 / www.canonpress.org

07 06 05 04 03   9 8 7 6 5 4 3

Cover design by Paige Atwood Design, Moscow, ID

Cover painting: King Gustavus Adolphus of Sweden before the Battle of Luetzen, 1632: oil on canvas, 1891, by Ludwig Braun. The Granger Collection, New York.

Interior illustrations: Marcus Mashburn Illustrations

Printed in the United States of America.

Scripture quotations in this publication are taken from the *Holy Bible: A New International Version.* Copyright 1973, 1978, 1984 by the International Bible Society/Zondervan Publishing House.

ISBN: 1-885767-54-4

With love to my children:
Teri, Kelly, John, Kimberly, and Marie

Contents

Introduction 11

Early Church: Facing Persecution, Fighting Heresy

1. Polycarp
   Witness in the Arena (69-155) 17
2. Blandina
   Martyr of Lyons (155-177) 21
3. Constantine
   Defender of the Church (272-337) 25
4. Athanasius
   Against the World (296-373) 31
5. Ambrose
   Bishop of Milan (339-397) 35
6. Monica and Augustine
   Christian Mother and Son (354-430) 39
7. Patrick
   Missionary to the Irish (389-461) 45

Middle Ages: Light from Darkness

8. Pope Gregory I
   Servant of the Servants of God (540-604) 55
9. Boniface
   Missionary to the Germans (680-754) 61
10. Charlemagne
    Protector of the Church (742-814) 65
11. Alfred the Great
    Christian King (847-899) 71
12. Anselm
    Theologian, Monk, Archbishop (1033-1109) 77
13. Bernard of Clairvaux
    Lover of Christ (1090-1153) 83
14. Peter Waldo and the Waldensians
    Faithful to the Word (1130-1217) 89
15. Francis of Assisi
    The Lesser Brother (1181-1226) 95
16. Elizabeth of Hungary
    Servant of the Poor (1207-1231) 101

17. John Wyclif
　　Morning Star of the Reformation (1330-1384) 107
18. John Huss
　　Forerunner of the Reformation (1369-1415) 113

Reformation: The Gospel Clarified

19. Martin Luther
　　Father of the Reformation (1483-1546) 121
20. William Tyndale
　　Translator of the English Bible (1485-1536) 127
21. John Calvin
　　Theologian of the Reformation (1509-1563) 131
22. Anne Askew
　　The Lord's Bold Witness (1521-1546) 137
23. Latimer, Ridley, and Cranmer
　　The Bishop Martyrs (1485-1556) 141
24. John Knox
　　Scottish Reformer (1514-1572) 147
25. Jeanne d'Albret
　　Reformation Queen (1528-1572) 151
26. Renee
　　Duchess of Ferrara (1510-1575) 157

Post-Reformation:
Great Courage and Great Awakening

27. Gustavus Adolphus
　　Warrior King (1594-1632) 167
28. Richard Cameron
　　Lion of the Covenant (1644-1680) 173
29. The Two Margarets
　　The Solway Martyrs (1622-1685) 177
30. John Bunyan
　　Happy Pilgrim (1628-1688) 181
31. Jonathan Edwards
　　Great Awakening Theologian (1703-1758) 187
32. George Whitefield
　　Great Awakening Preacher (1714-1770) 193

33. John Wesley
      The World His Parish (1703-1791) 199
34. John Newton
      Slave Trader Saved by Grace (1725-1807) 205

Modern Missions:
The Gospel to the Ends of the Earth

35. David Brainerd
      Preacher to the
      North American Indians (1718-1747) 213
36. William Carey
      Father of Modern Missions (1761-1834) 219
37. David Livingstone
      Missionary Explorer (1813-1873) 227
38. John Paton
      Witness to the Cannibals (1824-1907) 233
39. Hudson Taylor
      The China Inland Mission (1832-1905) 239
40. Amy Carmichael
      Mother to Outcast Children (1867-1951) 245

Recent Times: Standing for Christ

41. Charles Spurgeon
      Prince of Preachers (1834-1892) 253
42. Chinese Christians
      In the Boxer Rebellion (1900-1901) 259
43. Abraham Kuyper
      Theologian and Statesman (1837-1920) 265
44. J. Gresham Machen
      Valiant for Truth (1881-1937) 271
45. C. S. Lewis
      Chronicler of Narnia (1898-1963) 277
46. Richard Wurmbrand
      Tortured for Christ (1908-) 283

Further Reading
for Parents, Teachers, and Older Children 293

Introduction

For Christians, this book is a family history. Our sister, Blandina, faced the snapping jaws of wild beasts rather than renouncing Christ. Our brother, Ambrose, gave away his vast wealth to the poor and proclaimed the gospel to emperors and paupers. William Tyndale, our father in the faith, lived on the run and died at the stake to give us the Bible in English that we might read it for ourselves. If we do not know about our Christian forebearers, we cannot draw inspiration and encouragement from their lives nor praise God for His grace and power at work in them.

The Psalmist calls us to praise the Lord and "tell of His works with songs of joy." God's greatest works are not the creation of the mountains and seas but His acts of saving love, which transform sinners into children of God. These stories were not written to exalt great Christian men and women. They were written to exalt the Lord who made them great.

The book of Acts tells the story of the growth of the church under the leadership of the apostles. Through great trials they spread the good news of Jesus throughout the Roman world. The stories found in this book are drawn from the lives of those who served God in the years after the apostles rested in the grave. Within these pages, you will encounter Christians from widely different places, times, and stations—from slaves laboring in chains to regal monarchs reigning over vast empires. The stories are not fiction but historically accurate, biographical sketches. The background events and actions of the subjects were drawn from the most reliable sources, and all quotations were taken directly from the subjects' own speeches and writings.

I wrote the sketches originally for my own children, but if other readers may, in some small way, find inspiration in these stories from church history, I will be pleased and grateful.

Ambrose withstanding Emperor Theodosius

Early Church

Facing Persecution, Fighting Heresy

The early church endured persecution from without and false teachers from within, but through every trial God proved faithful to bless and preserve His church. The first two stories portray the martyrdom of an old minister and a Christian slave girl, and it may seem odd to begin a book written to encourage young Christians with stories of believers suffering cruel deaths. The pagans hoped through brutal killings to wipe out Christianity, but God strengthened His children to stand firm in the face of death. The martyrs' faith and courage inspired many to follow Christ— "Precious in the sight of the Lord is the death of his saints" (Ps. 116:15).

- Polycarp
    - Witness in the Arena
- Blandina
    - Martyr of Lyons
- Constantine
    - Defender of the Church
- Athanasius
    - Against the World
- Ambrose
    - Bishop of Milan
- Monica and Augustine
    - Christian Mother and Son
- Patrick
    - Missionary to the Irish

Polycarp
Witness in the Arena

Polycarp c. A.D. 69–155

"I will build my church," Jesus said. "And the gates of hell will not prevail against it." And He built it with shocking and glorious power. Christ burst from the tomb, showed Himself alive, and sent the Spirit in tongues of fire. This transformed the cowardly and confused disciples into valiant soldiers of the cross. They healed the sick, raised the dead, and boldly proclaimed the gospel. Thousands streamed into the Kingdom of God. Nothing like it had ever been seen before.

The Jewish religious leaders flogged the disciples and warned them to stop speaking about Christ. "Judge for yourselves," the disciples answered, "whether it is right in God's sight to obey you rather than God, for we cannot help speaking about all we have seen and heard."

Fearing the growing number of Christians and hating their refusal to bow down to the pagan gods, the Roman emperors declared that following Christ was a crime punishable by death. They began blaming Christians for every calamity. One early Christian sighed, "If the rivers flood, or if there is drought or famine or plague, the pagans cry: 'Throw the Christians to the lions!'"

The Romans put to death many of the first disciples of Christ, beheading Paul, crucifying Peter, and killing others by fire, sword, and beasts. They died with the words of Jesus ringing in their ears: "If the world hates you, keep in mind that it hated me first. If they persecuted me, they will persecute you also."

In the face of terrible persecution, the church grew stronger, expanding to the four corners of the Roman Empire

17

and beyond. A new generation of Christian leaders arose to take the place of the apostles and disciples. One of the foremost of these was a man named Polycarp. Here is part of his story.

Crouching low, hugging the sand, a lion circled the young man standing in the center of the arena. The crowd watched without making a sound. From the imperial box in the grand-stands, the Roman governor looked on with a grin. The rulers of the Roman Empire called Christians "godless" because they refused to bow down to Roman gods or offer incense to the emperor. Here in Smyrna, the governor had ordered that any Christians unwilling to renounce their faith would be executed. So now this young man stood still, circled by the lion.

"Come now," the governor shouted to the man. "You are young. A lifetime awaits you. It's not too late. Some of your friends have just sworn the oath to Caesar. I will remove the beast, if you will do it. Swear the oath and you will live."

The young man shook his head and stood his ground as the lion crept nearer. The lion paused and then pounced. In an instant the two were intertwined, with the animal tearing at the man with powerful swipes. The lion closed his massive jaws, and the young man went limp. The crowd cheered. "Death to the godless!" some shouted.

One of the Roman leaders spoke up. "He was just a follower." Another shouted, "We want Polycarp, their leader! Death to the godless! Death to Polycarp!" Soon the chant sounded throughout the arena, "Death to the god-less! Death to Polycarp!" The order was given, and a small troop left to arrest Polycarp, the bishop of Smyrna.

Polycarp had been taught in his youth by the Apostle John, and he had led many people to faith in Jesus Christ. When the soldiers found Polycarp, they rushed him to the arena and hauled him before the Roman governor of the province. Upon seeing Polycarp, the crowd erupted with a roar, "Death to the godless! Death to Polycarp!"

Dressed in an embroidered robe of purple and gold, the governor stood in the imperial box, glaring down at Polycarp in his dusty tunic. He waved his hand and quieted the crowd. "Are you Polycarp, the teacher of the Christians?" the governor asked.

"I am," Polycarp answered.

"Have respect for the honor of your old age," the governor said. "Swear by Caesar and save yourself. Point to the Christian prisoners there and say 'Away with the godless.'"

Polycarp turned from the Christian prisoners, pointed to the pagan crowds, lifted his voice to heaven, and said, "Away with the godless."

The people gnashed their teeth at the insult. "How dare he call us godless!"

The governor tempted Polycarp a second time, "Swear the oath to Caesar and I will release you. Deny Christ!"

Polycarp stood straight and answered in a clear voice, "For eighty-six years I have been His servant, and He has done me no wrong. How then can I blaspheme my King who saved me?"

"Swear by Caesar!" the governor shouted.

"You try in vain to get me to swear by Caesar. Hear me plainly, I am a Christian!"

"I have wild beasts here," the governor said. "I will throw you to them unless you change your mind."

"Call for them," Polycarp answered.

"If you are not afraid of the beasts, I will have you burned alive."

"You threaten me with fire that burns for a little while and goes out," Polycarp said. "But you are ignorant of the fire of eternal punishment which is prepared for the ungodly. Why do you wait? Come and do what you want with me."

"This is the teacher of Asia," someone cried, "the

father of the Christians, who teaches many not to worship our gods. Burn him!"

Soldiers tied Polycarp to a post and surrounded him with straw, oil-soaked kindling, and timber. Polycarp prayed aloud, "O Lord God Almighty, the Father of your beloved Son, Jesus Christ, through Whom we have received the knowledge of you: I bless You for granting me the honor of this day and hour that I might be numbered among the martyrs. You are the faithful and true God. To You be glory both now and for the ages to come. Amen."

A long torch ignited the bonfire and a mighty flame leapt upward.

Polycarp's courage in the face of death emboldened persecuted Christians throughout the empire to remain faithful to Christ.

• • •

Blandina
Martyr of Lyons

Blandina c. 155–177

The young slave woman, Blandina, gasped for air as she lay shaking on the damp, stone floor. Several fellow Christian prisoners had suffocated during the night, and Blandina closed her eyes to shut out the sight of their pale, lifeless faces. Suddenly the cell door creaked open, and a Roman soldier shouted, "Get up, godless! Come with me!"

Blandina and the other prisoners were dragged out of their cells and into the arena. Shielding their eyes from the brilliant sunlight, the Christian men, women, and children huddled together in the center of the arena. The spectators shouted curses at them. Towering over them on a raised platform stood the Roman governor of Gaul, a laurel wreath crowning his head.

"Listen to me, you godless," the governor said. "You Christians offend our gods and bring down their wrath upon us. But if you will just swear by Caesar, I will release you." Silence fell over the arena. Squeezing the hands of two friends, Blandina trembled and pled with God for strength. Then a few Christians stepped out of the huddle and with downcast faces swore the oath to Caesar. They were permitted to leave the arena, but most stood their ground. "Very well then," the governor said, "you have chosen the beasts, the fire, and the sword." Pulling several Christians from the group, soldiers beat them with whips and slashed at them with swords. The crowd roared its approval.

Then, from the group of prisoners, a young man, Vettius, moved toward the governor's platform. "Your Excellency, I humbly seek permission to speak in defense of the Christians.

I can prove to you that there is nothing godless or wicked in us."

The pagan spectators howled at him. Ignoring Vettius's request, the governor asked with disdain, "Are *you* a Christian?"

"I am," Vettius answered loudly, standing unbowed before the governor.

With a wave of his hand, the governor signaled the guards. They drew swords and cut Vettius down on the spot. Then the governor summoned Sanctus, a deacon of the church, from the crowd in the arena and asked, "What is your name?"

"I am a Christian," Sanctus answered.

"Where were you born?" asked the governor.

"I am a Christian," Sanctus said.

"Are you slave or free?"

"I am a Christian," Sanctus answered. The soldiers started to whip and beat him, but still his answer to every question remained: "I am a Christian." The enraged governor ordered his body crushed between two red-hot copper plates. He died standing firm in his faith.

Blandina and the other Christians were returned to prison. From morning to night, jailers punished frail Blandina. They pierced her body with daggers and crushed her limbs upon the rack. "Curse Christ!" they taunted. "Tell us all the wicked deeds the godless do."

"I am a Christian," Blandina answered. "We do nothing to be ashamed of."

At the close of day, the jailers could scarcely believe she was still breathing; her body was so broken. "Who are these Christians?" the jailers said to one another. "They go willingly and cheerfully to their deaths."

The next day soldiers again brought Blandina and some other Christians to the arena. She was hung on a wooden post, intended as food for wild animals. Blandina lifted her eyes to the Lord and prayed aloud, "O Father, strengthen us as we suffer for the glory of Christ."

Her faith gave fresh courage to the others. One by one the believers died, torn to pieces by the beasts. But to the crowd's amazement, Blandina remained untouched by the animals, and the guards hauled her back to prison. A few days later, she was again returned to the arena, now with Ponticus, a Christian boy of fifteen.

"Stand firm, dear Ponticus," Blandina urged him. Again, they were whipped and attacked by animals, and soon Ponticus lay dead. But Blandina, her body bloodied and broken, yet survived, her face radiant with the peace of Christ. "She looked," one eyewitness said, "as if she were invited to a wedding feast, not thrown to the beasts."

Her persecutors, frustrated and angry, wrapped her in a net and threw her to a bull that tossed her around the arena. Finally, a soldier reached down and slew her with a sword. The pagans said they had never seen a woman suffer so much or so long. The bodies of Blandina and the other Christians lined the streets of Lyons. Guards stood watch, preventing their friends from giving them a decent burial.

"Why won't you let them bury their dead?" the guards were asked.

"So they may have no hope in the resurrection," they answered. "It is this hope that gives them such courage."

After six days, the bodies were burned to ashes and thrown into the Rhone River. "Now let's see if they'll rise again," the guards said. Some Christians in Lyons survived the persecution. They wrote an account of the martyred believers and sent it to churches throughout the Roman Empire, encouraging them to hold fast to the faith.

• • •

Constantine
Defender of the Church

Constantine the Great c. 272–337

In 299, Emperor Diocletian ordered the Great Persecution and shattered a long period of peace for the Christian church. Believing that Christians angered the pagan gods, Diocletian sought to destroy Christianity once and for all. He demanded that everyone in the empire sacrifice to the pagan gods or risk loss of property, imprisonment, or death. The emperor's men tore down churches and confiscated Scriptures, burning them in the middle of public squares. They jailed Christian leaders and subjected them to flogging, the rack, and tortures of every kind; many were butchered with the sword, drowned in the sea, devoured by wild animals, or cast into fire.

When Diocletian left the throne in 305, the persecutions eased but did not end. For years, prominent men battled for control of the empire. In the West, it came down to two commanders, Maxentius and Constantine. Maxentius, a black-bearded pagan, who was distrustful of Christians, controlled Rome and Italy. Challenging his rule was Constantine, a tall, broad-shouldered supporter of Christianity, who in 312 crossed the Alps with his army and began a march of conquest. Forbidding his men to plunder captured cities, he won the support of the Italian people.

One day, as the army marched south, the sun, filtering through the noon sky, formed a cross of light in the sky. Constantine believed he saw the words, *By This Conquer*, under the cross and took it as a sign from God. For the rest of the day, Constantine pondered the meaning of the sign. He went to bed puzzled. As he slept he dreamed Christ appeared to him with the same cross of light he had seen in the sky. Christ commanded him to make a likeness of the sign and use it as a safeguard in battle.

At dawn Constantine awoke, informed his officers of the dream, and called together his goldsmiths. He described the sign to them and instructed them to recreate it in gold and jewels. The craftsmen overlaid a long spear with gold and joined a cross bar to it near the top, giving it the shape of a cross. At the top, they fixed a wreath of gold studded with precious gems. Inside the wreath they placed the Chi-Rho sign, ✱, a monogram formed from the first two Greek letters of Christ's name. This became the military standard carried into battle at the head of Constantine's forces.

When Constantine displayed the standard to his army and described his dream, the soldiers rejoiced. Inspired by the confidence of their commander, they believed they could not fail. He ordered his men to paint crosses on their shields, and they set out to do battle with the enemy. Hearing of the approach of Constantine's forces, Maxentius consulted pagan priests and oracles to discover if the gods were with him. Goats were sacrificed and their bowels examined for omens. A fortune-telling book predicted that on the day of battle, "The enemy of the Romans would perish." Buoyed by these good signs, Maxentius made his stand nine miles from Rome on a flat, low-lying plain on the Tiber River. To block Constantine's way to Rome, he destroyed the Milvian Bridge, an ancient multi-arched bridge of stone. In its place, his army built a bridge of wooden boats linked together with iron chains which could quickly be broken apart if the enemy tried to cross the river.

Maxentius, outfitted in ornately engraved armor, placed his cavalry on either side and massed his infantry in the center of the plain. Constantine, his long, dark hair flowing to his shoulders, rode at the head of his cavalry and charged headlong into the enemy's horsemen, hurling them back in disarray. They battled fiercely and pressed Maxentius's army to the river bank. Fleeing soldiers, including Maxentius, rushed across the boat bridge, which collapsed under their weight. Hundreds drowned, unable to stay afloat with their heavy military gear. Maxentius's splendid armor pulled him to the bottom like a rock. The citizens of Rome threw open the gates and welcomed Constantine as a deliverer, hailing him emperor of Rome.

Constantine broke from Roman tradition by refusing to offer a sacrifice to Jupiter at the Capitol. One of his first acts as emperor forever freed Christians from Roman persecution. In a decree known as the Edict of Milan, Constantine declared: "We grant both to Christians and to all men freedom to follow whichever religion he chooses. All previous orders against Christians are completely set aside. Anyone wishing to follow Christianity should freely hasten to do so without any worry or interference." The Edict called for the return of all property confiscated from Christians during the Great Persecution and the rebuilding of destroyed churches at government expense. Constantine recognized the legal rights of Christians, including the right to own property.

Later, Constantine declared Sunday a legal holiday, making Christian worship on the Lord's Day possible for everyone. He exempted church property and salaries from taxes. Seeking to bring a godly influence to the empire, he appointed Christians to high ranking posts. Throughout the empire, Christians breathed a sigh of relief. For the first time, an emperor was a friend, a defender of the church.

"I sought," Constantine said, "to draw the human race to observe the holy laws of God and prosper our most holy faith under the guidance of His Almighty hand." Constantine donated land and large sums of money to the church and began a massive church building program. To bring glory to God and draw pagans to the faith, he built ornate churches with huge marble columns, stained glass windows, and walls gilded in every color of the rainbow. Gold and silver chandeliers hung from ornately painted ceilings and multicolored mosaics decorated the floors. Constantine often advised the architects, engineers, and designers, sometimes complaining that there were not enough of them in the empire to meet the needs of his building plans.

Once, when Constantine was praised for his accomplishments, he answered, "God is the cause of all I have performed, for it belongs to God to do whatever is best, and to man to perform the commands of God." Constantine lived in royal splendor and dressed in gold embroidered purple robes, which glistened with precious gems. He wanted this splendor for the Christian bishops too and gave them jeweled robes and stately homes.

Above all, he sought to promote the peace and unity of the church. When strife broke out in Alexandria over the teachings of Arius, who said that Christ was created by the Father and inferior to Him, Constantine called a church council to decide the issue and make clear the church's teaching, for a few years earlier two separate church meetings had reached different conclusions regarding Arius and his beliefs. Three hundred bishops and hundreds of other churchmen attended the council at Nicea on the Black Sea. Constantine paid all the expenses to bring this about.

At the first public session of the council, all the churchmen rose when Constantine arrived wearing his imperial robe ornamented with gold and precious stones and a crown of pearls. With a wave of his arm and a smile, he said, "My dear friends, it was my cherished wish that I might one day enjoy the sight of this council. I give thanks to God, the ruler of all, who has granted me the greatest of all blessings to see you gathered together and united in your minds."

For two months, the men debated the place of Christ in the Trinity and other important teachings. Often Constantine sat in the sessions and joined in the discussion. In the end, the council decided the Bible taught that Christ was not inferior to the Father but was equal in power and glory with the Father and the Spirit. They wrote a creed summarizing basic Christianity. Constantine enthusiastically supported the creed, believing it to be true to Scripture, honoring to Christ, and helpful in uniting the church.

Constantine's influence in the church was not always positive. He assumed the power of appointing and dismissing bishops and exiling men who did not follow his instructions, including Athanasius, the great defender of the faith. He called church councils on his own authority, and his strong hand in church affairs led many Christians to look to the emperor for guidance instead of the leaders of the church. The wealth he brought to the church corrupted many ministers who loved riches more than Christ. Before long, church offices were being bought and sold for the power and riches that came with them.

In 337, with his health failing and at the age of sixty-five, Constantine requested baptism. Laying aside his imperial clothes, he confessed his faith in Christ when he answered the baptism questions. "Do you believe in God the Father Almighty and Jesus Christ, the Son of God, who was born by the Holy Spirit from the Virgin Mary, who was crucified under Pontius Pilate and died, and rose again on the third day from the dead, and ascended to the heavens, and sat down at the right hand of the Father, and will come to judge the living and the dead?" After the priest baptized him with water, he put on a white robe, traveled to a villa in the country, and died a few days later.

Constantine's embrace of Christianity affected the church in tremendous ways. The protection he granted and the wealth he lavished upon her brought many unforeseen changes to Christian life and worship. For centuries, some Christians have questioned the genuineness of Constantine's faith. Some think he used Christianity to strengthen his hand in ruling the empire, and they point out deceitful and ruthless actions he did while emperor. Others believe that Constantine, despite his many shortcomings, put his trust in Jesus Christ for the forgiveness of his sins. In this life, we will never know for sure. Perhaps Constantine himself said it best: "I myself await the judgment of Christ."

• • •

Athanasius
Against the World

Athanasius c. 296-373

On a sunny day around the year 306, a group of boys played church and pretended a baptism by the seashore. One of them, Athanasius, taking the role of minister, said over another boy, "I baptize you in the name of the Father, and the Son, and the Holy Spirit." Unknown to the boys, Alexander, the good bishop of Alexandria, had been watching them. Surprised by how accurately Athanasius performed the service, Alexander called him over to question him about his faith. Athanasius gave some very thoughtful answers that greatly impressed the bishop.

With encouragement from Alexander, the parents of Athanasius agreed that he should come under the care of the bishop to begin a rigorous course of study in the Bible, the writings of the early church fathers, and the classics of Greek and Roman literature. Athanasius, a fine student with a deep love for Christ, soon became Alexander's chief assistant.

At that time, the church was in the midst of great change. Emperor Constantine had openly embraced Christ and made it legal for Christians to worship freely, declaring Sunday a weekly holiday, and he even granted gifts of land and money to the church.

Although safe from persecution, the church faced grave dangers from within. False teachers attacked the Bible's message about God the Father, Jesus Christ, and the Holy Spirit. One attack started in Alexandria, as Bishop Alexander lectured a group of churchmen on the Trinity. A priest named Arius stood and interrupted the bishop saying, "You are in error, Alexander. The Father, Son, and Holy Spirit are not equal in glory. Jesus Christ is not God as the Father is." Arius's comment drew a gasp of shock from everyone. The room fell silent as all eyes looked to Alexander for his response.

Startled by the outburst, Alexander looked Arius in the eye and said, "Brother, the Scriptures plainly teach us that Jesus Christ is God."

"No," Arius shot back, "the Son was created by the Father, and therefore, he is lesser than the Father. There was a time when the Son was not."

Alexander called for a meeting of church leaders to examine Arius's teaching. They condemned his doctrine and forbade him to teach it to others. But Arius refused to obey. Traveling far and wide, preaching and writing, he spread his views across the churches of the empire. Before long, most Christians at that time accepted the Arian saying, "There was a time when the Son was not."

The Christian church divided over this matter. Working with Bishop Alexander, Athanasius grew to become the chief spokesman for the truth of Christ. In some places, arguments, fights, and riots erupted as Christians argued over whether or not Jesus was God. In order to bring peace to the church, Emperor Constantine called a meeting of church leaders. Over three hundred bishops and priests gathered from every corner of the Roman world to attend the Council of Nicea.

Emperor Constantine hosted a lavish welcoming banquet, greeting the churchmen in purple robes ornamented with gold and precious jewels. This was a strange experience for many of the Christians because for the first time they stood before an emperor to be honored rather than condemned. Constantine warmly embraced the churchmen who had lost limbs or suffered other tortures for their faith. He kissed the hollow eye socket of one whose eye had been gouged out.

Constantine opened the council saying: "I rejoice to see you here, yet I should be more pleased to see unity and love among you. I urge you, therefore, beloved ministers of God, to remove the causes of disagreement among you and to establish peace." Many weeks of intense and sometimes bitter debate took place. In the end, the members of the council agreed with Alexander and Athanasius. They wrote a statement of faith, the Creed of Nicea, which explained what Christians were to believe about God. Arius and his followers refused to sign it and were banished from the church. But they did not leave quietly. The Arians returned to their home cities and continued to teach their false doctrines in defiance of the council's decision.

After a time, Arius and a number of his followers, anxious to return to their leadership positions in the church, sought help from Emperor Constantine. They confessed their wrongs to the emperor, but they had not really changed their beliefs. Constantine, without consulting the leading bishops, agreed to reinstate the Arians and wrote a threatening letter to Athanasius, who had become bishop after Alexander died, telling him to restore Arius and his followers in the church. "As you know my wishes," Constantine wrote, "admit freely any who wish to enter the church. If I hear you have stopped anyone, I will immediately send an official to depose you and send you into exile."

When Athanasius refused, Constantine ordered Athanasius to face a number of strange charges which the Arians had concocted. They accused him of breaking sacred furniture, cutting off the arm of an Arian, torturing people, and trying to starve the people of faraway Constantinople! Constantine stripped Athanasius of office and banished him. Two years later, when the emperor died, Athanasius returned as Bishop of Alexandria.

In the meantime, the Arians won thousands to their side, including the new emperor Constantius, the son of Constantine. The Arians convinced him to exile Athanasius again, along with other church leaders who held to the Creed of Nicea. The Christians of Alexandria would not accept the Arian bishop sent to replace Athanasius until they were forced to by Roman soldiers.

Athanasius endured banishment from his church five times over the years as he struggled with the Arians. Once word came to him that two murderers had been paid to kill him, so Athanasius lived in hiding for several years in the Egyptian desert with Christian monks. Another time he escaped death by hiding for four months in the tomb of his father. Once word came that he had been exiled again, members of his church clung to him weeping. Athanasius comforted them saying, "Be of good cheer. It is only a cloud which will soon pass over."

Often the future looked very dark as the Arians gained more followers. Although it appeared that the whole church might accept their false teaching, Athanasius never lost hope. He pressed on, preaching and writing that Jesus was fully God and fully man. He has ever after been known by the Latin saying, "Athanasius contra mundum" which means, "Athanasius against the world." Even if the whole world would turn from the truth of the Bible, Athanasius would hold to it firmly.

He died at the age of seventy-five. Not long after his death, the Arians were finally defeated. Today, Christians all over the world believe the biblical teaching of the deity of Christ. Thanks be to God who raised up a faithful man like Athanasius to help make it so.

I believe in one God, the Father Almighty, Maker of heaven and earth, and of all things visible and invisible; and in one Lord Jesus Christ, the only begotten Son of God, begotten of His Father before all worlds, God of God, Light of Light, very God of very God, begotten not made, being of one substance with the Father. . . .

Nicene Creed

• • •

Ambrose
Bishop of Milan

Ambrose 339–397

In 374 a great stir arose at the cathedral in Milan. Men and women and boys and girls overflowed the cathedral. Red-faced men poked fingers at their neighbors' chests, and the shouts echoed off the stone walls. The people were deeply divided over who should become the new bishop. The Arian group among them— those who believed that Jesus was not truly God—wanted an Arian bishop. The others demanded a bishop who upheld the truth of the Trinity. Argument soon gave way to threats, shoves, and blows. It appeared impossible that the two sides could agree upon a new bishop.

Fearful that a riot might break out at any moment, Ambrose, the Roman governor of the province, rose to speak. Out of respect for their governor, the people quickly quieted down. For though Ambrose came from one of the wealthiest and most powerful families in the Roman Empire, he did not lord it over the people. Fairness and kindness so marked his reign that they looked to him more as a father than as a ruler and judge.

Ambrose called them to order and chastised them for their lack of charity. He urged them to elect a new bishop calmly and peacefully. A hush fell over the gathering. Many exchanged embarrassed glances. Most stood dumbfounded with their eyes downcast. No one spoke until a child's voice broke the silence. "Let Ambrose be bishop!" Then a few others shouted, "Let Ambrose be bishop!" Everyone agreed and soon the whole assembly chanted in unison, "Let Ambrose be bishop!"

Ambrose, with arms upraised, tried in vain to stop them.

"Brethren, I cannot be your bishop," he cried. "I am untrained for the ministry. I have not yet even been baptized." The people were convinced, however, that Ambrose was just the man for the job, and they unanimously elected him Bishop of Milan. Ambrose did everything in his power to escape from this duty. He hid in the home of a friend and wrote a letter to the Roman Emperor asking to be excused from serving as bishop. But the emperor, delighted with the choice of Ambrose, urged him to stand. Believing that it must be God's will, Ambrose was baptized, and eight days later, he was ordained bishop.

From that day forward, Ambrose lived to serve the Lord. He took to heart Christ's command to the rich young ruler: "Go sell everything you have and give to the poor, and you will have treasure in heaven. Then come, follow me." Ambrose sold his large estates and all of his worldly treasures and gave it all to the poor. He welcomed anyone who wished to see him at anytime, often spending the night praying with a troubled soul or seeing to the needs of a beggar.

Pouring himself into the study of the Scriptures, he discovered the Bible's clear message that the Father, the Son and the Holy Spirit are one God, equal in power and glory. Through his daily sermons and extensive writings, he defended the doctrine of the Trinity and the deity of Christ, protecting the church from the false teachings of the Arians. He also saw the importance of music in worship and wrote many hymns himself. *O Trinity Most Blessed Light* celebrates the unity of the Father, Son, and Holy Spirit:

> All praise to God the Father be,
> All praise, eternal Son to thee,
> Whom with the Spirit we adore
> Forever and forever more.

His warm, joyful spirit proved as effective in showing the truth of the gospel as his preaching. The Church Father, Augustine, came to Milan an unbeliever, but Ambrose's sermons and loving friendship drew him to a living trust in the Lord. "That man welcomed me as a father," Augustine said. "I began to love him first not as a teacher of the truth but simply as a man who was kind and generous to me."

Although loving and kind, Ambrose could also be stern and bold as later, his friend, the Roman Emperor Theodosius, discovered. Theodosius often stayed in Milan and worshipped at Ambrose's church. Although an earnest Christian, Theodosius was also a hothead. At times his anger carried him away into rash and unfair judgments. One such fit of rage erupted when Theodosius, learning of a riot in Thessalonica, ordered soldiers to retaliate violently. Without regard to guilt or innocence, seven thousand men, women, and children were massacred.

Ambrose, outraged at the slaughter, wrote boldly to Emperor Theodosius, exposing his wicked deed and commanding him to repent. The next Sunday, the emperor went to church expecting to receive holy communion. As he climbed the steps of the cathedral, he found Ambrose standing at the door barring his way saying, "How will you lift up in prayer the hands still dripping with the blood of the murdered? How will such hands receive the body and blood of the Lord? Get away and do not heap crime upon crime."

Theodosius stiffened, his shocked expression revealing his surprise at Ambrose's harsh words. The emperor said, "But King David committed murder and God forgave him."

"Well, you have imitated David in his sin," Ambrose answered. "Now imitate him also in repentance." Shamefaced, the emperor returned to his palace. But Theodosius did repent. He confessed his sin before the whole church and promised to check his anger by observing a thirty-day cooling off period before sentencing anyone to death. Theodosius grieved over the sinful massacre for the rest of his life. "Ambrose is the first man who told me the truth," Theodosius said. "He is the only man I know who is worthy to be a bishop." When Theodosius lay dying, he called for Ambrose and passed away in his arms.

Once, Ambrose challenged another emperor. Emperor Valentinian ordered Ambrose to turn over a church to the Arians. When Ambrose refused, imperial soldiers rushed to take the church by force. Ambrose and his congregation barricaded themselves inside for more than a week, passing the time with hymn singing and prayer. Ashamed to harm Ambrose or his flock, the emperor backed down. As the soldiers departed Ambrose declared, "The emperor is in the church, not over it."

When Ambrose lay gravely ill, fear gripped the Christians of Milan. If Ambrose should die, they worried, fighting and division might soon return. The elders of the city visited his sickbed, pleading with him to pray for healing and long life. Ambrose urged them to trust in God and said, "I do not fear to die for we have a good Lord." A few days later, on Good Friday evening, he died. His congregation buried him on Easter morning in the church so that they might always be close to their beloved bishop.

> O Trinity, most blessed Light
> O Unity of sovereign might,
> As now the fiery sun departs,
> Shed thou thy beams within our hearts.

• • •

Monica and Augustine
Christian Mother and Son

Augustine 354–430

In 354 Monica gave birth to her future pride and joy, a son to be named Augustine. Her lap became the center of learning and worship for him. The name of the Lord was often on her lips as she explained the story of salvation or sang hymns of praise to Jesus, the Savior of her soul. Monica's pagan husband, Patricius, was no help in pointing Augustine to God, so she alone taught him to love and serve the Lord. She held fast to the promise of God's Word: "Train up a child in the way he should go and when he is old he will not depart from it" (Prov. 22:6).

As Augustine grew, his father, recognizing his gifted mind said, "Our small town is no place to educate a boy of these talents. He must become cultured to do great things." So at the age of sixteen, Augustine was sent away to study under the best tutors in Carthage, the largest city in that part of North Africa. Monica urged him to cling to Christ and live a holy life, but once he was away from home in an exciting city of the Roman Empire, the temptations of sin overpowered him. Though he dearly loved his mother, he fell into the wicked ways of his new friends. "I despised my mother's advice and went headlong on my way," Augustine later admitted.

Stealing, carousing, watching evil entertainments, and sins of every kind became his habit. "I even used to pretend that I had committed sins which I had not done in order to impress my friends," Augustine said. Rejecting Christianity, he embraced the popular philosophies of the day, and Augustine grew proud. "I will make a great name for myself," he said.

Seized with fear at such news, Monica warned him, "My son, I fear the crooked path you are walking, for that way is walked by those who turn their backs toward God and not their faces." Seeking out her bishop for help, Monica pleaded, "Will you please speak to Augustine? Show him the error of his ways and teach him what is good."

The bishop shook his head, for he knew well Augustine's heart and mind at the time. "He is not yet ready to be taught," the bishop told her. "He is full of self-conceit with the novelty of these new ideas. But leave him alone for a while. Only pray to the Lord for him; he himself will find out by his reading what his mistake is and how great is its sinfulness." Monica, unwilling to take no for an answer, wept and gripped the bishop's hand, begging him to speak with Augustine. "No," he said firmly. "Now go away and leave me. It is impossible that the son of these tears should perish." The bishop's words, "It is impossible that the son of these tears should perish," sounded to her as if they had come from heaven. Monica wept and prayed for Augustine, never losing hope that God would save his soul. "Augustine," she often told him, "the son of these tears shall not perish."

The years passed, and Augustine became a respected teacher, but he continued to reject the Lord. At age thirty, he moved from North Africa to Milan in Italy to become one of the head instructors of the city, bringing his widowed mother with him. At that time, the great preacher, Ambrose, was bishop of Milan. Augustine went to hear his sermons not because he wanted to know Jesus but to listen to his eloquent words. Augustine told Ambrose that he did not believe in Christ. To Augustine's surprise, Ambrose accepted him in love. "That man welcomed me as a father," Augustine said. "I began to love him first not as a teacher of the truth but simply as a man who was kind and generous to me."

Gradually, Augustine began to hear the truth of God in Ambrose's sermons, and he started to read the Bible for himself. A friend gave him a book on the life of St. Antony. In it, Augustine saw how the grace of God could transform a life. Through it all, Monica prayed for his salvation and urged him to trust in Christ. As Augustine's doubts about the truth of Christianity faded, fears came in their place, fears that his many sins could never be forgiven. One day, overcome with guilt, he went into the garden to pour his heart out to God. His friend, Alypius, came with him. Suddenly a storm rose up within Augustine's heart, bringing with it a downpour of tears. To avoid embarrassment, he ran alone to the far end of the garden, flung himself down under a fig tree, and cried out to God. "How long, O Lord? Will You be angry with me forever? O Lord, remember not my many sins."

As Augustine wept and prayed, he heard the voice of a child singing the words, "Take and read. Take and read." He had never heard a children's song with those words before. Taking it as a message from God to read the Scriptures, he grabbed his Bible, opened it at random, and read the first verse he saw: "Clothe yourselves with the Lord Jesus Christ, and do not think about how to gratify the desires of the sinful nature" (Rom. 13:14). At once the Lord opened Augustine's eyes to see that only Christ's goodness could cover his sins. He did not read any further; he did not need to. The Lord had changed his heart. He praised God for the forgiveness of his sins and the gift of faith.

Calling to Alypius, he said, "When I read the verse, it was as though my heart was filled with a light of confidence in Christ and all the shadows of my doubt were swept away."

"Show me the passage you read," Alypius said.

Augustine showed him but Alypius's attention was drawn to the next verse: "'Accept him whose faith is weak.' This verse is for me," he said. "My faith is weak, but Christ can make me strong."

Falling to his knees, Alypius put his trust in God too. The two friends rushed inside and told Monica. Overjoyed, she threw her arms around her son saying, "This is what I have prayed for all these years." With eyes brimming with tears, she lifted her hands to heaven and prayed, "Praise to You, O Lord, for You are able to do far more than we can even imagine. You have turned my mourning into joy."

From that day an overpowering hunger gripped Augustine to know the Bible and worship God. "I can't have enough of the sweetness of meditating upon the depth of Your Word," he prayed. "What tears I shed in Your hymns and how I am moved by Your sweet singing church!"

Dressed in a white robe, Augustine was baptized by Ambrose along with many other converts in a candle-lit Easter-eve service. He resigned his teaching job in Milan and planned to serve God back in North Africa. One evening as they were preparing to leave, Monica and Augustine talked late into the night. "The greatest delights on earth," Monica said with a broad smile, "cannot be compared with the joys of heaven."

"As we talked of God and eternal life with the saints," Augustine later wrote, "our hearts thirsted for the heavenly streams—it was as if we had lightly touched the first fruits of the Spirit in heaven."

"My son," Monica said, looking into her son's eyes, "I don't know why I am still here on this earth. The only reason I wanted to stay a little longer in this life was to see you become a Christian before I died. Now God has granted me this beyond my hopes; for I see that you despise the pleasures of this world and have become God's servant."

A few days later she fell deathly ill. "You may lay this body of mine anywhere," she told Augustine and the others holding vigil at her bed.

"Aren't you afraid to die and be buried so far from home?" someone asked her.

Lifting her head, she answered in a weak voice, "Nothing is far from God."

Augustine knelt by her bedside, overcome with grief, and held her hand and prayed until her spirit slipped away to be with God. "I closed her eyes," Augustine said, "and a great flood of sorrow swept into my heart."

After burying his mother, Augustine returned to North Africa and eventually became the most important leader of the church in that region. Using the Word of God as his sword, he fought many battles against false teachers in the church. His greatest challenge came from Pelagius and his followers. The Pelagians taught that Adam's sin did not effect all mankind and that it was possible to live a sinless life through their own free will. They believed salvation was not the gift of God but was earned by men. Augustine recognized that these beliefs conflicted with the central teaching of the Bible that man is saved by God's mercy alone. "For it is by grace you have been saved," wrote Paul to the Ephesians, "through faith—and this not from yourselves, it is the gift of God—not by works, so that no one can boast." Augustine poured all his energies into combating the Pelagians and lifting up the grace of God. He wrote letters, called church councils, and traveled widely, speaking to packed churches. "Man was lost by free will," Augustine preached, "but the God-Man, Jesus Christ, came by freeing grace. See in Jesus Christ the freeing grace of God." After years of struggle, Augustine's message of God's grace and mercy won the day.

For the last forty years of his life, Augustine taught, preached, organized charities for the poor, and wrote books in defense of Christianity. His book, *The Confessions*, told the story of his life and the saving love of Jesus Christ. The entire book is a prayer to God, making it clear that he owed his salvation to the grace and mercy of God alone: "O Lord," he wrote, "You made us for Yourself and our hearts are restless until they rest in You."

Throughout his long life, Augustine never stopped showing people the way of God, and he always thanked the Lord for his mother: "God of my heart," he said, "I joyfully thank You for all those good deeds of my mother—for they were Your gift to me to save and guide me."

• • •

Patrick
Missionary to the Irish

Patrick c. 389–461

The cry "Pirates!" struck terror in his heart. Patrick leapt out of bed, slipped on his tunic and sandals, and ran outside. His mother and father were away in town, leaving sixteen-year-old Patrick to oversee the servants and the whole country estate. Red-bearded men waving swords and clubs came running from all sides. They seized Patrick and the servants and bound their hands. When everyone was captured, the pirates marched them down to the sea. Several thousand people, snatched from the surrounding countryside, were massed at the waters edge. Their kidnappers packed them tightly into the holds of waiting ships.

The pirates spoke a strange language which Patrick couldn't understand. But he knew who they were; everyone living on the west coast of Britain knew these were Irish raiders. Ever since the Roman legends abandoned Britain, Irish slave raids had grown common. Overwhelmed with anger and despair, Patrick trembled in the hull of the ship alongside men, women, and children. He believed he was bound to live out his days as a slave in Ireland, never to see his family or homeland again.

One week later, Patrick stood on the rocky hills of northern Ireland, tending sheep for an Irish chieftain. Poorly clothed and barely fed, Patrick's joints ached from the frost and wind. Homesickness twisted his stomach in knots. He hated the Irish, and this fueled his will to live. He vowed one day to repay them for their cruelty.

A year passed and then another and gradually Patrick discovered a strange change coming over him. It began with a painful guilt for his sins and unbelief. But just as the weight of his troubled conscience drove him to despair, he sensed the Spirit of God drawing near: "I turned with all my heart to the Lord, my God," Patrick said. "He guarded me before I knew Him and comforted me as a father comforts his son." His bitterness and loneliness began to melt away as he came to realize that God was with him. He tried to recall sermons from church and stories from the Bible. He chided himself for his boyhood lack of interest in the Lord. Although Patrick's family attended a Christian church and he knew of Christ and the commandments, he didn't care. "Take heed to your soul," the priest had warned him. But Patrick ignored his advice and went his own way.

But now as a slave in a distant land, the little he had learned as a boy came flooding back to him. He didn't have a Bible so he couldn't read the Word of God, but he could pray. He got up before daylight to pray and as many as a hundred times a day he lifted his voice to the Lord. If he awoke at night, he prayed before falling back to sleep; "The love and fear of God came to me more and more and my faith was strengthened," he said.

As his love for God grew, his hatred for the Irish died. He learned their language, Gaelic, and came to understand their ways. The Irish not only raided other lands but also fought constantly among themselves. Superstitions and strange rituals ruled their lives. Their heathen priests called Druids, believed to have magical powers, held sway over the people. Druids decorated themselves with bird skins and feathers, performed animal sacrifices, and predicted the future. They taught that spirits dwelt in trees and the souls of men came back after death and lived in other bodies. They had never heard the good news of Jesus Christ, so Patrick began to pray for the salvation of his captors.

Then one night in the sixth year of his captivity, he had a dream. In it a voice said, "Soon you will return to your own country. See, your ship is ready now." When Patrick awoke from the dream, he took it as a message from God and made hasty plans to escape. Early the next morning, he fled. Knowing that captured runaway slaves might face torture and even death, Patrick traveled back roads by night. He walked two hundred miles to a seaport and found a ship about to depart. "Captain, I would like to sail with you," Patrick said.

But the captain, seeing that he was a slave, answered him harshly, "It is no use for you to ask to go along with us. Get out of here!" Patrick turned to leave, and as he did he prayed for guidance. Before he ended his prayer, one of the sailors in the back of the ship said, "Come, hurry, we shall take you on." Patrick leapt aboard and was soon on his way to freedom. He pitched in with the work of the crew, hoisting sails and hauling cargo. He boldly told them of the Lord's power and goodness. After a short journey, the ship landed in a desolate place, and they searched many days for food. The haggard, half-starved men grew weak. The captain fixed his fiery eyes on Patrick and said, "Tell me, Christian, you say that your God is great and all powerful; why then do you not pray for us? We are suffering from hunger; it is unlikely that we shall ever see a human being again."

Patrick smiled. "Be truly converted with all your heart to the Lord, my God, because nothing is impossible for Him. This day He may send you food until you are satisfied, for He has abundance everywhere." That deserted place seemed more desolate than ever. But then a few minutes later, a herd of pigs crossed the path in front of them. They would feast on the ham for days.

Eventually, Patrick made his way home to Britain. His family and friends rejoiced to see him and received him as one returned from the dead. Patrick recounted the story of his life as a slave, his new faith in Christ, and his escape. "You have suffered so much," they said, "settle down here in peace and never leave us again." He told them not to grieve over his hardships. "God snatched me from my homeland and parents," he told them, "so that I might know and love Him."

Patrick tried to resume his old life, but he couldn't get

the people of Ireland out of his thoughts. One night as he slept, a vivid dream filled his mind. He saw the vision of a man coming from Ireland and heard many voices speaking in unison. Patrick recognized them as the voices of the Irish he knew as a slave. In Gaelic they cried, "We ask you, boy, come and walk among us once more." Another night, he dreamed again and heard the Irish calling to him and then the voice of the Lord saying, "He that has laid down His life for you, it is He that speaks with you." Patrick awoke full of joy, determined to proclaim the good news of Jesus Christ to the Irish.

When Patrick told his family and friends, they were shocked. "Don't do this!" they pleaded. "If you go back there you will be made a slave again or killed. Surely God would not require this from one who has suffered so much already." The elders of the community also tried to stop him, saying it was pure foolishness. His parents and family offered him many gifts, pleading with tears that he remain home. "I am prepared, most gladly for His name, to give even my life without hesitation," he said. "It is in Ireland that I wish to serve until I die, if the Lord would grant it to me."

After several years of preparation in the monasteries of France, Patrick was ordained and commissioned as a missionary to Ireland. With some helpers, he sailed up an arm of the Irish sea on the east coast of the island. "Let us fish well," he told his partners in the work, "for the Lord called us to be fishers of men and preach the gospel to every creature."

Almost immediately, Dichu, a local ruler, welcomed them, accepted Patrick's teaching, and was baptized. Many of his clansmen followed his example. Dichu gave Patrick a piece of land upon which stood a big barn. Patrick converted the barn into his first Irish church. "Thanks be to God," Patrick said. "Those who worshipped idols and had no knowledge of God are now made people of the Lord and are called sons of God."

His family and friends had been right about the danger. He soon faced great opposition. The Druids hated him for leading the people away from their idols. His opponents robbed, beat, imprisoned, and tortured him. Once he was taken as a slave again. Twelve times his enemies nearly killed him, but always the Lord rescued him—"Daily I expect murder, fraud, or captivity," Patrick once wrote, "but I fear none of these things. I have cast myself into the hands of God Almighty, who rules everywhere, as the prophet says: 'Cast your cares upon God, and He shall sustain you.'"

The greatest trials that Patrick faced were not attacks on him, for he was always ready to die for the faith, but on his new converts. The most tragic event of all came the day after a baptism. Patrick had been preaching to a number of villages clustered together, and many had turned to the Lord. After several months of instruction in the Christian faith, they were ready for baptism. On the great day of the baptismal service, all the converts arrived wearing white robes. "I baptize you in the name of the Father, and of the Son, and of the Holy Spirit," Patrick said with joy as he baptized each new Christian. A community feast followed the service, a wonderful celebration of new life in Christ. But the following day disaster struck.

As the early morning sun cast its first rays of light, soldiers of Coroticus, a notorious slave-trading chieftain, attacked the villages. They cut down men with the sword, killed children who got in the way, and sold the women into slavery. Immediately, Patrick intervened to free the women, but his efforts were met with jeers from Coroticus and his men. Without fear for his own life, Patrick publicly condemned the murderers: "You, sons of the devil, dripping with blood," he said, "you will perish with all the wicked at the judgment day of the Lord. I testify before God and His angels that it will be so unless you repent of this heinous deed and set free the captives."

It is unknown whether Coroticus released these captives, but Patrick's persistent condemnation of slavery rocked the foundations of the Irish slave trade.

For forty years Patrick labored among the Irish. They came to Christ by the thousands. Many Irishmen followed Patrick's example and went into the ministry, bringing Christianity to the farthest corners of Ireland and beyond. Near the end of his life, when asked if all the hardships had been worth it, Patrick answered, "The greatest gift in my life has been to know and love God; to serve Him is my highest joy."

St. Patrick's Breastplate:

I bind unto myself today
The strong name of the Trinity,
By invocation of the same,
The Three in One, and One in Three.

• • •

BONIFACE FELLING THE OAK TREE

Middle Ages

Light from Darkness

From A.D. 500–1500, Christians struggled mightily to shine the light of the Gospel in the deep and brutal darkness of the pagan world. It was a time of great successes and lingering immaturity. Though the church advanced God's kingdom on many fronts, her battle wounds from struggling with paganism left their mark in false traditions and abusive practices.

- Pope Gregory I
  Servant of the Servants of God
- Boniface
  Missionary to the Germans
- Charlemagne
  Protector of the Church
- Alfred the Great
  Christian King
- Anselm
  Theologian, Monk, Archbishop
- Bernard of Clairvaux
  Lover of Christ
- Peter Waldo and the Waldensians
  Faithful to the Word
- Francis of Assisi
  The Lesser Brother
- Elizabeth of Hungary
  Servant of the Poor
- John Wyclif
  Morning Star of the Reformation
- John Huss
  Forerunner of the Reformation

Pope Gregory I
Servant of the Servants of God

Pope Gregory I c. 540-604

Late in the sixth century, a bald monk, with bright eyes and a narrow, slightly crooked nose, wound through the bustling open-air market of Rome. Without a glance at the merchandise, ignoring vendors' calls, this monk—Gregory—hurried to the slave market, eager to see the newly arrived, unusual looking captives. Making his way through the throng, he saw some slave boys who were fair-skinned and light-haired with handsome features.

"From what part of the world do they come?" Gregory asked the slave trader.

"They come from the island of Britain," he was told, "where all the people look like this."

"Are the islanders of Britain Christians or pagans?" Gregory asked.

"Pagans," the slave trader answered.

"Alas," groaned Gregory with a deep sigh. "How sad that such bright-faced folk are still in the grasp of the author of darkness and that such graceful features conceal minds empty of God's grace!" Gregory looked long into the eyes of these poor boys and asked, "What race of people do they belong to?"

"They are called Angles," the trader said.

"Not Angles but angels," Gregory said with a smile, "for they have angelic faces and it is right that they should become joint-heirs of heaven with the angels. And what is the name of their king?" Gregory asked.

"Alle," he was told.

"Alleluia," Gregory cried, thrusting his arms heavenward. "God's praise must be heard there!" Overcome with pity for the lost souls of Britain, Gregory asked God to send him to the Angles and begged Pope Benedict for permission to set out at once. Benedict was reluctant because Gregory was no ordinary monk; he was an important church official in charge of charity to the poor of Rome. A descendant of one of the richest and most powerful families of Rome, Gregory was famous throughout the city. Before becoming a monk, Gregory served as the prefect of the city. As prefect he had dressed in silk robes glittering with gems, yet he ruled Rome with wisdom. But at the height of his power and wealth, Gregory resigned his office, sold his lands and homes, and gave the money to the poor and the church. "Good men," Gregory said, "dread riches in this world more than hardship." He built a monastery and entered it not as its abbot but as a simple monk.

The pope called him out of the monastery to coordinate care for the people of Rome. But Gregory sensed a strong call to Britain and pressed the pope. "It would be a wretched thing," he pleaded, "for hell to be filled with such lovely people." Seeing his zeal, Benedict granted him permission to go. Gregory quickly began his journey, but when the local Romans heard about it they were greatly distressed at the thought of Gregory's departure from Rome. A huge crowd stood along the road by which Pope Benedict went to St. Peter's Church. As he passed, they shouted, "You have destroyed Rome, you sent Gregory away!" After hearing their ongoing cries, Benedict sent horsemen to fetch Gregory back to Rome. Gregory resumed his duties, but he continued in prayer for the salvation of the Angles.

Great problems confronted Rome. Overrun by wave after wave of barbarian invaders, Rome lay in ruins. The people looked to the church to maintain peace and order. It fell to the bishop of Rome, the pope, to see to the defense of the city, supply assistance to the poor, and make treaties with the barbarian kingdoms. The outlook grew bleaker in the autumn of 589 when heavy rains pelted northern Italy for weeks, swelling the Tiber River until it burst its banks, drowning hundreds and wiping out the grain warehouses. Plague followed in the flood's wake. Thousands died, and the city reeked of death as piles of unburied bodies lay in the streets. After even the pope died in the plague, representatives of the church and people unanimously elected Gregory as pope. But he refused, preferring to return to the monastery. Gregory wrote a letter to the emperor in Constantinople asking him not to accept the election and made plans to go into hiding. But the people seized him, carried him to St. Peter's Church, and consecrated him pope on September 3, 590.

"I am heartsick," he wrote a friend, "for I have lost the deep joy of my quiet, and while I seem to outwardly have risen, I am inwardly falling down." Some months later though, he wrote, "Seeing it is God's will, I have recovered a more cheerful frame of mind." Maintaining a cheerful spirit was not easy in the midst of a terrible plague and continuing barbarian threats. Throughout Italy, the Lombards had slain churchmen and burned homes, monasteries, and churches. "Everywhere we see tribulation," Gregory said in a sermon. "The cities are ruined, the villages empty, the fortresses torn down, the fields laid waste, the land made desolate. Idolaters are daily glorying in cruelly shedding the blood of the faithful. Yet no repentance takes place under this scourge." For three days Gregory led prayer processions through the city, singing hymns, confessing sins, and imploring God's mercy.

Despite the brutality of the Lombards, Gregory did not hate them but did all in his power to lead them to Christ. He told the bishops of Italy, "With all your might, by the power of persuasion, hurry the Lombards on to the true faith; preach to them the kingdom of God without ceasing." Gregory organized an army for Rome's defense, strengthened the walls for a siege, and sent messages of peace to Ariulph, the Lombard chief. The invaders swept aside the Roman forces and advanced to the city gates. Gregory could see captured Romans with ropes around their necks, like dogs, being led away as slaves. Gregory walked outside the walls and met Ariulph. Ariulph's head was shaved up the back and his hair, parted in the middle, hung long on the sides of his face. Gregory reasoned with him and offered him payment and a truce if Ariulph left the city unharmed. Impressed by Gregory's eloquence and character, Ariulph promised never to lead an army against Rome as long as Gregory was pope in the city.

Remarkably, in the midst of the burdens of ruling Rome, Gregory worked tirelessly: preaching, writing commentaries on Scripture, reforming the church, and spreading the gospel to distant lands. He sent God-fearing monks under their abbot, Augustine (a later man, not the son of Monica), to bring the good news of Jesus to the Angles and Saxons of Britain. But as the monks journeyed through France on their way to England, they heard frightening reports about the Angles. "They are fierce barbarians, babbling in a strange language," the monks were told. The fearful monks decided to halt and sent Augustine back to Gregory. Augustine pleaded with him to call off their dangerous mission, but Gregory sent Augustine back with firmness and compassion: "My very dear sons," he wrote, "it is better never to undertake any great work then to abandon it when once begun. So with the help of God, you must carry out this holy task which you have begun. Do not be deterred by the troubles of the journey or by what men say. May God Almighty protect you with his grace and grant me to see the result of your labors in our heavenly home." Their courage revived, the monks sailed to Britain, where soon the Angles converted to Christianity. When word reached Gregory he praised the Lord and wrote Augustine, "Glory be to God in the highest. Who can express the joy of all faithful hearts that the English nation, through the grace of God and your labors, shines the light of the holy faith."

Gregory stood against heresies, proclaiming the deity of Christ, the Trinity, and the bodily resurrection of the dead. He wrote hundreds of letters and several books, including a guide for pastors. He urged them to teach the Bible to rich and poor, to educated and ignorant. "The Word of God strengthens the understanding of the wise and nourishes the simple," he wrote. Gregory knew that sinful church leaders unfamiliar with the Word of God devastate the flock, and He demanded that church leaders be godly, able to teach, and faithful in everything. "Every preacher's deeds," he said, "should speak louder than his words. He should, by his good life, make footsteps for men to follow." Above all, Gregory urged churchmen to root out their pride and serve humbly. "Love humility with all your heart," Gregory told a bishop, "humility brings harmony and unity to the whole church."

When the Bishop of Constantinople claimed the title of "Universal Bishop" and tried to elevate himself above other church leaders, Gregory resisted him with all his might. "He proudly puts his name above others," Gregory wrote, urging church and state rulers to reject the Bishop of Constantinople's claims. Gregory did not believe that one church leader was supreme over others as later bishops of Rome would teach. He refused the proud and vain title of "Universal Bishop" and preferred to call himself, "The servant of the servants of God."

Gregory also firmly opposed simony, the sale of church offices, and forbade churchmen from accepting fees for their service. Gregory wrote hymns, poetry, and music, and formed a school for singers to improve the sung worship of the church. One of the most lasting types of praise singing bears his name —the Gregorian chant. Sadly, Gregory accepted and expanded some church teachings contrary to the Bible on purgatory and the veneration of saints and relics. It took a thousand years before Christians in large numbers rejected these errors.

On his deathbed, Gregory received word that the queen of the Lombards, a Christian woman, persuaded the Lombard king to allow their infant son to be baptized. "We share in your joy," he wrote her, "that by the grace of God, your son has been given to the Christian faith. Raise the future king in the fear of the Lord." At the very last, he wanted to honor God. "Pray for me," he said to a friend, "lest I give way to impatience through my sufferings, and lest my sins be increased by my complaining." He died on March 12 in the year 604 and was buried in St. Peter's Church.

• • •

Boniface
Missionary to the Germans

Boniface 680–754

With the sun reflecting off the shaven crown of his head, Boniface challenged the Hessians to forsake pagan gods and the worship of their sacred oak tree and turn to Christ. The long-haired Hessians shook their heads, grumbling at his words, angry at his mocking of their gods. The oak of which Boniface spoke was a gigantic oak tree atop Mt. Gudenberg, a gathering place for pagan feasts, idol worship, and animal sacrifice. The Hessians held it in deepest awe, believing it sacred to Thor, the god of thunder and lightning. They believed Thor was a fierce, red-haired god who rode through the sky and carried a gigantic hammer. Boniface then dared them to come back a few days later to see who was stronger, Thor or the Lord God.

"Thor will strike you dead, you fool," a chief shouted. Yet a few days later, the Hessians did return, boiling with rage, and gathered on the mountain top around the sacred tree. As they waited for Boniface to arrive, their anger grew. "Who does this babbler think he is? When Thor wields his mighty hammer, he'll feel the lightning of his wrath!" One of the chieftains stood up and said, "Where is this boastful Christian? Perhaps he is too afraid to come near."

Just then Boniface, along with some of his Christian brothers, marched out of the forest and up to the tree. Boniface had an axe slung across his shoulder, and the crowd stubbornly parted, murmuring curses and threats. Boniface stood before the great oak, axe in hand. A tribesman shouted, "How dare you defy the power of Thor!" Boniface firmly gripped the axe handle and prepared to strike.

"Stand back," the people warned one another, fearful

of being struck by Thor's lightning bolts. Boniface lifted his axe, and the people gaped as Boniface struck the tree with all his might. They looked expectantly to the heavens, but no lightning bolts flashed. Time and again the iron axe head hit its mark, and soon the huge oak cracked and leaned. The tribesmen scattered as it crashed to earth with a thundering blast and splintered into large chunks. Now the people stood bewildered. Boniface looked into their faces but said nothing.

Then a pagan chief stepped forward, raised his chin, and with a trembling voice declared, "Our fathers and grandfathers came here to win the favor of the gods and so have we. But if our gods are powerless to protect their own holy places than they are nothing." He paused and pointed to Boniface, "Tell us, holy man, about your God."

Motioning with his arms for the people to draw near, Boniface said, "We speak to you as messengers of the Lord who cannot be appeased by sacrifices or gifts of money. You are bound to Him by the blood He shed." A few tried to bow down to him, but Boniface stopped them with a wave of his hand. "My beloved," he said, "we are men covered with sin as you are, but we believe that the Son of God took our sin upon His own body when He died on the cross. If you are to be saved, you must believe in Him and follow Him only."

Boniface sensed their openness to Jesus Christ as they listened intently to all he told them. Seizing the moment, Boniface ordered that a church be built using the timber of the fallen tree. As the Hessians became more open to Christianity, Boniface wrote to Christians back in England, his homeland, urging them to join him in the work. Hundreds came. "Let us give our lives for the Word of God," he told them. "Let us not be hirelings who flee from the wolf but faithful shepherds, watchful for the flock of Christ. Let us preach the whole counsel of God to the high and to the low, to the rich and to the poor, to every rank and age, as far as God gives us the strength." Through their efforts, tens of thousands of Hessians joined the Christian church.

Boniface made it clear to the converts that each was committing their whole life to the Lord. "Listen, my brethren," he told them, "and consider well what you have solemnly renounced in your baptism. You have renounced the devil and all his works. The devil's works are pride, idolatry, envy, murder, lying, stealing, adultery, abortion, belief in witches and other such evil things. You have promised to believe in God the Father, Son and Holy Spirit, one almighty God in perfect trinity. And you have promised to obey all His commandments." Working closely with the pope in Rome, Boniface organized churches throughout Germany and established monasteries for training clergy, caring for the poor, teaching children, and copying the Scriptures. Boniface studied the Bible daily using a copy with large handwritten print because his eyes were weak. He sought to instill in the illiterate tribesmen a reverence for the Bible. "Behold the Word of God," Boniface would say before preaching, holding up a large New Testament with gold letters.

Sadly, Boniface could sometimes be unkind to Christians who did not agree with all the teachings of the Roman Church, even though many of those teachings were contrary to the Bible. There were fine Christian missionaries in Germany from Ireland, Scotland and other lands, but because they permitted ministers to marry and did not acknowledge the pope as the head of the church, Boniface spoke against them and refused to work with them. He believed that Christianity would triumph over the warring pagan tribes only if it were strong, unified, and closely linked to the Roman Church.

As Boniface grew old, the fire in his heart to convert the pagans did not grow cold. At the age of 73, he decided to leave Germany, sail down the Rhine with some companions to Fresia (Holland), and preach to the pagan tribes there. Boniface knew he was heading into danger. As he packed a few belongings for the journey into a wooden book-chest, he pulled from the closet his burial shroud. He folded the long white cloth, tucked it into the chest, and boarded the boat for Fresia. Through the preaching of Boniface and his helpers, many Frieslanders were baptized, tore down their pagan shrines, and built in their place Christian churches. Pagan chieftains and priests, enraged that Boniface had turned so many people away from idolatry, threatened to kill him and his friends if they continued their missionary work. But Boniface and his brothers pressed on.

In the late spring of 754, Boniface and his helpers set up camp on the banks of the Burda River near Dukkum and prepared for a large gathering of new converts. Early on the morning of June fifth, when the first rays of sunlight reached the grassy plain, Boniface, who sat reading the Bible in his tent, heard the distant sound of a large crowd approaching. As he joyfully rushed outside, expecting to welcome the new converts, he saw a wave of pagan warriors with flashing swords racing across the open field toward the camp. The friends of Boniface ran for their weapons to defend themselves, but he stopped them saying in a calm voice, "Take courage, my beloved, trust in God, they can only kill our bodies, they can't harm our souls. The Lord's promises are true; today we shall be with Him in everlasting glory." Moments later, the pagans swarmed in, slaughtering Boniface and most of his companions.

By God's grace, he left behind a great legacy, firmly rooting Christianity in Germany and establishing a strong, well organized church. This is why Boniface is known as the "Apostle to the Germans."

• • •

Charlemagne
Protector of the Church

Charlemagne c. 742-814

Around the year 780, shoppers in a public market on the west coast of Frankland beheld a strange sight. Above the cackling of the chickens and the cries of the hawkers of fish, they heard two Irish monks calling, "If anyone wants some wisdom, let him come to us and receive it: for it is wisdom which we have for sale." The Franks gaped wide-eyed at the strangers from the famed monasteries of Ireland where the Scriptures and ancient writings were preserved and studied. For several days, they showed no wares and displayed no books but only cried out, "Wisdom for sale, come to us for wisdom!" Most of the onlookers laughed and thought them crazy, but one man, knowing that the king admired and pursued wisdom, sent word to the royal palace. King Charlemagne summoned the Irishmen at once.

The monks went to the palace and were led into the throne room, their palms sweating, for Charlemagne was known as a fierce warrior, a man of iron. Charlemagne's six-foot, muscular body towered over them. His thick, white hair fell to his shoulders, and his large, piercing eyes seemed to gaze right through them. His legs were wrapped in bands of white cloth, and he wore a long blue cloak and a shimmering black vest of otter skin. Strapped to his side hung a long, golden-hilted sword.

"Is it true," the king asked, "as everyone is saying, that you have brought wisdom with you?"

Bowing low, the Irishmen answered, "Yes, we have wisdom, and in the name of God, we are prepared to teach it to any worthy people who seek it."

Charlemagne ran his eyes over the strangers from the

crown of their shaved heads to the tips of their deer-skinned boots. "And what payment do you want for your wisdom?" he asked.

"We make no charge, great king. All we ask is a suitable place to teach and talented minds to train. Of course, we will need food to eat and clothes to wear, for without these our work cannot be accomplished." Charlemagne flashed a broad smile, clapped the strangers on the back, and welcomed them into the royal palace. In time, he sent one of these Irish monks to Italy to organize a monastery and school. The other he placed in charge of the palace school. Here boys from the noblest families studied, and also boys from poor homes who demonstrated interest and ability in learning. Charlemagne challenged the students to use their minds to the fullest and to work hard.

Shortly after the palace school began, Charlemagne rode off to battle and did not come home for a long time. When he returned victoriously, he called all the students to the throne room to review their writings and poems. Charlemagne delighted in the excellent compositions of the boys from poor homes, but the children of noble parents presented careless, foolish work. Then Charlemagne rose from his throne and called to his right hand those who had worked well. The smiling king stooped down and said, "My children, I am grateful to you, for you have tried your very hardest to carry out my commands and to learn everything which will be of use to you. Continue to study hard and to strive for perfection, and I will give you bishoprics and fine monasteries, and you will always be honored in my sight."

Then Charlemagne turned to his left, frowning at the wealthy, lazy students. "But you young nobles," he thundered, "you pleasure-loving sons who trust in your high birth and your wealth, and care not a straw for my command, you have neglected the pursuit of learning and have indulged yourselves in time-wasting follies and idleness." Charlemagne raised his right hand toward the heavens and declared an oath against them, "By the King of heaven," he shouted, "I think nothing of your nobility! Know this for certain, unless you immediately make up for your previous idleness by diligent study, you will never receive anything worth having from Charlemagne!"

When word spread that Charlemagne welcomed men of learning, scholars from across Europe offered their services to him, including Alcuin, an English monk, one of the greatest living scholars of the Bible, literature, and science. Alcuin created a new palace school, which tutored Charlemagne's children.

"I dispense the honey of the Holy Scriptures," Alcuin said of his work, "the old wine of the classics, the fruit of grammar, and the dazzling splendor of the stars." Charlemagne himself sat in on lectures and during meals he ordered the public reading of great books, his favorite being Augustine's *City of God*. He mastered material quickly and learned to speak many languages.

Charlemagne ordered schools established throughout his vast kingdom. "The priests are to have schools in the towns and villages," read the royal decree, "and all who wish to have their children instructed, the priests must teach without charging a fee." He built monasteries and paid for the copying and translating of the Scriptures and ancient manuscripts gathered from the far flung monasteries of Europe, Ireland, and Britain. Charlemagne instructed bishops to train the priests under their care. Once, in an angry letter to the archbishop of Mainz, he wrote, "I am surprised that while you labor, with God's aid, to win souls, you take no care at all to teach good reading to your clergy. All around you, people dwell in dark ignorance. When you could enlighten them with your own knowledge, you let them live in their own blindness." Literacy and scholarship revived in Western Europe through his leadership and example.

Charlemagne sought to rule his kingdom for the glory of God. He signed his name: "Charles, by the grace of God, King of the Franks." "Remember," he often said, "we must all appear before the Judgment Seat of Christ." He went to worship service every day and attended early morning and late evening prayer vigils. Charlemagne's decrees at times sounded more like sermons than royal proclamations. Once his heralds read in public squares throughout the kingdom, "Be humble and kind to one another. Envy, hatred, and violence keep men from the kingdom of God. Confess your sins and give to the poor." He took great pains to insure the well being of the needy. "The poor, widows, orphans and pilgrims," he said, "shall have consolation and protection. No one shall refuse shelter, warmth, or water to those traveling through the land, for God Himself said, 'I was a stranger and you took me in.'" Charlemagne gave away great amounts of his treasure to the poor.

Clad from head to toe in iron armor, Charlemagne often led his troops into battle. For nearly all of his forty-six year reign, he waged war—more than doubling the size of his kingdom. Eventually his rule extended from the Baltic Sea to Italy, a kingdom whose size had not been seen since the days of the Roman Empire. His greatest military challenge came from the Saxons in the north. The Saxons, a fierce, warlike people, clung to their pagan gods. "It is my duty, by the grace of God," he said, "to defend the church of Christ against the assaults of pagans." When Charlemagne's army defeated the Saxons in battle, they promised peace and friendship, but when his army returned home, they destroyed monasteries, tore down churches, and slaughtered Christian converts. Missionaries fled to Frankland from the northern territories. Some resumed their work at once when Charlemagne's forces marched north again. One trembling missionary, full of doubts and fears about returning to the Saxons, flung himself before Charlemagne and asked, "What should I do?"

"You should," Charlemagne barked, "go back to your mission field in the name of Christ." He did and brought many Saxons into the Christian church.

Eventually, after thirty-three years of fighting, Charlemagne completely defeated the Saxons and firmly established the rule of his kingdom among them. In the wake of his victories, he sent missionaries to proclaim the good news of Jesus Christ and to build churches, monasteries, and schools. At times he forced the conquered people, under the threat of violence, to accept Christianity and submit to baptism. Naturally, many of these people resented Christianity because of it. Alcuin advised Charlemagne to win the people to Christ through faithful preaching and kindness. "If the light yoke of Christ were preached to the stubborn Saxons as much as the duty to give money," he told Charlemagne, "perhaps they would not reject the sacrament of baptism. What is the use of baptism without faith," Alcuin said. "A man can be forced to baptism, but not forced to believe." Later in his reign, Charlemagne heeded Alcuin's advice and presented Christianity more gently to conquered people.

In the winter of the year 800, Charlemagne came to the aid of Pope Leo III, who had been attacked by a mob and deposed. Charlemagne investigated the incident and reinstated the pope. On Christmas day, Charlemagne worshipped with the pope and a great crowd at St. Peter's Church in Rome. The church, decorated with gold and purple embroidered tapestries, glimmered from the light of a thousand candles. Toward the close of the service, when Charlemagne rose from prayer, the pope placed a gold crown on his head, draped a purple imperial robe around his shoulders, and knelt before him, kissing the hem of the robe. Then the whole congregation in one voice burst into the cry, "Long life and victory to Charles Augustus, crowned by God, the great Emperor of the Romans!" From that day, Charlemagne took the title of Roman Emperor.

Though there was much in Charlemagne's life to commend, yet it was also a life marred by serious sin. At times he was very cruel. Once, he ordered the execution of over four thousand unarmed, captured soldiers. As a young man and then again in his old age, he married and divorced several times, rebelling against God's commandments for marriage.

A few days before he died, Charlemagne crowned his son, Louis, emperor in the presence of a large crowd of churchmen and nobles. Charlemagne urged him to love and fear God, to govern and defend the church, to care for the poor, and to rule justly. As he placed the golden crown upon his son's head he said, "Blessed is the Lord God who allowed me to see this day a son of mine upon my throne."

Not long after, he fell gravely ill. On the morning of his death, he feebly raised his trembling right hand and made the sign of the cross, then closed his eyes and sang in a soft voice, "Into Your hands, O Lord, I commit my spirit."

After the rule of Charlemagne, the church in Europe was never the same. He protected the power and influence of the pope, brought Christianity to pagan lands, and encouraged Christian education. And his reign raised questions. Should the king be a spiritual leader and rule the church? What should be the relationship between the church and state? For centuries after, kings and churchmen wrestled for control of both earthly and spiritual power.

• • •

Alfred the Great Christian King

King Alfred the Great 847–899

Long ago in the days of the Saxon kings of England, when marauding Vikings pillaged the land, the monks of Crowland Abbey one day labored, loading boats with silver utensils, works of art, hand-written manuscripts, and other treasures. Thirty of these monks paddled down river to safety with their precious cargo. Abbot Theodore remained with a few aged monks and small boys. "The Vikings will see we are utterly defenseless," he thought, "and this will curb their wrath."

Theodore and the others concealed the remaining valuables, donned their priestly robes, and worshipped in the chapel. The Vikings, inflamed by their hatred for Christianity and their lust for treasure, burst into the monastery chapel with broadswords flashing, cutting down Theodore where he stood. They slew the others too, stacked all the bodies, and set them ablaze. After ransacking the monastery, they left it in flames and marched away to plunder neighboring homes, churches, and abbeys.

"O Lord, deliver us from the fury of the Northmen," cried the Christians of England, but the carnage and destruction continued for years. The weak and divided Saxon kingdoms proved no match for the invaders. The Saxons of England were descendents of the pagan Saxons of Germany, who settled in Britain and converted to Christianity. Not even Alfred, the daring king of Wessex, land of the West Saxons, could dislodge the Vikings from his realm, although he sought to with prayer and fasting and battle. For seven years he fought scores of battles and endless skirmishes against the better-armed Vikings with slim prospects for ultimate victory. Every year brought hundreds of Viking ships loaded with fresh troops to the English coast. Many Saxons fled overseas, and the rest were subdued to the Vikings' will—all but Alfred the king. Eventually, the Vikings drove Alfred from his stronghold into the marshes at the remote western edge of his kingdom where most of his countrymen gave him up for dead. There, with a few loyal men, cold and half-starved, he raided small Viking outposts and made plans to rescue his kingdom from ruin.

Throughout these months of trial, Alfred continued his practice of daily worship. Arising before sunup, without his household knowing, he would slip away to a church to pray. Lying prostrate before the Lord on the cold stone floor, he pled for God's mercy and direction. Certainly the words of the Psalms, many of which Alfred knew by heart, filled his prayers during these dark days. "Save me, O God, I sink in the miry depths. The chariots of God are tens of thousands and thousands of thousands. Surely God will crush the heads of His enemies. Come quickly to me, O God. You are my help and my deliverer; O Lord, do not delay."

He did not have to wait long, for in early spring of 878, a window of opportunity opened. The Duke of Devonshire, a friend of Alfred, finding his castle surrounded by Vikings, crashed through the Viking lines at dawn, taking them by surprise, slaying their chief, and putting the enemy to flight. The stunning victory revived hope for deliverance in the hearts of the Saxons. Alfred seized the moment, sending messengers throughout the land calling on Saxon nobles, freemen, and peasants to gather in the Selwood Forest at the Stone of Egbert. On the appointed day in early May, thousands of Saxons traveled the backwoods under the cover of darkness to meet their king. The sight of the handsome and muscular thirty-year-old Alfred brought tears to their eyes for they beheld him as one raised from the dead. Horn blasts and shouts of joy resounded through the forest as they saluted King Alfred. Alfred led them in prayer, unfurled his war banner, the golden dragon, and called them to arms. With whoops and back slaps the order passed from man to man, "Tomorrow, we march on the invaders."

The Vikings, hearing rumors that the Saxons were rising, massed their forces at Edington under Guthrum, their greatest chieftain. After a two-day march, Alfred, his chain mail and sword shining in the afternoon sun, led his army to the field of battle, forming them into a tightly-packed shield wall. They repelled wave after wave of charges from enemy horsemen and infantry. When the enemy began to waver, the Saxons unleashed a furious attack, slaughtering the Vikings until they broke and ran. Alfred, with his men in hot pursuit, hacked them down, chasing Guthrum and the remnant of his army into a nearby castle where they lay siege to it. After fourteen days spent suffering thirst and hunger, the Vikings asked Alfred for his terms of surrender, fearful that death awaited them all.

But Alfred, moved by Christian compassion and hoping to establish a lasting peace, offered terms with unheard-of generosity and kindness. Alfred granted life and freedom to Guthrum and his men on the condition that they depart peacefully from his kingdom with the pledge never again to wage war against Wessex. In addition, Guthrum agreed to convert to Christianity and be baptized. Three weeks later, after the remainder of the Viking army left Wessex, Guthrum, with thirty of his best officers, came to Alfred's headquarters where he welcomed the Vikings as friends and honored guests. At his baptism, Guthrum, dressed in a long white robe, stood next to Alfred, who served as his sponsor. After the priest baptized him in the name of the Father and the Son and the Holy Spirit, Alfred embraced his old enemy and received him as his adoptive son. Twelve days of feasting followed, and Alfred showered Guthrum and his men with many gifts. In the coming years many Vikings turned from paganism to Christianity.

With the defeat of the Northmen, Alfred directed his energies to rebuilding his kingdom. From childhood Alfred

was inspired by Charlemagne, the great Christian king of
the Franks. Charlemagne's religious zeal and his love of justice and Christian learning helped shape Alfred's vision for
his kingdom. But Wessex lay in ruins, the cities defenseless, with churches and monasteries destroyed. Most educated Saxons were dead or in exile. Law and order had dis-
integrated and Viking hordes, unconnected to Guthrum,
posed a constant threat. "I did not strongly desire at all this
earthly kingdom," Alfred said, "but felt it to be the work
I was commanded to do." He fortified the cities and garri-
soned them with troops to defend against surprise attack.
Alfred increased the number of soldiers equipped to fight
on horseback in order to confront the fast-moving Vikings,
and he built a fleet of large rowing ships to push back invaders before they reached land.

"We were all despoiled by the heathens," Alfred wrote
as he surveyed the spiritual decay of the people and the col-
lapse of law and order. Using the Word of God and some
old Saxon laws as a guide, he compiled a new law code for
his kingdom. Alfred, knowing that God is the supreme law-
giver and judge, began his code with these words: "Thus
says the Lord, I am the Lord your God, who brought you
out of the land of Egypt, out of the house of bondage. You
shall have no other gods before me." He included the remainder of the Ten Commandments, other chapters from
Exodus of the Law of Moses, and Christian duties from
the New Testament. The code concluded with a list of spe-
cific crimes and punishments.

Alfred often sat at judicial hearings to monitor the wisdom and justice of his judges. He reviewed many judgments,
especially in cases concerning the care of the poor for whose
welfare he felt a divine obligation. If a decision appeared
unfair, he would summon the judge to his royal chambers
and ask, "Why did you pass so unfair a sentence? Did you
lack information? Did you favor one party over the other?
Did you take a bribe?" Many confessed that they had acted
unwisely, and Alfred chastised them: "I am astonished at

this arrogance of yours, since through God's authority and my own you have enjoyed the office and status of wise men, yet you have neglected the study and application of wisdom. I command you either to relinquish immediately your office or else apply yourselves much more attentively to the pursuit of wisdom." The officials pledged on their knees to apply themselves to wisdom and justice. If they failed to do so, the king removed them from office.

Alfred bemoaned the ignorance of his people. "It very often comes into my mind," he wrote a friend, "before everything was ransacked and burned, what wise men there formerly were throughout England and how happy the times were then. Churchmen fulfilled their service to God with zeal. Foreigners came to this land in search of wisdom and instruction. Now we shall have to find wise men from abroad if we are to have them. When I came to the throne, I cannot remember a single man in the kingdom who could translate a letter from Latin into English." So Alfred sent for educated men from across Britain and Europe, paying them handsomely for their labors. He devoted large sums of money to rebuild monasteries and churches, and he challenged the monks and priests to dedicate themselves to the work of education. "My desire," Alfred said, "is that all the freeborn youths of my people may apply themselves in learning until they can read English writings properly."

Young people who demonstrated academic promise were taught to read and write Latin, and they studied the classics of Greek and Roman literature and the writings of the Church Fathers. Alfred modeled the love of learning himself. One day when Alfred and his learned friend and advisor, Asser, were sitting together discussing all sorts of topics, Asser read aloud a Latin passage. Alfred, delighted with the passage, asked Asser to copy it down in a little handbook which Alfred always carried with him. Asser discovered that Alfred had filled all the blank pages of the book with prayers, Bible passages, and poetry. Finding no empty space in which to copy the passage Asser said, "Would it meet with your approval if I were to copy out the passage separately on another sheet of parchment?" The king agreed and Asser folded together several long sheets of parchment into a booklet. All the while Alfred looked on and prodded him to hurry. Before the day was out, Asser copied four Latin passages into the booklet, and Alfred set at once to translate them into English.

"I stretched out my hands to the heavens," Asser later wrote, "and gave mighty thanks to Almighty God who had sown such great enthusiasm for the pursuit of learning in the king's heart."

As Alfred expanded his translation work, he formed a plan. "Then I recalled," Alfred said, "how the Bible was first composed in the Hebrew language, and when the Greeks learned it they translated it all into their own language, and all other books as well. Similarly all other Christian peoples turned them into their own language. Therefore it seems good to me that we should turn into the language that we all can understand certain books which are the most necessary for all men to know." Alfred led the way by translating into English books by Augustine and Gregory and works of history and poetry. Alfred's efforts revived and expanded education in England.

As Alfred's reforms succeeded and the kingdom prospered, he resolved, in thanksgiving to the Lord, to give half of his yearly income to God. With cheerfulness, Alfred dedicated half of the royal income to support churchmen in their work of caring for the poor and building churches, monasteries, and church schools. He made a solemn vow to give half of his time and energy both by day and night in service to God. During his reign Alfred wrote this prayer: "O Wise One, I have sought to live worthily while I have lived, and after my life to leave to the men that come after me a memory of me in good works." God wonderfully answered King Alfred's prayer. For centuries mankind has honored the memory of this good and godly man, and he alone among all the kings and queens of England is called "Great."

• • •

Anselm
Theologian, Monk, Archbishop

Anselm 1033-1109

Around the year 1040 in Aosta, a small town in northern Italy, lived a young boy named Anselm. Aosta, nestled at the foot of the Alps, was a green place alive with the sound of streams rushing off the mountains. Anselm used to stare for hours at the great snow-capped peaks. When his mother told him about the one true God who reigns on high, Anselm thought she meant the heights of the Alps. He looked at the jagged mountains and wondered which of the steep, icy trails led to God.

Then one night he dreamed that God called him to the mountain top. In his dream, as he approached the foot of the mountain, he saw servants of God reaping in golden fields of grain. But the servants were careless and idle. Anselm, indignant at their laziness, determined to report their slothfulness to God. He hastily climbed the mountain and approached the grand throne room. The Lord greeted him with a smile, invited him to sit at His feet, and spoke with him in a pleasant and friendly way. Anselm told Him all that was on his heart. While basking in the love of God, he forgot all about the ill report he intended to make about the lazy harvesters. Then God called His steward, who brought the whitest bread Anselm had ever seen. Anselm ate the delicious bread in God's presence and was refreshed. When he awoke in the morning, Anselm believed that his mountaintop experience had really happened. He told his family, his friends and the townspeople, "I have been to heaven," he cried, "and feasted on the bread of God." As Anselm's knowledge of God grew, he never lost his childlike enthusiasm and joy for the Lord.

Anselm's mother taught him the Christian faith, and when his friends tempted him to sin, his love and reverence for her kept him from evil. But his mother died when he was a teenager, and his cruel father, who tormented him, made life in the home miserable. Anselm labored to do exactly as his father ordered, but the more obedient he was the sharper his father's anger grew. With his spirit crushed, and fearing something terrible might happen, Anselm fled his home and country and began a new life in a strange land.

After a few years of wandering through Europe, Anselm came to the Abbey of Bec in Normandy. The stone abbey was new, built on the bank of a stream which flowed through a meadow, hemmed in on both sides by wooded hills. The abbot, Lanfranc, a great scholar and teacher, turned Bec into the most important center of learning in the region. Monks copied manuscripts, Lanfranc wrote books, and they all pursued their work and prayer. Lanfranc attached a school to the abbey, and when Anselm was about twenty-years old, he became a student there. Lanfranc's brilliance and devotion inspired Anselm to pursue God and knowledge. At Bec, Anselm decided to give his life in service to God. He said to himself, "Well then, I shall become a monk. But where?" He ruled out monasteries with severe discipline that would hinder his studies and writings.

He considered entering the abbey at Bec but said, "No, at Bec I would be condemned to insignificance because of the outstanding ability of Lanfranc. I shall go somewhere I can both display my knowledge and be of service to others." But soon Anselm recognized his sinful pride. "Why," he said, "should a monk desire to receive more honor and glory than others? Far from it. Set aside your rebelliousness and become a monk where you will be lowest of all." And so Anselm shaved the crown of his head, put on a monk's cowl, and entered the abbey at Bec. His hard work, devotion to God, and love for others won him the admiration of the brothers. Later, when Lanfranc left Bec for another work, the monks unanimously chose Anselm to lead them.

When Anselm was not directing worship, keeping the hours of prayer, guiding the monks, or teaching the boys, he wrote. Anselm excelled in the study of and meditation on Scripture, and he wrote a now famous book explaining how Christ's death on the cross satisfied the justice and honor of God. His writings were highly prized throughout Europe and forced theologians and philosophers to re-think their understanding of many things.

"I do not seek to understand in order that I may believe," Anselm said, "but I believe in order that I may understand." The monks and churchmen thought Anselm, because of his gifted mind, should devote most of his time to writing and leave off teaching the boys in the abbey school. "Why do you give so much of your time to the training of the older boys and young men?" he was asked.

"A youth is like a piece of wax," Anselm answered. "If the wax is too hard or too soft it will not receive a perfect image when pressed with a seal. So it is with the ages of men. Old men, untrained in the truth of God, are like hardened wax, and young boys, unable to understand spiritual things, are like soft, liquid wax, incapable of receiving a seal. But the young man is pliable. If you teach him, you can shape him as you wish. Knowing this, I watch over the young men with great attention, taking care to nip all their faults in the bud, so that afterwards, being properly instructed in the practice of holiness, they may form themselves in the image of spiritual men."

Once a visiting abbot complained to Anselm about the difficulty of training boys. "What, I ask you, is to be done with them? They are incorrigible ruffians. We never stop beating them day or night, and they only get worse and worse," he said shaking his head in disgust. Anselm was astonished. It brought back memories of his father's cruelty.

"You never stop beating them?" he asked. "And what are they like when they grow up?"

"Stupid brutes," the abbot answered.

"You raised them to be brutes," Anselm said. "But tell me, if you planted a tree in your garden, and hemmed it in on all sides so that its branches could not stretch out in any direction, what sort of tree would it become?"

"A useless one, with its branches all twisted and knotted," the abbot answered.

"And would not the whole fault be your own, who forced it to grow so unnaturally? So it will turn out also with boys treated with severity and without love or kindness." Anselm counseled him to use love and discipline to train boys' hearts for God. The abbot hung his head and knelt on the ground saying, "We have indeed wandered from the way of truth." He left determined to train the boys with love.

Anselm often used everyday occurrences to teach spiritual truths. Once when he and some of the monks were out riding on horseback, a rabbit being chased by dogs fled between the feet of Anselm's horse. Anselm drew in the reins and kept his mount still so that the rabbit, quaking in fear, might hide safely under the horse. The dogs barked loudly and pawed the ground, but they could not make the rabbit run from under the horse. Some of the monks laughed and made fun of the cornered animal.

"You laugh, do you," Anselm said, bursting into tears. "There is no laughing for this unhappy animal. His enemies stand round about him, and in fear of his life he flees to us for help. So it is with the soul of man: evil spirits stand ready to seize it and carry it off to everlasting death. So the soul looks around in great alarm, looking for a protecting hand to defend it. But the demons laugh and rejoice when they see the soul without any help." Anselm chased off the dogs, and the rabbit hopped away to safety. The monks, no longer laughing, had learned a lesson in compassion.

During Anselm's years at Bec, William, Duke of Normandy, invaded England and defeated the Saxons at the

Battle of Hastings. William built a stone cathedral at Canterbury and called Lanfranc to be the archbishop of Canterbury, head of the church in England. After William the Conqueror died, his son, William Rufus, used the church and kingdom for his own pleasure and greed. "God shall never make me a good man," he boasted. The king sold church offices to the highest bidder and refused to replace bishops who died so that he could take the church's money for himself. "The church of Christ is rich," he said, "why shouldn't I try to get some of it for myself." When Lanfranc died in 1089, the king did not appoint a new archbishop for Canterbury.

In 1093, Anselm came to England to start a monastery and school. When he arrived at Canterbury, the churchmen and people hailed him archbishop. Anselm wanted to remain a simple monk, so he fled the city to escape them. Not long after, Anselm met King William Rufus to inform him of his plans for the monastery. When he came to the royal court, the king rose from his throne and greeted Anselm at the door. After a cheerful conversation, Anselm asked to speak to the king in private and rebuked him for his wicked abuse of the church. The king was furious and determined that Anselm would not meddle in his affairs.

Soon, a serious illness struck the king, pulling him to the brink of death. His nobles convinced him to appoint Anselm archbishop of Canterbury. Churchmen, and the people, hearing the news, erupted in shouts of joy and clapping. But Anselm resisted with all his might. "I am old and unfit for the work," Anselm pleaded to the nobles and bishops, "how can I bear the responsibility of the English church? I am a monk, do not entangle me in what I have never loved and am unfit for."

He did not accept the appointment, but before he could escape, the people seized him and forcibly carried him to the church. With great rejoicing and hymn singing, Anselm was ordained archbishop of Canterbury. Downhearted and longing to return to Bec, he began his work. The king

recovered and resisted Anselm's efforts to end the sale of
church offices and to stop corruption in the church. Anselm
sought to protect the church from the greedy king and preserve the church's right to govern itself.

The king, believing that he owned the church's land, told
Anselm, "Are they not mine to do with as I please?"

"Yours," Anselm fired back, "to protect, not to waste
and destroy." Eventually, the king exiled Anselm from the
country. After the death of William Rufus, the new king,
Henry I, returned Anselm to England. But when Anselm
refused to accept bishops and abbots appointed by King
Henry without church approval, the king threatened him
with force. "I am not afraid," Anselm said, "of banishment,
or poverty, or torture, or death, for God strengthens me."
King Henry also threw him out of England. But after three
years, Henry relented and agreed that the power of bestow-
ing church offices rested with the leaders of the church.
Anselm returned to Canterbury to a tumultuous welcome.
He installed godly bishops and abbots to guide the English
church. The sovereignty of the church had been preserved.

Anselm served as archbishop and continued meditating
on Scripture and writing to the day of his death in 1109.
As he lay dying a friend said to him, "We think you are
going to leave this world for your Lord's heavenly courts."

"If it is His will," Anselm answered, "I shall gladly obey
His will." Anselm was buried in Canterbury Cathedral next
to his old friend and teacher, Lanfranc.

• • •

Bernard of Clairvaux
Lover of Christ

Bernard of Clairvaux 1090–1153

Father and son stood on the terrace of the family castle at Fontaines. Before them lay the beautiful hills and valleys of Burgundy, France, in the glow of an autumn day. The father, Tescalin Sorrel, a nobleman and knight, turned to his gifted son, Bernard, a twenty-two-year-old scholar and natural leader. Tescalin hoped his son would serve the Grand Duke of Burgundy in a high ranking government post.

"Now, Son, what is it you wanted to tell me?"

"Father," Bernard said, "I have decided to devote my life to God. I am going to become a monk." Tescalin was unaware that Bernard was even considering going to a monastery. "A monk!" he said, the color rising in his cheeks. "And where do you plan to be a monk?"

"Citeaux," Bernard answered.

"Citeaux!" His father exploded. "That hovel in the marshes where the men looked half-starved and work like slaves?" Bernard looked into his father's eyes and reminded him that his mother had always wanted him to serve the church. He was making this decision out of devotion to God and loyalty to his mother. At the mention of Bernard's mother, Tescalin quieted down. His wife, Aleth, had been dead for seven years and the pain of her absence still hurt deeply. Together they had raised their six sons and one daughter to love the Lord and serve others. Aleth had often took her children with her as she did acts of mercy and kindness for the sick and poor.

"Last month," Bernard said, "when I went to visit Guy and Gerard as they were besieging the castle at Grundy, I rode along weighed down by my sin and worried about my

future. Then these words from Mother came back to me
over and over again: 'My Son, was it for this that I brought
you into the world?' Soon I came to a small, wayside chapel.
I entered, fell to my knees weeping, and prayed. In a moment, the Lord swept away my doubts and fears. I left the
chapel certain of God's love and forgiveness and ready to
serve him as a monk." Just then, Bernard's brothers, Guy,
Gerard, Bartholomew, and Andrew appeared on the terrace.

"Father, we too have decided to serve the Lord at
Citeaux." They paused. "Will you give us your blessing?"
Tescalin slumped a little and then stretched out his arms
and embraced his sons, saying quietly, "May the Lord bless
you." Then Tescalin smiled and added, "Now be moder-
ate, I know you; nothing can hold back your zeal!" The
brothers bid farewell to their father and as they left the castle,
they saw their youngest brother, Nivard, playing in the
courtyard. "Goodbye, little brother," Guy called, "we leave
you all our lands and worldly goods—see how rich you will
be!"

"That's not fair," Nivard said, "you take heaven and leave
me the earth." When Nivard was of age, he joined his brothers at the monastery. Bernard had not only persuaded his
brothers to join him, but also an uncle and over twenty other
friends. They walked through the woods and marshlands
and arrived at the wooden gate of Citeaux. Bernard clanged
the iron knocker. The white-robed abbot appeared and asked,

"What do you seek?"

"God's mercy and yours," they answered.

To Bernard, the hard labor, coarse clothing, meager food,
and bare surroundings were not a sacrifice but a joy. Soon
the abbot recognized Bernard's devotion and leadership and
chose him to lead a group of monks out from Citeaux to
begin a new monastery. When he was just twenty-five, Bernard and twelve monks, walking two by two, headed north,
singing hymns as they went. In late June of 1115, they arrived at a clearing wedged between two thickly forested hills.
It was a dark and forbidding place called the Valley of

Wormwood. But once the brothers began to shine the light of Christ there, the people round about renamed it Clairvaux, which means "clear valley."

"We must root out our personal will," Bernard told them, "the will that is purely our own, that which is not in tune with the will of God." Following a strict, daily schedule of prayer, meditation, worship, work, and rest, they cleared the land, prepared the soil for planting, and erected a simple building which served as chapel, sleeping room, and dining hall. They slept on rough-cut boards with dried leaves for mattresses and blankets. Bernard delighted in studying and meditating upon Scripture.

"He who is filled with the love of God," he said, "is easily moved by everything in the Word." His sermons seemed like tapestries woven together with threads of verses gathered from all of the Scripture. He dug deeply into the Scriptures, spending over twenty years studying and preaching through the Song of Songs alone. "Brothers," he told them, "know how immeasurably God deserves to be loved. The Lord, who is so great, first loved us who are so little and so wretched! What then, I ask you, could be the limit of our love?"

William, an abbot of a nearby monastery, told what it was like to visit Clairvaux: "At first glance," he said, "as you enter, after coming down the hill, you can feel that God is in the place. The silent valley speaks in the simplicity of its buildings and the true humility of the men of Christ living there. The silence is only broken by the music of singing or the sound of the hoe in the garden. I marveled and thought I saw a new heaven and a new earth."

As word of Clairvaux spread, many flocked to it. Rich and poor, even bishops and princes, renounced their places of honor to wear the white robe. The most welcome arrival of all was Tescalin, Bernard's father. As their numbers grew, Bernard sent monks off to start new monasteries in other lands, eventually starting over one hundred new houses. The monks of Clairvaux did not hide from the world but fed and lodged travelers, nursed the sick, and cared for the poor. Once when a terrible famine swept across France, Bernard emptied the storehouses of all the monasteries and sent out the monks to give away the food until nothing remained.

Bernard's reputation as a wise and fair man spread throughout Europe. Kings, nobles, popes, and bishops sought his advice and asked him to settle disputes. He hated to leave Clairvaux, but many times he traveled away to help others. "God's business is mine," he said. These journeys were often long and dangerous. Three times he crossed the Alps in the dead of winter, enduring frigid snow and treacherous mountain passes. Many lives were saved by Bernard's help in getting warring groups to agree to peace. He did not fear to speak the truth boldly. Although Bernard was faithful to the pope, once he wrote to him, "You are despicable . . . . In all circumstances you know no law but your pleasure, you never think of God nor do you fear Him."

Bernard showed great courage when he stood up to his own king, Louis VII of France, when he acted cruelly. "I urge you to stop your evil ways," Bernard told him. "If, Sire, you continue in this way, your sin will not long remain unpunished. I am resolved to stand firm. Lacking shield and sword, I shall use the arms of my estate—prayers and tears."

One great mistake of Bernard's came in 1145 when he joined the call for a crusade to free the Holy Land from the Muslims. Crusades always led to the deaths of many innocent people. As men of every station rallied to fight, problems immediately broke out. A German monk, Rudolf, traveled up and down the Rhineland preaching, "Death to the Jews!" Men preparing for the crusade were turned aside by him. "Soldiers of Christ," he told them, "before you fight the infidel in the Holy Land, rid our homeland of the Jews, the God-killers."

Rudolf whipped them into a frenzy of hatred and hundreds of Jewish men, women, and children across Germany were massacred. A few brave people did what they could to protect the Jews, but most did nothing. When word of the killing reached Bernard, he rushed to stop it. Facing angry mobs, he spoke out boldly, "Defend the Holy Land," he said, "but do not hurt the Jews. The Scriptures will not allow you to push them out from your midst. Their conversion will come some day and God will turn upon them again His eyes of mercy. Now stop this murdering and do no harm to these people." The crowds obeyed him. The massacres came to an end.

Above all else, Bernard is remembered as a lover of Christ. "My God, my love," he often prayed, "how You love me!" Perhaps his favorite verse in the Bible was Psalm 73:26: "My flesh and my heart may fail, but my God is the strength of my heart and my portion forever." He told the brothers of Clairvaux: "I serve the Lord with freedom, since love brings freedom. I invite you, dear brethren, to serve in love." Bernard wrote hymns of love for Christ which the brothers of Clairvaux sang in chapel and while at work in the fields, making the valley echo with beautiful harmonies of praise. His hymns have been sung ever since. "Jesus Thou Joy of Loving Hearts" and "O Sacred Head Now Wounded" are the most loved.

Through the centuries, Bernard's life and writings have guided Christians to a deeper devotion to Jesus Christ. John Calvin, the Reformer of Geneva, said that often "Bernard speaks as though the very truth itself were speaking." And Martin Luther said of him: "Bernard loved Jesus as much as any one can."

> Jesus, Thou Joy of loving hearts,
> Thou Fount of life, Thou Light of men,
> From the best bliss which earth imparts
> We turn unfilled to Thee again.

• • •

Peter Waldo and the Waldensians
Faithful to the Word

Peter Waldo c. 1130–1217

Around 1170, at a gathering of the rich and powerful of Lyons, France, Peter Waldo, a wealthy merchant, delighted himself in the prestigious company and feasting. Everyone who was anyone was there: heads of the government, leaders of the church, knights, nobles, and men of business. As Waldo laughed and talked with one of the leading men of the city, the man collapsed to the floor, dead. Shocked and bewildered, Waldo stood trembling, staring down at the man's ghostly white face. The sudden death struck Waldo like a lightning bolt. "That could have been me," Peter kept saying to himself. "Am I prepared to die?"

He could think of nothing but the shortness of life and the state of his own soul. Not long afterward, while walking through the town square, he heard a minstrel singing a ballad about St. Alexis who gave away all his riches to seek God and serve others. Peter Waldo wondered if God was calling him to do the same. Now Waldo found himself dissatisfied with hearing only a few Bible verses read in Latin each Sunday. So he hired two well-educated men to translate the Gospels and some other parts of the Bible into French. As he read the Bible for himself for the first time, he was awed by the beauty and power of the words. Christ's message to the rich, young ruler seemed to have been written just for him: " Go sell all you have and give it to the poor, then come follow Me."

So Peter Waldo did. He sold all his property, gave the money away to the needy, and began to teach others the good news of Jesus Christ. Those who joined him in following the teachings of the Bible were called by some "the poor men of Lyons," and others called them Waldensians. Traveling about in twos—barefoot, clad in plain robes, without money, they preached to the poor and read from copies of the New Testament in French.

Waldo and his friends had no intention of breaking away from the church. They saw their work as helping the church return to the beliefs of the Apostles and the first Christians. But when the archbishop of Lyons told Waldo and his companions to stop teaching the Bible and preaching to the people, they refused saying, "We must obey God rather than men."

Seeking the permission of Pope Alexander III to preach and teach, a few Waldensians journeyed to Rome to explain their work and present the pope with a copy of the French New Testament. The pope formed a commission to study the matter. Walter Map, an English churchman who headed the commission, said of the Waldensians, "They have no settled home, like the apostles, they follow the Lord who had no place to lay his head." But their simple faith and humble lives did not win the respect of the commission. "They are ignorant and foolish men," Map said.

The churchmen roared with laughter at their simple answers to complicated questions. Although they mocked the Waldensians, they saw in their childlike faith and zeal something to be feared. Map said, "Right now they are just beginning and have not yet gained any firm footing, but if we give them the approval of the church, eventually we ourselves will be driven out." The pope forbade them to teach the Bible, and when they continued telling others about the good news of Jesus Christ, he declared them heretics and enemies of the Church of Rome. Not long after, church leaders passed a law which said that only priests could read the Bible, and they added common-language Bibles to the church's list of forbidden books.

Church officials began fiercely to persecute the Waldensians, burning thousands at the stake, along with their copies of the Bible, and driving them from Lyons.

Fleeing across southern France into Germany, Switzerland, Italy, and beyond, they gathered secretly for worship in out-of-the-way places or in small groups in homes. Not all Frenchmen cooperated with the persecution. Once a French bishop asked a knight, "Why don't you drive out the Waldensians from the province as the church has ordered?"

"We cannot do it," he answered, "for we have grown up with them and have family members among them; besides, we see them living good and honest lives." Wherever they settled the Waldensians lived simply, supporting themselves through manual labor and farming. Some became traveling peddlers as a way to spread the gospel. After buying some clothing or jewelry, the customers would ask,

"Have you nothing more to sell?"

"Yes," the Waldensians would answer, "we have jewels still more precious than anything you have seen; we would be glad to show them also. We have a precious stone, the Word of God, it is so brilliant that by its light a man may see God." And so they told those who would listen about Christ's love, often leaving behind a handwritten copy of some part of the Bible. The Waldensians so loved the Bible that they memorized large portions of it. Some could recite the entire New Testament by heart.

Over the centuries, as the Church of Rome drifted farther from the Bible's central message, the Waldensians held fast to Scripture as God's supreme guide to His people. They rejected the Church of Rome's teachings on indulgences, prayers to saints, purgatory, and other unbiblical ideas, and they endured persecution because of it. Not until the Protestant Reformation, begun by Martin Luther in the 1500's, would large numbers of Christians believe as the Waldensians did.

The coming of the Protestant Reformation, however, did not end the Church of Rome's persecution of the Waldensians but intensified it. In 1655, the cruelest attacks of all crashed down like an avalanche upon the Waldensians living in the mountain valleys and fertile plains of Savoy in northern Italy. With the promise of the pope's blessing, the ruler of Savoy issued a terrible decree.

"Within three days, all Waldensian families living in the lower plains and valleys must leave their homes and move up into the Alpine valleys. Within twenty days, all Waldensian property must be sold." Anyone willing to follow the Church of Rome was permitted to stay. This order came in the middle of winter. Little children and the elderly and the sick and the lame were forced to cross ice-covered mountains and valleys through bitter winds and snow. Huddling together for warmth, they encouraged one another to continue. Their icy trail was stained with blood. Anyone of them could have avoided this disaster by simply giving up their beliefs and following the Church of Rome.

"I was a pastor of a congregation of nearly two thousand people," one man wrote later, "and not one of them chose to deny the faith. I wept for joy as well as for sorrow when I saw that all the fury of these wolves was not able to shake one of these lambs from the faith. I blessed God to see them bear this heavy cross so nobly." Many died from cold and hunger, but those who survived received a warm welcome from their Waldensian brothers in the higher valleys. They invited them into their homes and shared all they had with them. The persecutors, however, were not content with forcing them out of the lower plains and valleys; they wanted to destroy them altogether.

When spring came, an army of 15,000 men was outfitted for war and sent to the Alpine valleys. The soldiers attacked without mercy. They were not satisfied with simply killing. They tortured their victims in the cruelest ways imaginable. Parents were forced to watch the killing of their children. Little ones were torn from their mothers' arms and dashed to pieces. Some were thrown alive into bonfires. One father was marched to his death with the heads of his slain sons hung around his neck. Bodies lay everywhere. Those still alive fled. Several hundred hid in a large cave up a steep mountainside on the edge of a cliff. But the soldiers tracked them down. Some were tied up in balls and rolled down the mountain. Women and children were thrown over the cliff. The attackers set fire to everything: churches, houses, farms, and orchards.

"Our valley," one man said, "was like a paradise, but it was changed into a raging volcano spewing fire and cinders. Daylight was turned to darkness from the smoke." The survivors gathered together in the mountains grief-stricken, but they did not waver in their trust in God. Armed with courage and knowledge of the land, they decided to fight back. They pushed back the soldiers in many places though at times they were outnumbered nearly a hundred to one.

The Waldensians sent letters to the Protestant leaders of Europe. Appeals for help went out to England, Germany, Switzerland, and beyond. "Our tears are no longer of water," they wrote, "they are of blood and choke our very hearts." Protestants were horrified to learn of the massacre. The English and the Swiss threatened to fight for the Waldensians if the rulers of Savoy did not end the persecution. Peace was restored, but the Waldensians never regained all of their lost homelands. Through the years, they continued to suffer many persecutions, but they remained faithful to the Lord.

• • •

Francis of Assisi
The Lesser Brother

Francis of Assisi 1181–1226

All the citizens, town fathers, and churchmen of Assisi packed the piazza and cheered as their young men rode off to battle against Perugia, a rival city-state to the west. One knight, Francis Bernardone, stood out as the most impressive. His father, Pietro, had seized the opportunity to show off his wealth and spent a small fortune outfitting his son with the finest horse, armor, and weapons. He wanted Francis to help Assisi to victory and hoped that a taste of combat would rid Francis of his romantic dreams of greatness and make him content to settle down and work in the family business.

"Take care, Francis, fight nobly!" one man shouted. Francis smiled and bowed low in the saddle. It was not only the splendid outfit which attracted attention to him; his wit and charm had made him a town favorite for years. The young ladies waved bouquets, wondering what their parties would be like without Francis, the fun-loving poet and singer, whom they called "the King of the Feasts." As the warriors rode out of the city gates, Francis, his armor gleaming in the sunlight, raised his lance high into the air, reared his horse, and shouted, "I shall return a great prince."

But the war went badly. The Perugians defeated the army of Assisi, captured Francis and forty other lancers, and threw them into prison. There, in chains, they endured filth and disease until a ransom for their release was paid. More than a year passed before Pietro Bernardone managed to buy his son's freedom. Francis returned home bedridden and with a high fever. During several long months of illness, he thought about the state of his own soul and trembled at the thought of Judgment Day.

One day when Francis regained some strength, he went for a walk dressed in his finest clothes. He met a poor man wearing a ragged tunic. Suddenly a compassion that he had never felt before overwhelmed him. Francis traded clothes with the man on the spot. Not long afterward, as Francis rode his horse on the plain below Assisi, he saw a man walking toward him on the road. Filled with terror, Francis pulled back hard on the reins and stopped. The man, a beggar and a leper, was pleading for alms. White oozing sores covered his outstretched hand. Horror gripped Francis, but as he tried to back his horse away, he felt compelled to go forward. He leapt from his horse, hugged the leper, and kissed his deformed hand. After giving the beggar all the money in his bag, he rode away full of joy, singing praises to God.

In church the next Sunday, the Gospel reading was from Matthew 10. In this passage, Christ is sending out his disciples to preach and says, "Do not take along any gold or silver or copper in your belts; take no bag for the journey, or extra tunic or sandals or a staff." As soon as the verse was read, Francis rejoiced, certain of God's calling for his life.

He said, "This is what I want; this is what I long for with all my heart." From that day forward, Francis was a changed man. Forsaking all worldly comforts, he wore a coarse brown robe tied at the waist with rope. He walked barefoot and lived among the lepers, begging alms for them, washing their wounds, and easing their pain. Francis saw them as children of the King of kings and treated them with courtesy and respect like a servant to his master.

The people of Assisi, however, did not like the change in Francis. They thought him a dirty madman. When he first walked through town in his humble clothes, they ridiculed him. "Get out of here you fool," they shouted. They pelted him with dirt and insults, but he did not return evil for evil. He found comfort in the Lord's promise: "Blessed are you

when people insult you, persecute you and falsely say all
kinds of evil against you because of me. Rejoice and be glad,
because great is your reward in heaven." His father was the
loudest mocker of all. He couldn't bear it that his son had
turned his back on a life of wealth in order to serve the
poor. He seized Francis, beat him, and chained him to a
cellar wall. There Francis remained until his mother released
him while his father was away on business.

Francis traveled about preaching Jesus Christ. "Repent,
my brothers and sisters, and look to our blessed Savior,"
he said. "Know that he who comes to Christ will have all
his sins forgiven. Take heart, repent and find your joy in
the Lord." Always at the center of his teaching was the
wonder of the Incarnation—God enfleshed. He wanted
everyone to marvel at the mystery of God becoming a man.
In order to encourage devotion to Christ and deepen the
celebration of His birth, Francis organized an outdoor
Christmas service complete with manger, hay, ox, and don-
key. All the worshippers held candles and sang hymns. This
began a tradition of Christmas nativity scenes.

As word of Francis spread, some men wanted to join
him in his work. Francis read to them a verse from the Gospel of Matthew: "If anyone would come after me, he must
deny himself and take up his cross and follow me" (Matt.
16:24).

"This is our life and rule," Francis said, "and the life
and rule of all who wish to join our company. We shall follow
our Lord's example by preaching to the poor and caring
for the sick." Soon men by the hundreds and then thousands flocked to join him. They shaved the crowns of their
heads as a sign of humble submission to God and wore
simple brown robes like Francis. He called his group the
Lesser Brothers. He said, "My brothers are called lesser so
they will not presume to become great men." Although
Francis and his followers owned nothing and worked hard,
their lives were marked by thanksgiving, joy, and song.
Francis often sang psalms and hymns. He wrote poetry about

God's love and the beauty of creation, putting the words to music and teaching the brothers to sing them.

Francis loved nature and saw the glory of God in everything that God had made. Even the lowliest of creatures showed His wonderful handiwork. They, too, were created to bring praise and glory to the Lord. One day Francis approached a flock of birds and said, "Oh birds, my brothers, you have a great obligation to praise your Creator, who clothed you in feathers and gave you wings to fly with and cares for you without any worry on your part." Once he said to a chirping cricket, "Sing, my sister cricket, praise the Lord Creator with your joyful song."

When the Lesser Brothers grew to over five thousand, Francis sent them out to the four corners of the world. He told them to preach faithfully and live holy lives. "Cast your cares upon the Lord," he told the brothers as they left, "and he will support you." The brothers went to the eastern end of Europe, north to Germany, south to the Muslim lands of Africa, and west to Spain and England. Wherever they went, they served the poor. Their humble lives of poverty and service set a fine example for the priests and monks to follow, for the church had become full of selfish and lazy men.

Although Francis's humility and love serve as an example to all Christians, some of his beliefs do not. For example, Francis accepted the teachings of the church, which encouraged the adoration of Mary, prayer to saints, and other unscriptural teachings. It was not until the Reformation, three hundred years after Francis, that many Christians turned from these errors.

Through the years, Francis suffered illness and pain. Near the end of his life he was practically blind. As he lay dying at the age of forty-four, he said, "Welcome, Sister Death."

"It is in dying," he told the brothers, "that we are awakened to eternal life." His friends said, "He met death singing."

The Prayer of St. Francis

Lord, make me an instrument of your peace.
Where there is hatred, let me sow love;
Where there is injury, pardon;
Where there is doubt, faith;
Where there is despair, hope;
Where there is darkness, light;
Where there is sadness, joy.

O Divine Master, grant that I may not so much seek
To be consoled, as to console;
Not so much to be understood as to understand;
Not so much to be loved as to love;
For it is in giving that we receive;
It is in pardoning that we are pardoned;
It is in dying that we awaken to eternal life.

• • •

Elizabeth of Hungary
Servant of the Poor

Elizabeth of Hungary 1207–1231

Famine gripped the German states of Thuringia and Hesse in the summer of 1226. The famished poor wandered the fields and forests, searching for wild nuts and berries, clawing at the earth for roots, stripping the bark from trees, and devouring every kind of dead animal encountered in their desperate search for food. Many starved to death, covering the roads with corpses. The ruler of the region, Duke Louis, and most of the fighting men were away on a military campaign in Italy. When desperate crowds hiked the steep road to Wartburg Castle and clamored at the gates for food, nineteen-year-old Duchess Elizabeth, wife of Louis and daughter of the King of Hungary, heard their pleas.

The beautiful olive-skinned duchess threw her energies by day and by night into relieving the suffering of her people. The duke's advisors, fearing an uprising, cautioned the duchess to keep a tight rein on finances and a strong guard at the royal granaries. Instead, Elizabeth emptied the royal treasury, giving the money to the poor and depleted the granaries to feed the hungry. She instructed the castle's kitchen staff to bake bread and cook soup from sunrise to sundown, and she even served the people with her own hands.

Coordinating her efforts with the monks, nuns, and priests, she organized food distribution across the land with money gained from the sale of most of her jewels and other property.

"Stop it," the advisors warned. "You'll bankrupt the royal house!" But Elizabeth pressed on, grateful for God's call to help the needy.

"O Lord," she prayed, "how can I sufficiently thank you for having given me the opportunity to serve these poor ones, who are your dearest friends." She fed nine hundred people who came to the castle each day. To those too weak or ill to ascend the mountain to the castle, she carried food herself. Elizabeth began a hospital and two houses for the poor in Eisenach, the town nestled below the massive, gray-stoned castle. Laying aside her royal robes, she twice daily donned a peasant's cloak and walked down to Eisenach to make beds and comfort the sick. She gave new clothes and shoes to able-bodied men and women and set them to work in the fields, preparing the ground and planting seeds in the hopes of raising a small crop by harvest time.

When her money failed, she gave the poor her veils, silk scarfs, and other articles of clothing saying, "Sell these to satisfy your wants and work as your strength allows, for the Bible says, 'He who does not work does not eat.'" When word of the famine reached Duke Louis in Italy, he hastily returned home. As he drew near to Wartburg, his officials went out to meet him. They denounced Elizabeth's reckless spending and the emptying of the granaries.

"We warned her," they protested, "but she wouldn't listen."

The duke stopped their complaining and said, "Let my good little Elizabeth give to the poor as much as she pleases, so long as she leaves me Wartburg and Naumburg, alms will never ruin us." When Louis arrived home, Elizabeth threw herself in his arms and showered him with a thousand kisses. As he held her in his arms he asked, "Dear sister, what has become of your poor people during this terrible year?"

With a gentle voice and broad smile she answered, "I gave God what was His, and God has kept for us what was yours and mine."

In her youth, Elizabeth's father told her about Francis of Assisi. His decision to honor Christ by turning away from riches and loving the poor inspired her to follow in his steps. She often met the lepers, kissing them, easing their pain, and praying for them. She bathed them, cutting up castle curtains and linens for towels to dry them.

"O, how happy we are," she told a fellow worker, "to be able by this work to cleanse and clothe our Lord." Once when her husband was away, she discovered a poor leper whose body was so diseased that no one would help him. She took him into the castle, bathed him, rubbed medicine on his sores, and laid him in her own bed, much to the consternation of her mother-in-law and the royal officials. When the duke returned, his mother ran to him and said, "Come with me, dear Son, and I will show you what your Elizabeth does. You will see one she loves much better than you." Taking Louis by the hand, she led him to his bed chamber saying, "See! Your wife puts lepers in your bed and I can't stop her. You can see for yourself that she wants to give you leprosy."

Louis did not rebuke his wife but praised her for her loving kindness and built at her request a home for lepers on the castle road. When affairs of state called Louis from the castle, Elizabeth wore plain dark clothes and spent her time in works of mercy, prayer, and fasting. But when Louis came home, she dressed in her finest jewelry and her most colorful gowns.

"It is not vanity or pride that leads me to dress this way," Elizabeth told her maidens, "for I would not give my husband any occasions of discontent or sin by having anything in me to displease him." God blessed Louis and Elizabeth with four children. A few days after her first child, Herman, was born, she wrapped herself in a gray robe, took her newborn son in her arms, and slipped secretly out of the castle. She walked barefoot to the town church and lay the baby on the altar saying, "My God and my Lord, with all my heart I give my child to You as You have given him to me. Please receive this child, all bathed in my tears, into the number of Your servants and friends and bless him."

In the autumn of 1227, Louis packed his armor and sailed off for a crusade to the Holy Land, leaving Elizabeth and the children in the care of Henry, his brother. But this trip would bring great sadness. Not long after he left, Louis caught a fever from which he finally died. In the meantime, court officials who despised Elizabeth's religious zeal and her use of the royal treasury to help the poor, turned Henry against her. To strengthen his own claims to the throne, Henry ordered the expulsion of Elizabeth and her children from Wartburg Castle and from all royal lands.

A court official declared to her, "You ruined the country, wasted the treasury, and dishonored your husband. By order of Duke Henry, you must leave the castle immediately." Astonished by the sudden, cruel demand, Elizabeth asked if she might have some time to prepare her departure.

"No," he answered firmly, "leave this place at once." It was a late winter afternoon, and a bitterly cold wind wiped across the mountainside when guards pushed Elizabeth, and her children, and two companions outside the castle walls, slamming the great metal gates behind them. She carried her baby daughter in her arms and the other children wept as they trod the narrow path to Eisenach. By the light of the moon she walked the streets seeking shelter, but Duke Henry forbade the citizens to help Elizabeth in any way, and the cowardly people of Eisenach obeyed him. After her years of selfless devotion to them, no one opened his home to her.

"They have taken from me all that I had," she said weeping, "now I can only pray to God." Finally an innkeeper let her rest the night in a backyard shack where he kept his pigs. At midnight, her children fast asleep, Elizabeth heard the bell ringing for matins at the Franciscan convent which she and Louis had founded. She arose and worshipped with the brown-robed friars. She asked them to sing a hymn of thanks to God for the tribulations he had sent her. Then she prayed aloud, "O Lord, may Your will be done. My children are born of royal race, and behold them hungry, and without a bed to lie on. Yesterday, I was a duchess in strong castles and rich domains; today I am a beggar and no one takes me in." For many nights they slept in the church. "This is God's house," Elizabeth said, "at least from here no one can drive me away."

To feed her children, she resorted to begging and later earned her livelihood by spinning wool. In her poverty, she reserved a portion of food from every meal to share with the needy. Remembering the sufferings of Christ, she did not complain but accepted her lot with thanksgiving. "O yes, Lord," she prayed, "If You will be with me, I will be with You, and I wish never to be parted from You."

Later, outraged knights, friends of the late duke, forced Henry to give Elizabeth part of the estate. She used these resources to build a hospital and care for the poor. Later she gave away all her money to the poor and took a vow of poverty. She spun wool and ministered to outcasts.

When her father, the King of Hungary, heard that his daughter was living in poverty, he dispatched an ambassador at once to bring her to him. When the finely dressed and jeweled ambassador found Elizabeth spinning wool in a dark hovel, he burst into tears and cried out, "Did anyone ever before see a king's daughter spinning wool?" He pleaded on bended knee with her to return to Hungary where she would be treated as a royal princess.

"I am a poor sinner," she said, "who never obeyed the law of God as I ought to have done."

"Who has driven you to this state of misery?" he asked.

"No one," she answered, "but the infinitely rich Son of my Heavenly Father, who has taught me by example to despise riches."

"Come, noble Queen," he said, his arms outstretched to the frail Elizabeth. "Come with me to your dear father, come, possess your kingdom and your inheritance."

"I hope indeed," she replied, "that I already possess my Father's inheritance—that is to say, the eternal mercy of our Lord Jesus Christ." As the ambassador left she arose from her spinning wheel and gently took his hand saying,

"Tell my dearest father that I am more happy in my life than he is in his regal pomp, and that far from sorrowing over me, he ought to rejoice that he has a child in the service of the King of heaven."

A short time later, Elizabeth was bedridden with a high fever. For two weeks she suffered, wracked with pain, but she remained peaceful and prayerful. In her last words to friends she said, "Let us speak of Jesus who came to redeem the world. He will redeem me also." She died on November 19, 1231, at the age of twenty-four.

• • •

John Wyclif
The Morning Star of the Reformation

John Wyclif c. 1330–1384

Great trouble engulfed Oxford University during the winter term in 1378, for John Wyclif, the leading philosopher and theologian of Oxford, stood condemned by the Church of Rome. Enraged by Wyclif's ideas, Pope Gregory XI had sent sealed documents declaring Wyclif a heretic to the king of England, the archbishop of Canterbury, and the chancellor of Oxford University. "John Wyclif," he wrote, "is vomiting out of the filthy dungeon of his heart most wicked and damnable heresies. He hopes to deceive the faithful and lead them to the edge of destruction. He wants to overthrow the church and bring ruin to the land. Arrest Wyclif immediately and hold him until a church court can be convened to pass final sentence."

Everyone knew that such strong words from the pope meant that soon Wyclif would be burned at the stake. The only way to save himself would be to recant—to say his teachings were wrong and ask forgiveness. But would Wyclif recant? If not, would he be arrested and executed? These were the questions which cast dark clouds over the students and teachers of Oxford.

Though small and frail, John Wyclif was Oxford's most powerful preacher and teacher. The "wicked heresies" of which the pope wrote were these: Wyclif said the pope and all church leaders should be subject to the Word of God. They should give up seeking their own pleasures and live simple lives of humble service. He argued that the bread and wine of the Lord's Supper was not the physical body and blood of Jesus but were signs and seals of Christ's spiritual presence with His children. But foremost of all he taught that Scripture was the supreme guide of the church and that Scripture was for everyone. "Jesus taught the people simply and in their own language," Wyclif said. "At Pentecost, the Holy Spirit gave the apostles the gift of tongues so that everyone could hear the good news in his own language."

So Wyclif and his followers labored for eleven years translating the Bible into English. "Press on in this work," he told his helpers, "for if the people of England will read the Scriptures for themselves it will be the surest road for them to follow Christ and come to heaven."

But this violated the laws of the church. "It is heresy to have the Holy Scriptures in English," a churchman declared. "Giving the common people the Bible is like throwing pearls before swine." Church officials did not want the people studying the Bible for themselves for fear they would lose influence and the unity of the Church of Rome would be broken.

The pope hoped to stop John Wyclif and his ideas once and for all by condemning his writings and putting him to death. What would Wyclif do? Would he try to save his own life by saying that he had been wrong? Would he tell his followers to put aside the Bible and submit to the leaders of the church? John Wyclif did not retreat an inch. "The pope has no more power to judge than any other minister," he said. "His words should be followed only so far as he follows the words of Christ. I am under obligation to obey the law of Christ."

"Master Wyclif," one of his students said, "What will become of you? What about your place in the university? What about your life?"

"When I came to Oxford nearly thirty years ago," he said, "I was enticed by the wisdom of the world. Above everything else, I wanted fame; I wanted men to honor me. But praise be to God who saved my soul and showed me the glories of His Word! I am ready to follow the teachings of Scripture even unto death if necessary."

Pope Gregory XI died suddenly before he could see to

Wyclif's execution. A great struggle ensued over who should be his successor, a struggle which enabled Wyclif to continue teaching, writing, translating, and training young men to go out and preach the whole truth of the Word of God. "Live a prayerful, holy, and honest life," he told them. "Let your deeds be so righteous that no man may be able to find fault with you. For the example of a good life stirs men more than true preaching alone."

Hundreds of young men set out dressed in simple brown robes with a handwritten copy of the English Bible in hand. They traveled across Britain reading from the Scriptures, proclaiming the good news of Christ, and singing psalms of praise. Students came to Oxford from all over Europe, and many returned to their homelands to translate the Bible and preach Jesus Christ to their countrymen in their own languages. They were called Lollards, though no one is quite certain how they got this name. Perhaps it came from the old word "lollen" which meant to sing.

"After your sermon is ended," Wyclif told his traveling preachers, "visit the sick, the aged, the poor, the blind, and the lame, and help them as you are able." By so doing, the Lollards won the hearts of the people. Many came to faith in Christ and began to learn the Word of God for the first time in their lives. The local priests would have none of this and obtained a law to stop the evangelists. They waited to fall upon the preachers when the travellers entered a town. But the people often sided with the preachers, forming a strong ring around them to protect them from harm.

In 1382, the Archbishop of Canterbury, fuming over the growing influence of Wyclif and his preachers, called a church council to crush them. But as the council proceeded to write up the sentence of condemnation against Wyclif, an earthquake rocked London, violently shaking the stone building in which they met. The alarmed churchmen hesitated to proceed, believing that God was angry with their work. But the archbishop hardened them saying, "Don't you know that the earth is releasing its noxious vapors which loose their power when they burst forth? Well, in the same way if we rid the wicked men from our community, we shall put an end to the troubles of the church." Wyclif declared that the Lord had sent the earthquake as a rebuke of the heresies of the churchmen "as the earth trembled when Christ died on the cross." The council condemned Wyclif, and the archbishop pressed the king to seize him at once. "If we permit this heretic to continue," he told the king, "our destruction is inevitable. We must silence these Lollards—these psalm-singers." The king ordered the arrest of Wyclif and the Lollards. But the House of Commons, angry that the persecuting order was approved without their consent, called for its repeal.

Ignoring the House of Commons, the archbishop convened a church court at Oxford and summoned Wyclif—whose health was failing—to stand before it. Wyclif's friends urged him not to appear. "What!" Wyclif said, "Should I live and be silent? Never! Let the blow fall. I await its coming." Wyclif faced his accusers, rebuking them for failing to follow the Word of God, for leading the people astray, and for using church office for selfish gain. "In the end," he said in closing, "the truth shall prevail." He left the court. His enemies dared not utter a word. Wyclif was banished from Oxford University, but divisions in church and state prevented his arrest and execution. Wyclif did not retire quietly. "The church law has no force," he said, "when it is opposed to the Word of God." He continued preaching, writing, and translating the Scriptures. "I intend with my whole heart," he said, "by the grace of God, to be a true Christian and as long as breath remains in me to proclaim and defend the law of Christ."

Two years later, Wyclif died of a stroke, but his followers carried on the work. But the leaders of the church were determined to crush the Lollards. They ordered all copies of the English Bible and the writings of Wyclif to be burned, along with many of the Lollards themselves. This fierce persecution failed to snuff out the gospel light which the Lord lit through John Wyclif. His writings later influenced the leaders of the Protestant Reformation. Because of this, Wyclif is known as the "Morning Star of the Reformation."

In 1428, forty-four years after his death, the leaders of the church had the bones of Wyclif dug up. As a sign of condemnation, John Wyclif's remains were burned and his ashes were dumped into a stream called the Swift. Many years later, an English historian wrote: "They burnt his bones to ashes and cast them into the Swift, a neighboring brook running hard by. Thus the brook carried his ashes into the Avon, the Avon into the Severn, the Severn into the narrow seas and they into the main ocean. And so like his ashes the message of Wyclif has spread throughout the world."

• • •

John Huss
Forerunner of the Reformation

John Huss 1369–1415

On October 2, 1412, the priests of Prague, Bohemia, finally possessed what they had long petitioned the pope to provide: an order to seize John Huss, forbid his preaching, excommunicate him, and destroy Bethlehem Chapel. The leading theologian and preacher of Prague, John Huss, had been a thorn in the side of the priests for years. His church, Bethlehem Chapel, overflowed with people for its services. Huss conducted services in Czech, the language of the people, and not Latin as required by the pope. He preached the Word of God and condemned laziness and greed in the clergy. Now, with the prodding of the priests and some leading men of the city, a large crowd assembled outside the senate house.

"Come on, men," their leader shouted, "we'll march to Bethlehem Chapel, arrest that heretic, Huss, and level the building to the ground." The people of Bethlehem Chapel rallied to the defense of their pastor and church.

"Brothers and sisters," Huss told them, "they want to block God's Holy Word and tear down a chapel built for His service." The friends of Huss met the mob with such determination that the angry townsmen left without Huss and without harming the chapel. But his enemies kept up the attack. The pope placed all of Prague under interdict, forbidding any church services until authorities arrested Huss. The city was divided between supporters of Huss and supporters of the pope. Tensions mounted, and fights even broke out. John Huss did not obey the pope's ban but continued to preach the good news of Jesus. "Christ commanded his disciples to go into all the world and preach," he said.

"No pope can stop what Christ taught to be done."

Although expelled from Prague by the king of Bohemia, huge crowds flocked to hear him speak in fields, forests, villages, and castles. He stayed in touch with his congregation by sending letters and sometimes sneaking into the city to visit them. "My greatest comfort," he wrote them, "is to see you earnestly following the Bible. Please pray that the Word of God may not be kept back in me." Some of his friends, worried for his safety, asked whether he could give in to the pope but a little. "I will confess Christ as long as he gives me grace to do so," Huss said. "I will resist to the death all agreement with falsehood. A good death is better than a bad life."

For two years he wrote, preached, and resisted the ban of the pope while growing numbers of Bohemians sided with Huss. As the unrest grew, the German Emperor Sigismund feared it would spread into his empire. So he encouraged the king of Bohemia to send Huss to appear before the church council meeting in the Swiss city of Constance. The emperor promised Huss protection from harm, giving him a letter of safe conduct to and from Constance. Huss gladly agreed to go because he longed to defend his teachings before the council. "Under the safe conduct of your protection," he wrote the emperor, "I shall appear before the council. I hope that I shall not be afraid to confess the Lord Christ and, if need be, to die for the truth of his Law."

Many in Huss's congregation warned him not to trust the emperor's safe conduct. One man, eyes brimming with tears, gently took Huss's hand and said, "God be with you; I am afraid you will not return again unharmed. Dearest Master John, may the King of Heaven reward you for the good and true instruction that I received from you."

Huss bid farewell to his flock saying, "Remember, Christ suffered for the sake of his chosen. If my death can glorify His name, than may He give me grace to endure with good courage whatever evil may befall me. May the Lord watch over you and bring you into eternal peace and glory."

With two knights armed for battle, riding beside him for protection, he set out for Constance. For three weeks he traveled across Germany to Switzerland. Large crowds came out to see and hear him. Wherever he went he left behind a handwritten copy of the Ten Commandments, for the people knew next to nothing of the Bible.

Not long after his arrival and despite the emperor's promise of protection, soldiers arrested him and threw him into a putrid dungeon cell next to an open sewer. The stench and foul air ruined his health, giving him severe headaches and throwing him into vomiting fits. Though deprived of his books and Bible, ill and nearly starved, chained day and night, he prepared his defense. But the council had no intention of letting Huss explain himself, deciding in advance that he could either recant or be burned. Huss requested an advocate to speak on his behalf.

"We do not grant such privileges to heretics," they told him.

"Well, then," Huss said, "let the Lord Jesus be my advocate, who also will soon be your judge." Finally, after months of imprisonment, suffering from headaches and stomach pains, Huss was brought to the cathedral before the council to hear the charges against him. They sat him on a tall wooden stool in the middle of the cathedral, where he was surrounded by princes, bishops, cardinals, and theologians. Emperor Sigismund sat on a throne. The smell of incense lingered from the high mass celebrated before his arrival. A stack of books and papers were laid on the table before him. "These are your writings. Will you admit they are full of false teachings?" they asked.

"I am ready to retract anything in them," Huss said, "if I am shown from Holy Scripture where I am in error." A councilman came forward and picked up one of the books.

"Burn it!" shouted several men in the assembly. The councilman called for quiet and then read aloud a short chapter. "Do you retract this?" he asked. As Huss attempted to quote passages from the Bible and the writings of the

Church Fathers to defend the chapter, a loud howling like wolves erupted from the council. "Away with your arguments," they shouted, "say yes or no." Each time he tried to speak they interrupted him with howls. When he managed to say that Christ alone and not the pope was the head of the church, the councilmen shook their heads and laughed.

They called on him once more to accept the judgment of the council and recant. "It would be better for me," Huss said, "that a millstone were hung around my neck and that I should be cast into the sea before I should deny the truths of God." Soon the judgment was read: "The holy council, having only God before its eye, condemns John Huss as a stubborn and open heretic."

"I never was stubborn," Huss said, "I only demand that you show me from Scripture where I have erred." Huss looked to the emperor who had promised him protection. The emperor's cheeks flushed red; he turned his head and said nothing. Falling to his knees, Huss prayed aloud, "O Christ, the council has condemned your Word. Lord Jesus, forgive my enemies; as You know I have been falsely accused by them. Forgive them for the sake of Your great mercy."

A roar of laughter pealed from the councilmen who pointed at Huss and mimicked his prayer. The Council turned Huss over to the secular rulers who condemned him to death by fire. Before he was executed, six bishops wrapped priestly robes around his shoulders and placed a eucharistic cup in his hands. Then they stripped him of his robes, saying he was no longer a minister in Christ's church. Snatching the cup from him, one said, "We take from you, condemned Judas, the cup of salvation."

"But I trust in God," Huss replied, "that today I shall drink of the cup of salvation with my Lord Jesus Christ in His kingdom." While cursing him, they set on his head a hat painted with devils and the word "archheretic." "My Lord Jesus," Huss said, "wore a crown of thorns for me; why should I not be willing, for His sake, to wear this."

A bishop called out, "Now we give over your soul to the devil."

Huss looked to heaven and said, "And I commit my soul to Jesus." A guard of a thousand armed men led Huss through the city, holding back the people who thronged the streets. A large crowd followed close behind to the place of execution. There Huss dropped to his knees and with tears in his eyes prayed lines from the Psalms and said, "Into your hands, Lord, I commit my spirit. Lord, help me to endure this cruel and shameful death for preaching Your holy gospel." With an old chain, brown and flaking, they bound his hands behind his back and strapped his neck to the stake. "My Lord Jesus." he said, "was bound with a harder chain than this for my sake, and why then should I be ashamed of this rusty one?"

As they piled wood and straw around him to his neck, a nobleman called out, "There is still time. Recant."

"What error," Huss answered, "should I recant. I shall die with joy today in the faith of the gospel of Jesus Christ which I have preached." When the fire was lit he sang out with a loud voice, "Jesus, Son of the living God, have mercy on me." They threw his clothes and shoes into the flames and later scooped up the ashes, casting them into the Rhine River.

His death inspired tens of thousands of his country-men to boldly follow Christ. And one hundred years later, his stand on the Word of God encouraged Martin Luther and the other Reformers in their belief that Scripture is the supreme standard of truth. Luther praised Huss's courage and faithfulness. "If he is to be regarded as a heretic," Luther wrote, "then no person under the sun can be looked upon as a true Christian."

• • •

LUTHER TRANSLATING THE NEW TESTAMENT

Reformation

The Gospel Clarified

The Reformation was a great spiritual revival that swept across Europe in the 1500s. Reformers rediscovered the central truth of the gospel: sinners are justifed by the righteousness of Jesus Christ. Many brave men and women risked their lives to proclaim that truth.

- Martin Luther
  Father of the Reformation

- William Tyndale
  Translator of the English Bible

- John Calvin
  Theologian of the Reformation

- Anne Askew
  The Lord's Bold Witness

- Latimer, Ridley, and Cranmer
  The Bishop Martyrs

- John Knox
  Scottish Reformer

- Jeanne d' Albret
  Reformation Queen

- Renee
  Duchess of Ferrara

Martin Luther
Father of the Reformation

Martin Luther 1483–1546

On a late summer day in 1517, the sun cast a golden glow over a German town near the border of Saxony. A great assembly of peasants, merchants, lords, and ladies waited in eager expectation. Trumpet blasts announced the approach of a grand procession making its way to the town square. At the head of the parade strode the mayor, then marched the priests, monks, and friars hoisting brilliant banners of red, white, and purple emblazoned with the cross of Christ and the golden keys, symbolizing the power of the pope. The traveling preacher, dressed in a white robe, rode in an ornate carriage. At the end came a churchman lifting high a gold embroidered velvet cushion upon which rested a great parchment, the pope's Bull of Indulgence— a papal letter offering forgiveness. As the banners were set in place around a platform in the square, the murmuring of the crowd died down and the preacher, Tetzel, rose to speak.

"Take care to listen, dear children, for God and St. Peter are calling you," he said, pointing his finger and making eye contact with people in every corner of the square. "Do you know that your life is like a small ship caught in a terrible storm? Sin and temptation toss you about. Are you ever going to make it to the safety of heaven?" Downcast eyes revealed to Tetzel that his message was hitting the mark. "Today is the day," he continued, "and this is the hour to have all your sins removed, for the Holy Father, Pope Leo, has declared a special indulgence. Confess your sins, drop some money in the box, and you will be forgiven."

Tetzel preyed on their fear of purgatory, a place which

the Roman church taught existed between heaven and hell and where Christians after death were punished for their sins and purified for heaven. "And, my children," Tetzel added, "do not forget your dear dead relatives. Listen, can't you hear them calling to you from the pains of purgatory? 'Pity us! Pity us! We are in terrible torment, but you can free us for a pittance. Will you not drop a few coins into the box and open the door of heaven to us?'" He closed his appeal shouting: "As soon as the coin in the coffer rings, the soul from purgatory springs!"

Many people rushed forward, emptied their pockets, and returned home with joy, clutching the letters of indulgence, the guarantee of forgiveness, to their breasts. Some from Wittenberg excitedly told their priest, Martin Luther, about Tetzel's message and showed him their indulgences. Thirty-four-year-old Martin Luther, the crown of his head shaved as a sign of his monastic order, frowned and sighed deeply. Luther used to buy indulgences, too. In search of forgiveness, he painstakingly performed every duty recommended by the church, but his sin and guilt continued to overwhelm him. Then, when studying Scripture, he read Romans 1:17, "For in the gospel a righteousness from God is revealed, a righteousness that is by faith from first to last, just as it is written: 'The righteous will live by faith.'"

The truth of God revealed in that verse transformed Luther's life. He discovered that a sinner is not made right with God by anything he does himself but only by trusting in what Christ has done for him.

"I felt that I was reborn and had gone through open doors to paradise," he said. "I saw that God had given me the righteousness of Christ through faith. Christ suffered all the penalty for my sin on the cross. By faith Christ's righteousness becomes my righteousness." This good news liberated Luther from striving to win God's grace through pilgrimages, indulgences, or relics. His service to God now flowed out of gratitude for his salvation.

Luther began preaching that sinners are made right with God by faith in Christ alone, but his congregation, ignorant of the Bible, accepted without question the Roman church's teachings. They believed they would find forgiveness through indulgences, prayers to saints, and the veneration of relics—bits of bones, hair, and teeth from the bodies of dead saints.

The Castle Church in Wittenberg housed more than 17,000 relics, the largest collection in Germany, claiming among them four strands of the Virgin Mary's hair, a piece of straw from the baby Jesus' manger, a nail from the cross, and a piece of bread from the Last Supper. The pope decreed that visitors to the Castle Church on All Saints Day who venerated the relics and gave a contribution could reduce their time in purgatory by over one million years.

Luther yearned to lead the people out of the darkness of superstition and vain works and into the light of faith in Jesus Christ. The thought of Tetzel's jingle "As soon as the coin in the coffer rings, the soul from purgatory springs," emboldened him to act. Martin Luther publicly declared Tetzel's teaching and the sale of indulgences a sham.

"Christ alone can forgive sins," he proclaimed. "The pope has no power to forgive or to free souls from purgatory. If he had such power why does he not release everyone from purgatory at once? Why does he not do it free of charge?"

Then Luther wrote a list of ninety-five arguments or theses against indulgences. On October 31, 1517, he nailed the ninety-five theses to the door of the Castle Church, challenging church leaders and scholars to debate the sale of indulgences. A printer published the theses and soon they circulated throughout Germany and beyond. What Luther had intended to be a discussion on indulgences among the university professors and churchmen of Wittenberg exploded into a spiritual struggle that engulfed all of Europe.

Believing that Scripture clearly taught man the will of God, Luther pointed out errors in the Roman church's teaching about many things, including relics, prayers to saints, and the rule of the pope. In response, Pope Leo called Luther a "child of the devil" and issued a papal bull declaring Luther a heretic, excommunicating him from the church, and condemning all his writings. A large crowd of students and professors gathered in the square at Wittenberg University before a great bonfire where Luther read aloud a copy of the papal bull.

"This bull condemns me without any proof from Scripture," he said. "If I am a heretic then show me from God's Word. It is better that I should die a thousand times than I should retract one word of what I have written about the sacred truth of God." Then Luther cast the bull into the flames. Everyone knew that the likely result of Luther's stand against the church would be death by burning. His friends urged him to slow down and keep quiet. But Luther said, "I cannot go against what the Scripture teaches. I am in God's hands."

Martin Luther's message deeply divided Germany. Some rejoiced to learn that salvation came by faith alone in Jesus Christ, while others remained loyal to the teachings of the Roman church. The German Emperor, Charles, wanted to settle the matter once and for all. In 1521, he called a meeting of the German princes at the city of Worms to hear from Luther and representatives of the pope in order to decide Luther's fate.

Before setting out from Wittenberg, a professor said to him, "Martin, don't go! The emperor hates your ideas. They will burn you alive like they did John Huss."

"I commend my cause to God," Luther answered. "He saved three boys from the fiery furnace, but if He will not save me, my head is worth nothing compared with Christ. This is no time to think about safety."

In Worms, princes, nobles, professors, scholars, and church leaders so packed the great hall to standing capacity that only Emperor Charles had room to sit. The eyes of all these powerful and learned men were fixed on Luther, who stood before them dressed in a coarse brown monk's robe.

"These are your writings," a churchman said, dropping a pile of books and pamphlets on a table in front of Luther. "Do you defend them or will you renounce them and admit your errors?"

"Most serene Emperor," Luther said, bowing at the waist, "most illustrious princes, most merciful lords, if I have not given some of you your proper titles, I beg you to forgive me. I am not a courtier but a monk. I cannot renounce these works unless I am shown from the Scripture where I am in error. If I am shown my error from Scripture, I will be the first to throw my books into the fire." Murmurs echoed around the hall and tensions mounted as it became clear that Luther had not come to recant but resist.

His accusers demanded that he accept the decrees of popes and church councils as superior to Scripture itself. "Martin, you claim that you only teach what the Scripture teaches. This is what heretics always say. This is what Wyclif and Huss said. Martin, how can you think that you are the only one to understand Scripture? Are you wiser than the pope and the great church councils? Now answer us simply, do you renounce your books and the errors which they contain?"

"Since your majesty and your lordships desire a simple reply, I will answer," Luther said, sweeping his gaze around the hall. "Unless I am convicted by Scripture and plain reason—I do not accept the authority of popes and councils alone, for they have contradicted each other—my conscience is captive to the Word of God. I cannot and will not recant anything. Here I stand, I cannot do otherwise, so help me God." Supporters of the pope hissed and shouted as Luther left the hall. "Away with him," some cried, following him out of the city, howling like wolves. Luther doubted that he would reach Wittenberg alive.

Meanwhile in the great hall, Emperor Charles rose and said, "A single monk cannot be right and the testimony of a thousand years of Christendom be wrong." The princes agreed, declaring Luther an enemy of the state and sentencing him to death. As Luther left Worms and headed into the countryside, a band of armed men on horseback charged out of the woods, seized him, and galloped away to an ancient castle perched on the edge of a mountain. His kidnappers were not enemies but friends. Prince Frederick of Saxony, Luther's friend and protector, fearful that Luther might be killed, arranged the kidnapping. Safe from his enemies, Luther began translating the Bible into German.

"I want the people to read the Scriptures for themselves," Luther said. Before long, printing presses cranked out tens of thousands of copies of the German Bible, and the people snatched them up, eager to discover the truths of God's Word.

Luther returned to Wittenberg to preach, teach, and write. And how he wrote! Besides his German translation of the Bible, he wrote commentaries on most of the books of the Bible, scores of books and pamphlets on the Christian faith, and a number of hymns. The greatest of these, "A Mighty Fortress Is Our God," became the anthem of the Reformation.

At the age of sixty-two, Luther died of a sudden illness. His last prayer was, "Father, into your hands I commit my spirit, for you have redeemed me." Luther's teachings and writings changed the thinking of a large part of the Christian world. He pointed people to the Scriptures as the only infallible guide to Christian faith and life, and God has used it to change individuals and societies throughout the world.

● ● ●

William Tyndale
Translator of the English Bible

William Tyndale 1485–1536

The outlaw, William Tyndale, being informed that agents of the church and king had discovered his whereabouts, stuffed his bags with as many books and papers as he could carry and fled, barely escaping capture. He was on the run again. The king of England, the emperor of Germany, and the pope of Rome all wanted him dead. What great crime had he committed? Tyndale wanted to translate the Bible into English, but church leaders did not want the people reading the Bible for themselves and in their own language; the leaders were fearful that this would undermine their authority. They decreed that the translating, publishing, and distributing of common language Bibles was an offense punishable by death.

As a university scholar, Tyndale came to a saving faith in Christ by reading the New Testament in Greek. As he studied the Scriptures for himself, he recognized that many of the Roman church's teachings were contrary to the Bible, clouding the sinner's path to Christ. Because most people couldn't read Greek or Hebrew or Latin, Tyndale determined to translate the Bible into English so that all the people of England could read the Bible for themselves.

Once, in Coventry, England, some parents were burned to death for teaching their children the Lord's Prayer and the Ten Commandments in English. Such atrocities drove Tyndale to tears. So he preached the Bible and encouraged the people to follow God's Word.

Once a rich and learned man, who was fed up with Tyndale's habit of quoting the Bible, shouted, "We would be better off without God's law than the pope's."

"I defy the pope and all his laws," Tyndale answered. "If God spares my life, in a few years a farm boy shall know more of the Scriptures than you do." Because of the great danger of attempting the translation in England, Tyndale secretly crossed the English Channel in 1524 to the mainland of Europe. Living life as a hunted man, he crisscrossed the lands of Western Europe, labored tirelessly on the translation, and stayed one step ahead of his pursuers.

Despite the danger and hardships, Tyndale completed the translation of the New Testament and had it printed and smuggled into England. Merchants hid the New Testaments among the cargo, sneaking it past the king's agents, who searched all ships for the contraband books. Thousands of copies slipped into the country tucked away in boxes of linen or barrels of grain. Church and government leaders knew that if they failed to stop Tyndale, a flood of inexpensive English Bibles would inundate the land, enabling the people to read God's Word for themselves. They seized many copies of the New Testament, publicly burned them, and declared him a heretic.

When word of their deeds got back to Tyndale, he said, "I expected they would burn the New Testament, and they may one day burn me also. I am content to do God's will." With the New Testament completed, Tyndale plunged into the difficult task of translating Hebrew, the original language of the Old Testament, into English. The agents of the king were hot on his heels.

In 1529, when word came that his enemies were near again, he packed the completed English manuscripts of the first five books of the Old Testament and fled to Antwerp, Belgium, boarding a ship bound for Hamburg, Germany. He thanked God for another safe escape as the ship sailed north to Hamburg. But off the coast of Holland a terrible storm broke out, whipping the waters of the North Sea to a frenzy, destroying the mast, and driving the helpless ship upon the rocks. Tyndale and the other passengers narrowly escaped drowning by jumping into the frigid water and scrambling to shore.

In a few minutes, waves battered the ship to pieces. As Tyndale stood shivering in the rain on the beach, he watched as all his books and the labor of three years of translation were swept out to sea. But right there, he resolved to begin again. Tyndale boarded the next ship for Hamburg and translated Genesis, Exodus, Leviticus, Numbers, and Deuteronomy all over again. When they were completed, he secretly returned to Antwerp to see to their publication and shipment to England.

The wealthiest port in Europe, Antwerp conducted a bustling trade with England; a large number of English merchants lived there. Invited to stay in the home of a godly English merchant named Thomas Poyntz, Tyndale decided to stay in Antwerp. The Poyntz family provided him with a comfortable bed, fine meals, and a study room where he carried on his translation work. One day Tyndale met a young Englishman, Henry Phillips, who encouraged him to press on with his work.

"The people of England need to read the Scriptures for themselves," he said. But Henry Phillips was a spy paid by church leaders in England to kidnap Tyndale and bring him to trial. One evening, Phillips asked him to be his guest at dinner. He led him into a narrow alley where two officers lay in wait. They pounced on Tyndale, tied him with ropes, and threw him into a damp dungeon cell in the castle of Vilvorde, a huge medieval fortress.

Although he faced execution, Tyndale did not despair. His one regret was that he had translated only one-third of the Old Testament. For eighteen months he languished in the rat-infested hole, while the authorities prepared their case against him. In the meantime, they tried bribery, threats, and abuse to get him to recant, but he stood firm in his faith, as immovable as the castle's massive stone walls.

In the darkness of his cell, Tyndale prepared his own defense by writing a paper entitled: *Faith Alone Justifies*

Before God. In it, he explained the good news of the Bible, showing from the Scriptures that all who trust in Christ are forgiven. While in prison, Tyndale, like the apostle Paul in Philippi, so impressed the jailer with his Christian character and sound arguments that the jailer and several members of his family believed in Jesus Christ.

When the trial finally began Tyndale stood alone. They charged him with heresy for teaching that sinners are made right with God by faith alone, that Christians do not need to go through a priest to have their sins forgiven, and that people should be able to read the Bible in their own language. Tyndale defended his teaching with Scripture and refused to recant.

The court pronounced him guilty on all charges and sentenced him to be burned at the stake. In October of 1536, guards chained William Tyndale to a wooden post and surrounded him up to the waist with kindling, straw, and logs sprinkled with gun powder. Church and state officials sat in front on cushioned seats of honor, and a large crowd of townspeople gathered to watch the execution. One last time, Tyndale raised his voice in prayer to God, "Lord, open the king of England's eyes."

A guard ignited the bonfire and William Tyndale died a painful death. But the Lord answered Tyndale's last prayer. Less than two years after the martyr's death, King Henry VIII granted permission for the publication of the Bible in English and decreed that a copy of the English Bible be placed in every church in the kingdom. Tyndale's translation was used nearly word for word in this first approved English Bible.

Not long after Tyndale's death, an English bishop declared to a gathering of churchmen, "The common people now know the Holy Scripture better than most of us." William Tyndale's life goal had been accomplished. The people of England were reading the Bible for themselves in their own language.

• • •

John Calvin
Theologian of the Reformation

John Calvin 1509–1563

In July of 1536, a young man with a long, sharp nose, pale face, and neatly trimmed black beard arrived in Geneva with a few traveling companions. He registered at an inn under the name Charles d'Espeville, went straight to his room, locked the door, and sat down, grateful for a chance to read and rest. But this was not to be; for as he entered the city he had been seen and recognized by someone who knew he wasn't Charles d'Espeville but John Calvin, a fugitive wanted by the king of France.

Calvin was a twenty-seven-year-old Protestant reformer and author of *The Institutes of Christian Religion*, a book which explained the central teachings of the Word of God. Church and state leaders condemned Calvin and his writings.

"I would have my own son beheaded," King Francis of France said, "if he followed these new heresies." Francis ordered the arrest, torture, and execution of French Protestant leaders, so Calvin fled France under an assumed name. His escape route led him through Geneva, Switzerland, a walled city of ten thousand people who had recently voted to become a Protestant city. There Calvin, settling in for the night, was startled by a knock at his hotel room door.

"Who's there?" he asked.

"William Farel," a strong voice answered. Farel, widely known as a bold preacher, was leading Geneva away from the traditions of the Roman Church and back to the teachings of the Scripture. Calvin invited him in. Although Farel's body was short and weak, he burst into the room like a thunderstorm. His sunburned face and red hair matched his fiery personality.

"Mr. Calvin," he said, pumping Calvin's hand vigorously, "thank God you're here. You must join me in the work at once!"

"I don't understand, Sir," Calvin said, "I will be leaving Geneva in the morning."

"No," Farel replied, "I'm afraid that won't do. We must have you here. The reformation of this city has just begun, and I need your help."

"But Sir," Calvin said, "I'm a scholar, not a minister. Besides, I'm too shy and inexperienced for such a work. I plan to devote my energies to private study and writing." Unwilling to take no for an answer, Farel pled with Calvin to stay and teach the people and organize the church. Calvin remained unmoved. "Mr. Farel," he said, "my plans are set. I must keep free from other duties to study and write."

Farel leaned forward in his chair, his eyes ablaze. Pointing his finger at Calvin he warned in a loud voice, "You are following your own wishes, and I tell you in the name of God Almighty, that if you do not help us in this work of the Lord, the Lord will punish you for seeking your own interests rather than His."

Calvin sat trembling in shocked silence, terror-struck. Farel's words came to him as if from an Old Testament prophet. "I felt," he later said, "as if God from on high had stretched out his hand and took hold of me." He agreed to stay in Geneva.

Shortly after Calvin arrived in Geneva, a religious debate was held in Lausanne. The citizens crowded into the cathedral to hear an open discussion between the Reformers and the Roman Catholics. One hundred seventy-four Roman clergymen attended. Farel, the chief spokesman for the Reformers, brought Calvin along. For three days they debated, but Calvin said nothing.

Farel poked and prodded him to speak but he said, "You

know well how to answer all questions. Why should I interfere?"

"But you have so much insight and knowledge," Farel said. "It's a shame your shyness keeps you from using it."

On the fourth day, a priest claimed the writings of Augustine and the early church fathers supported the teachings of the Roman Church. "You men," he said, pointing his finger at the Reformers, "stand against the church fathers." Farel, uncertain how to answer, prepared to stammer a reply when suddenly Calvin rose to speak. All eyes were fixed upon him.

"Honor the holy church fathers," he said, looking the priest squarely in the eyes. "If you read them more carefully you would not speak as you do." For over an hour he quoted from memory whole passages from Augustine, Tertullian, and others, arguing that the church fathers agreed with Scripture and the Protestants. "Judge for yourselves whether we are hostile to the Church Fathers," he said, "and admit that you hardly know what they taught." When Calvin finished, he had destroyed the arguments of the priests. The churchmen looked one to another, but no one said a word. Not a single man stood up to refute him. No one in the audience had ever heard anything like it.

After several minutes of awkward silence, a Franciscan friar, his brown robe tied about his waist with a rope, stepped forward. He was John Tandy, a preacher and sworn enemy of the Protestants.

"Based on what I have just heard," he said, "I confess that I have sinned against the Spirit and rebelled against the truth. Because of ignorance I have lived in error and spread wrong teaching. I ask God's pardon and the forgiveness of the people of Lausanne. I give up my role as friar; from now on I will follow Christ and His pure teaching alone." Not long after the debate, more than one hundred priests, monks, and friars became Protestants. Lausanne was won for the Reformation.

In Geneva, Calvin preached daily, visited the sick,

counseled the troubled, organized the church, started a college, and wrote commentaries on most of the books of the Bible. He slept just four hours a night. In all his teaching he emphasized God's sovereignty over all things and His love and mercy for His children. Many people turned to Jesus Christ for the forgiveness of their sins, and Geneva was transformed. It was said that prayer and psalm singing never ceased in the city. Fighting, cursing, drunkenness, and gambling nearly disappeared. A hospital, schools, and homes for the poor were built. Widows and orphans were cared for.

But some in Geneva hated John Calvin and his teachings. He preached obedience to God's commands. His main enemies, called Libertines, wanted to live as they pleased. They fired guns outside his home, sent death threats, and banished him from the city for a time. Because Calvin believed that Christ alone was the head of the church and that the church was free from state control, he was often at odds with the ruling council of Geneva. A crisis came when the council decided it would determine whether a person who was excommunicated or barred from the Lord's Supper by the leaders of the church should be restored and permitted to take the bread and wine again. Calvin refused to agree to this interference with the church.

Several Libertines who had been barred from the Lord's Supper for scandalous sins came to St. Peter's Cathedral one Sunday armed with swords, intending to take the Lord's Supper by force if necessary. Calvin led the worshippers who thronged the cathedral in prayer and psalm singing. Then he climbed the spiral staircase to the large raised pulpit.

"God has brought us into His family," he said. "As a most excellent Father concerned for His children, He gives us food to nourish us. Therefore through His Son, He gives us the bread and wine, the life-giving body and blood of Christ. But," he added, "this spiritual food is turned into deadly poison for those who partake unworthily, casting them down to greater ruin." He ended the sermon saying:

"I will not give the bread and wine to anyone whom the church has forbidden to receive it, and woe to any who tries to take it by force."

Then he came down and stood before the communion table. The Libertines, their swords strapped to their sides, pressed forward, determined to partake in the Supper. With his arms outstretched over the table and the loose sleeves of his black robe hanging over the bread and wine, Calvin looked straight at them and said: "You may break these arms, and you may take my life, but you will never force me to defile the table of the Lord." The Libertines halted red-faced, then withdrew in shame. The sanctuary fell silent. In awe and holy reverence, the Lord's Supper was celebrated.

Calvin's frail body often suffered from sickness, but this did not keep him from his work. Once when he was gravely ill, a friend found him sitting up in bed and writing a letter.

"You need to rest. Put away your work."

"What!" Calvin said. "Would you have the Lord find me idle when He comes?" When Calvin lay near death, his last visitor was his old friend, William Farel. "William," Calvin said to him, "Christ is our reward in life and death." John Calvin's writings continue to point sinners to Jesus Christ and instruct Christians in the deepest truths of the Bible.

• • •

Anne Askew
The Lord's Bold Witness

Anne Askew 1521–1546

Late in the reign of King Henry VIII, when the Church of England still clung to many false beliefs, an enraged husband burst into his home shouting for his wife, Anne. A priest had just taunted him saying, "Your wife is a heretic! She openly renounces the teachings of the church."

Anne Askew, a beautiful young woman, came running to her husband. Grabbing her by the arm, he dragged her to the front door and violently threw her out of the house.

"Get out and never return," he cried. Banished from her home and uncertain where to turn, Anne went to live near her brother in London. Her brother, a soldier in King Henry VIII's bodyguard, introduced her to the Queen, Catherine Parr, and several devout Christian ladies of the court. Catherine was Henry's sixth wife. Henry divorced two of his previous wives and had two others beheaded.

Before long, Askew and the Christian ladies were meeting daily in the queen's private rooms to hear a sermon, pray, and study the Bible. Although the king had decreed all such religious meetings illegal, he did nothing to stop her. This was a difficult time for the Protestants of England. For although Henry VIII had separated the churches in England from the Church of Rome, he did so not because he embraced the ideas of the Protestant Reformation, but because he wanted a divorce, which the pope refused to grant. Henry and his supporters in the Church of England clung to the doctrines of the Catholic Church, many of which were against the clear teachings of the Bible.

The churchmen who hated the Reformation decided to make an example of Anne Askew. By attacking her, they hoped to scare the queen and others of the royal court away from the Protestant Reformers. Askew's outspokenness about her faith made her an easy target.

Once she said, "I would rather read five lines in the Bible than hear five masses in the church." She openly declared that the bread and wine of the Lord's Supper were not changed by the priest into the physical body and blood of Jesus as the Roman Catholics taught. For these beliefs, Askew was arrested and thrown into prison. The Lord Mayor of London and a judge questioned her at length.

"Why did you say that you would rather read five lines in the Bible than hear five masses?" the judge asked.

"Because the one helps me greatly," Askew answered, "and the other does nothing at all."

"Have you the Spirit of God in you?" he asked.

"If I don't," Askew replied, "I am unsaved and without hope."

"Do you think private masses help the souls of those who have died?" he asked.

"It is great idolatry to believe them to be of more value than the death that Christ died for us," she said.

Looking down his nose at Anne, the Lord Mayor said, "You foolish woman, in the mass after the priest says the words of consecration over the bread, does it not become the Lord's body?"

"No," Askew answered, "it is but consecrated or sacramental bread."

"What if a mouse should eat it after the priest's consecration?" the Mayor asked her. "What do you say, foolish woman, will become of the mouse?"

Askew replied, "What do you say will become of it, my Lord?"

"I say the mouse is damned," the Lord Mayor answered.

Anne Askew smiled and said, "Ah, poor mouse!"

Next came Edmund Bonner, Bishop of London, who visited Askew in prison, determined to drag a recantation out of her. Beforehand, he had drawn up a list of beliefs of the Catholic faith. Thrusting the list into Askew's hands, he ordered her to sign it. She carefully read it and then wrote at the bottom of the page, "I believe everything written here which agrees with the Holy Scripture." As Bishop Bonner read the statement, his cheeks flamed red. Snatching the pen from her hand, he scratched out her sentence and thrust the paper and pen back demanding, "Sign this document!" Askew wrote, "I, Anne Askew, do believe many things contained in the faith of the Catholic Church."

Enraged at Askew's refusal to comply, he hurried out of her cell saying, "She is a woman, and I am not deceived by her." Three months later, the bishop hauled Askew before a church court which declared her a heretic and sentenced her to death by burning.

"I have searched all the Scriptures," Askew said to the court, "yet I have never found that either Christ or His apostles put anyone to death." Back in her prison cell she wrote a poem of faith in Christ:

> Like as the armed knight
> Appointed to the field,
> With this world will I fight,
> And faith shall be my shield.

The court sent Askew to the Tower of London to be tortured in hopes that she would give them evidence against the ladies of the royal court. Soldiers shackled her wrists and ankles with chains, threw her on the rack, and turned two wooden cranks, pulling her arms in one direction and her legs in another. Askew grimaced in pain as ligaments and tendons in her arms and legs were pulled tight.

"Tell us who else defies the king and the church. Renounce your faith and you will be pardoned," they demanded.

"I will sooner die than break my faith," she answered. Seeing that she would not break, the guards returned her to her dungeon cell, where falling to her knees she prayed,

"O Lord, I have more enemies now than hairs on my head; yet, Lord, let them never overcome me with vain words, but fight Lord, in my place, for on You I cast my care."

On the sixteenth of July, 1546, a huge crowd gathered to view the execution of Anne Askew and three other prisoners in front of St. Bartholomew's church in Smithfield, London. Because of the torture, Askew was unable to walk and had to be carried to the stake.

Before the burning, the bishop delivered a sermon during which Askew pointed out statements contrary to the Bible by saying, "He errs and speaks without the Book." As soldiers chained Askew to the stake and made ready the bonfire, a messenger arrived offering the king's pardon if she would recant. "I did not come here," Askew said, "to deny my Lord and Master." Then she died for Christ in the flames.

A year later, Henry VIII died and the Protestant Reformation moved forward quickly. The beliefs that Anne Askew died for became the teachings of the Church of England. Anne Askew's bravery in the face of death still shines as a beautiful example of the faithfulness of God to uphold His children in the midst of great trial.

> On Thee my care I cast,
> For all their cruel spite
> I set not by their haste,
> For Thou art my delight.

• • •

Latimer, Ridley, and Cranmer
The Bishop Martyrs

Hugh Latimer 1485–1555
Nicholas Ridley 1500–1555
Thomas Cranmer 1489–1556

Mary Tudor, crowned Queen of England in the summer of 1553, mustered all her power to drag the Church of England back into the Roman Catholic Church, burning or beheading more than three hundred men, women, and children who refused to give up their faith. Because of her ruthlessness, the queen earned the nickname "Bloody Mary." Among the martyrs were the Bishops Cranmer, Ridley, and Latimer.

Thomas Cranmer, archbishop of Canterbury, brought the English Bible to every church in the land, and with the help of Nicholas Ridley, the brilliant bishop of London, wrote *The Book of Common Prayer* and the *Articles of Religion*, which laid down the biblical worship practices and beliefs of the Church of England. And Bishop Hugh Latimer preached the good news of Jesus Christ with greater boldness than anyone in England.

For over twenty-five years, Latimer, Ridley, and Cranmer labored to advance the Protestant Reformation in England. But in 1553, soldiers under orders from Queen Mary seized the three bishops, hauled them to the Tower of London, and threw them into the dungeon. A royal proclamation condemned their books as well as those of Luther, Tyndale, and others. After suffering for months in the dark cells of the Tower, they were sent to Oxford for trial.

A great crowd thronged St. Mary's Church in Oxford, eager to witness the trial of the famous bishops. Ridley and Latimer were tried first, before a tribunal of church officials and university professors. The chief accuser, putting on a concerned expression, rose and approached the white-haired, seventy-year-old Latimer saying, "Master Latimer, for God's love consider your position, you have had the office of bishop; you are a learned man. Consider that if you die now, you die without grace, for outside the Church of Rome there can be no salvation." Latimer's Bible hung from a leather strap on his belt; his spectacles, tied to a string around his neck, rested on his chest. Though Latimer's body was stooped with pain, he stood as straight as he could and answered.

"I know perfectly by God's Word that the true church is in all the world, but its foundation is not in Rome only as you say. The true church is ruled by the Scriptures."

The churchman pointed at Ridley and Latimer and demanded, "Swear allegiance to the pope, confess your heresies, and you will live." But Ridley and Latimer stood their ground and attempted to respond with biblical answers, though they were often interrupted with hisses from their accusers, who acted more like barnyard animals than scholars. After two days of hearings, the church court excommunicated them from the church and turned them over to the Crown for punishment. Queen Mary ordered their execution.

On Wednesday, October 16, 1555, most of Oxford gathered across from Balliol College, outside the town's north gate, to watch the executions. Ridley wore a black robe, Latimer a worn coat and buttoned cap. The two men warmly embraced when they met at the stake.

Ridley smiled and said, "Be of good heart, brother, for God will either ease the pain of the flames or else strengthen us to endure it."

Latimer nodded saying, "God is faithful. He will not let us be tempted beyond what we can bear." They knelt in the dirt and prayed, then spoke quiet words of comfort to one another. A priest delivered a sermon accusing Latimer and Ridley of terrible heresies, condemning them to the fires of hell.

At the close of the sermon Ridley asked, "May we say a few words to the people?"

"No!" thundered the priest, "You may speak only to recant your errors."

"Well then," said Ridley, "I commit our cause to Almighty God who shall fairly judge all." They removed their coats and prepared to die.

Ridley lifted his hands and prayed, "O Heavenly Father, I give to You most hearty thanks, for You have called me to be faithful unto death. Lord God, have mercy upon the realm of England and save her from all her enemies." Guards strapped the two bishops to the stake with a single iron chain, binding them tightly around the waist, and surrounded them with straw and wood.

As the bailiff stepped forward with a torch, Latimer said, "Be of good cheer, Master Ridley, and play the man. We shall this day, by God's grace, light such a candle in England, as I trust, will never be put out."

As the flames rose up, Ridley said in a loud voice, "Lord, receive my spirit."

And Latimer said, "Lord, receive my soul."

Meanwhile, Thomas Cranmer, stripped of his ministerial robes and dressed in rags, was threatened and abused. His persecutors scraped his hands and fingers raw, signifying that he was no longer a minister of the church. Through it all, Cranmer refused to condemn the Protestant Reformation or his writings. Then his persecutors changed tactics. They transferred Cranmer from his dank prison cell to a comfortable room in the home of an Oxford dean. Scholars and priests lavished him with kindness, urging him to return to the Church of Rome.

"Dr. Cranmer," they told him, "if you would just recant some of your views you would win the queen's favor and be quickly restored to your great office in the church." After enduring harsh treatment for three years, the kindness threw Cranmer off guard. Little by little, he agreed to change his mind, until at last he signed his name to a paper which read: "I, Thomas Cranmer, late bishop of Canterbury, do renounce all heresies and errors not in agreement with the Church of Rome. I acknowledge the pope as the supreme head of the church whom all must obey. I believe in the seven sacraments, purgatory, and prayers to the saints. I am sorry that I ever thought otherwise and led others away from the Church of Rome."

Hoping to discourage the Protestants, church leaders printed his confession and publicized it throughout England. Yet despite his confession, Queen Mary insisted on his death and sentenced him to burn at the stake. Church officials decided that on the morning of the execution, Cranmer should speak against the Reformation and warn everyone against the Protestant faith.

St. Mary's Church overflowed with spectators who had come to hear the old archbishop speak and to watch him die. All eyes fixed on Cranmer, who wore a torn, dirty robe and stood on a raised platform opposite the pulpit. He bowed his bald head as he listened to a preacher condemning the Reformation and Cranmer's part in it.

"But," the preacher added, his eyes scanning the assembled throng, "Dr. Cranmer has confessed his sins and recanted his errors and he will address you now."

Cranmer knelt, sighed deeply, and prayed, "O Father, have mercy on me, most miserable sinner. I have offended against both heaven and earth, more than I can say. Have mercy upon me, O Lord, for Your great mercy." Then he rose and faced the congregation, tears brimming in his eyes. "I desire to speak a few words before I die by which God might be glorified and you might be instructed in the faith."

In solemn tones, he urged them to love one another and care for the poor. "And now," he said, raising his voice for all to hear, "I come to the great thing which troubles my conscience more than anything I ever did in my whole life.

I now renounce the things written with my hand against the truth in my heart. I feared death. I wrote the recantation to save my life. And because my hand has offended, writing against my heart, therefore my hand shall be punished first, for when I come to the fire it shall be burned first. And as for the pope, I refuse him as Christ's enemy with all his false doctrines."

"Stop the heretic's mouth," someone cried. Murmurs and shouts erupted throughout the church. "Lead the heretic away!" came the order. As the crowd jeered loudly, guards pulled Cranmer from the platform and rushed him through the drizzling rain to the same spot where his friends, Ridley and Latimer, were killed.

As the fire began to rise, Cranmer, true to his word, stretched out his right hand, held it unflinchingly in the flames and said, "This unworthy right hand. This hand has offended." He too died in the flames.

The candle lit by Ridley, Latimer, and Cranmer was not put out. Their brave deaths strengthened the Protestants to press on. Within a few years, Bloody Mary died, and the Reformation was fully restored in England.

• • •

John Knox
Scottish Reformer

John Knox c. 1514–1572

In 1547, the French galley, *Nostre Dame*, cut through the rough waters of the English Channel. One hundred and fifty slaves, straining at the oars, pulled it forward. Chained night and day to the rowing bench, the slaves, suffering from sun, wind, and rain, barely survived on scanty rations of biscuits and water. Disease swept through the crowded galleys and many men died. These convicted criminals, sentenced to the galleys for life, were among the most violent and cruel men in France. But one slave aboard the *Nostre Dame* was neither a Frenchman nor a criminal. He was a thirty-three-year-old Scottish minister named John Knox.

Knox suffered the horrors of the galleys because he sought to reform the church in Scotland. But he had not always been a reformer. Growing up in a church which forbade the reading of Scripture and where ignorance and superstition abounded, Knox accepted the church's teachings without question. But when the ideas of Martin Luther and the Protestant Reformation crossed the North Sea, Knox and many other Scots began reading the Bible for themselves. John Knox put his faith in Christ after reading John 17, "Now this is eternal life: that they may know you are the only true God, and Jesus Christ, whom you have sent."

Reformation ideas divided Scotland. Church leaders arrested and killed a number of Protestants. Some Protestants wrongly sought revenge, destroying church property. A small band even murdered an archbishop. Fear and suspicion reigned, and people armed themselves and travelled in groups for safety. John Knox rallied to the Protestant cause, bought a long, two-handed sword, and volunteered to guard George Wishart, a friend and gifted preacher, who lived under the constant threat of death. Wishart, a peace-loving man, urged the Protestants to forsake violence. But still the church leaders seized him and burned him at the stake in St. Andrews.

"Never before in Scotland," Knox said, "was there a man of such graces." John Knox, taking up the work of his martyred friend, preached throughout Scotland. "By God's grace," Knox said, "I declare Jesus Christ, the strength of His death, and the power of His resurrection." Scots turned to Christ by the thousands. The rulers of Scotland, fearful of losing power to the Protestants, petitioned France for help. Ships of the French navy attacked the castle of St. Andrews where Knox served as minister and condemned him to a slave galley along with many of his countrymen. There, in prison rags and leg irons, Knox endured the un-relenting toil and the blistering crack of the slave driver's whip across his back. "The torment I suffered in the gal-leys," he said later, "brought forth sobs of my heart." Though battered and bruised in body and spirit, his faith in God remained unshaken.

Once when Knox lay near death from illness, James Balfour, a Scotsman and fellow slave, asked him, "John, do you think we will ever get out of here alive?"

Knox struggled to raise his head and answered in a faint but steady voice, "I know the Lord will deliver us. Don't forget that Satan made Joseph go into Egypt, but God meant it for good to rescue His people. Don't lose hope, brother. God is faithful. We will return to our homeland and God will give us the victory."

At one time, the *Nostre Dame* traveled across to Scot-land and James Balfour said to Knox, "Look ashore, can you tell where we are?" Knox, lifting himself from the rough wooden bench, craning his neck and peering over the deck, caught a glimpse of St. Andrews.

"Yes, I know it well," Knox said, "for I see the steeple of that place where God first opened my mouth in public to His glory, and I know, no matter how weak I am now, that I shall not die until I shall glorify His godly name there again."

After nearly two years in chains, France released him due to the intervention of English Protestants. Knox went to England to help advance the Reformation there. His knowledge of the Bible and dynamic preaching won the admiration of King Edward VI, who invited Knox to preach regularly before the royal court. Knox, who only a few months before rowed in a slave galley, now proclaimed God's Word to kings and princes.

When King Edward died suddenly, Mary Tudor took the throne, vowing to return England to the Catholic Church. "Bloody Mary" sentenced hundreds of Protestants to death. Knox fled to Switzerland, befriending John Calvin in Geneva. The Genevan church welcomed Protestant refugees from all over Europe and generously provided for their needs. "It is the most perfect school of Christ on earth since the days of the apostles," Knox said.

After twelve years in exile, Knox finally returned to Scotland. During his absence, church leaders condemned him as a heretic and the crown declared him an outlaw. Anyone who communicated with Knox did so under pain of death. Yet when John Knox arrived in Scotland, huge crowds rushed out to greet him and hear him preach. He spoke plainly, yet with great passion, inspiring the Scots to follow Christ and emboldening them to resist anyone who would deny their freedom to worship God as Scripture commands. "The voice of that one man," a Scot said, "is able in one hour to put more life in us than five hundred trumpets continually blustering in our ears." When Knox preached at the church in St. Andrews, he remembered the day he had seen its steeple from his ship so many years before and praised God for His faithfulness.

The rulers of Scotland, with the help of French troops, tried to crush the Protestants, but they fought back. Although shot at and threatened, Knox pressed on, inspiring the people to hold fast bravely to their faith. Several times the Queen of Scotland summoned Knox to appear before her. Convinced that she held absolute power to rule her subjects, she despised Knox and the Protestants who taught the people to follow God before any other.

"You are teaching the people to believe things I have not allowed," she told him. "How can this be right since God commands subjects to obey their rulers?"

"Madam," Knox answered, "Your subjects are not bound to follow what you feel is right but what God's Word declares to be true." The beautiful young queen expected doting submission from her people, and Knox's blunt remarks turned her creamy, white cheeks crimson.

"How dare you speak to me like that!" the queen said, fanning her flushed face. "I have put up with you for too long. I shall be revenged."

"I must obey God," Knox said. "His Word commands me to speak plainly and flatter no one on the face of the earth." Eventually the Protestants gained control of Scotland. John Knox, with other ministers, created a church grounded in Scripture. He wrote the Scots Confession which explained clearly the main truths found in the Word of God and laid out biblical guidelines for worship. Knox urged the churches throughout the land to build schools to educate every Scottish child.

As Knox grew older, he suffered greatly from stomach ailments that came from the harsh treatment he'd received in the slave galleys. Although so weak he had to be carried into the pulpit, he continued preaching to the day of his death. At his funeral a Scottish noble said, "Here lies one who never feared the face of man."

• • •

Jeanne d'Albret
Reformation Queen

Jeanne d'Albret 1528–1572

During the Reformation, the kings of France, fearing that the Huguenots, the French Protestants, would divide their kingdom, persecuted them without mercy. Though burned at the stake, drowned in rivers, and cut down by the sword, the number of Huguenots still grew. Many Huguenots, like John Calvin, fled the country for the safety of Switzerland. After Calvin became the chief minister in Geneva, the Genevan Church became a haven and model for the Huguenots.

In most places in France, the Huguenots worshipped in secret, gathering in fields or barns to sing God's praises from the Genevan Psalm book, read from Scripture, and hear a sermon. Huguenot ministers, many of them trained by Calvin in Geneva, disguised themselves and used false names to protect their identities. "Send us wood," Calvin told the Huguenots, "and we will send you back arrows." The arrows he referred to were well-trained preachers. These brave young men returned to France knowing they faced certain death.

On Christmas Day in 1560, a courageous and devout woman strengthened the Huguenot cause. Jeanne d'Albret, Queen of Navarre, publicly proclaimed, "I am a follower of the Reformed faith." With her husband, Anthony, Jeanne ruled Navarre, a small kingdom allied with France and located on the border with Spain. Anthony was a French nobleman in line to the throne of France. For years they had brought Protestant ministers to their court and sent money to support those who fled to Geneva. Yet they feared to declare themselves Protestant since their tiny kingdom was surrounded by powerful Catholic countries. But finally Jeanne believed herself compelled to stand for the truth, no matter the cost.

"The Reformation of the Christian faith is so right and so necessary," she said, "that I would be disloyal and a coward before God and my people if I failed to join it." Like other Protestants, she embraced the Reformed faith because the Roman Church had strayed far from God's Word. "I follow Calvin and the other Reformed preachers," she said, "only in so far as they follow the Scriptures."

The kings of France and Spain, along with the pope, sprang into action to prevent Navarre from leaving the Roman Church. They promised Anthony land and money if he declared himself and his kingdom loyal to the Roman faith. He agreed. Crushed by her husband's lack of spiritual courage, Jeanne noted, "He planted a thorn in my heart."

Anthony brought Jeanne to Paris and made her a prisoner in her own quarters, threatening to divorce her unless she returned to the Roman Church. She still refused. French officials urged her to follow the lead of her husband. "You may lose everything you have if you don't change your faith," they warned her.

"I would rather plunge my kingdom to the bottom of the ocean than do that," she said. Jeanne fled Paris for Navarre and used her power to promote the Reformed faith in her kingdom. She purified the churches in her realm of images, called Genevan pastors to preach to her people, and established Reformed seminaries. Jeanne herself wrote essays to defend and persuade others of the Reformed faith. She regularly used her personal funds, even selling her own jewels, to support Reformed schools, pay pastors' expenses, and print Bibles. She had the Bible translated into Bearnnois, the language of Navarre, and encouraged her subjects to study God's Word for themselves.

But the situation for the French Huguenots grew more perilous. In Vassy, soldiers massacred hundreds of Huguenots gathered in a barn for worship, and they slaughtered three thousand more at Toulousse. Finally, the Huguenots took up arms to defend themselves. Anthony led an army into battle against them, laying siege to a Huguenot city. Yet a musket ball fired from the wall ripped through his arm; he later died from the wound.

Jeanne, now ruling her kingdom alone, decreed that in Navarre both Roman Catholics and Huguenots were free to worship. The pope dispatched a French cardinal to persuade her to forbid Huguenot worship in her kingdom.

"Your majesty," he told Jeanne, "You are being misled by evil men who want to plant a new religion in Navarre. If you go ahead with this, you will never succeed. Your subjects will not stand for it and your enemies will stop you. You do not have an ocean to protect you like Queen Elizabeth of England." He called the Huguenots murderers, rebels, and heretics. "Madame," he said, "Don't let these people ruin your conscience, your goods, and your grandeur. I implore you with tears to return to the true fold."

Jeanne leaned forward, looked the cardinal squarely in the eye, and answered boldly, "Your feeble arguments do not dent my tough skull. I am serving God and He knows how to protect His cause. Our ministers preach nothing but obedience, patience, and humility. Keep your tears for yourself. I pray from the bottom of my heart that you may be brought back to the true fold and the true Shepherd."

Eventually the struggle between the Huguenots and the French Catholics exploded into war. Thousands on both sides perished. At the battle of Jarnac, when the leading Huguenot general was killed, the troops wavered, uncertain if they could fight on. Jeanne raced to the field with her son, Henry—an heir to the throne, and rallied the men to victory. But Jeanne, hating the bloodshed, sent a letter to the king of France. "I am confident in your natural goodness and fatherly love for your people," she wrote. "I beg you to take to heart the misery which this war has caused. If you will let your subjects worship as Catholics or as Reformed, your name will be celebrated by all nations."

At last, in 1571, both sides, exhausted from war, signed a peace treaty. In order to strengthen the peace, the Queen Mother of France, Catherine de Medici, suggested that Jeanne's son, Henry of Navarre, marry her daughter, Margaret, hoping that if a Huguenot prince married a Catholic princess that peace would be secured. Jeanne d'Albret stood firmly against it. But Huguenot leaders throughout France pleaded with her to accept the marriage for the sake of peace. "Perhaps it will lead to greater religious freedom," they told her.

Reluctantly, she finally agreed, but Jeanne warned her son to remain true to the Word of God no matter what his future wife might do. Jeanne traveled to Paris to make the wedding arrangements, but while there she fell gravely ill. Many believed she was poisoned. On her deathbed, she asked to hear some chapters in the Gospel of John read. She died with the words of Jesus sounding in her ears: "In this world you will have trouble. But take heart! I have overcome the world" (John 16:33).

Two months later, Henry of Navarre married Margaret in Paris. Huguenot leaders from all of France gathered for the royal wedding. But Catherine de Medici, scheming to destroy them once and for all, told her son, King Charles, that the Huguenots must be wiped out or he would never control France.

Full of anger, Charles shouted, "By God's death! I want all the Huguenots of France killed. See to it immediately!" A few days after the wedding, French troops received the order against the Huguenots. "Kill them all, the king commands it."

Archers, horsemen, and foot soldiers fanned out across Paris to attack the ten thousand Huguenots visiting the city. The Paris rabble joined in when the king's soldiers shouted: "Kill them! Massacre the Huguenots!"

Mobs ran wild through the streets, breaking into houses, killing Huguenots, running them through with daggers, or throwing them headlong from buildings. They knocked little children and old people senseless and cast them into the river to drown. Soldiers, trying to clear the streets of dead bodies, wheeled carts loaded with corpses to the river and dumped them in, turning the water red.

This happened on August 23, 1572, the Feast of St. Bartholomew, and so this terrible day is remembered as the St. Bartholomew's Day Massacre. The killing of Huguenots continued across France for weeks. Tens of thousands of men, women, and children were slaughtered.

Yet the massacre sparked a renewal of war which continued for many years until Jeanne's son, Henry, was crowned king of France. Although Henry did not hold to the Reformed faith as his mother had, he gave the Huguenots freedom of worship by issuing the Edict of Nantes, which granted religious freedom to both Roman Catholics and Huguenots.

One of Jeanne's favorite passages of Scripture was Psalm 31. Just before she died, she had it read to her, and it beautifully expressed her own struggles and faith: "For I have heard the slander of many, Terror is on every side; . . . They schemed to take away my life. But as for me, I trust in Thee, O Lord, I say, 'Thou art my God.' Make Thy face to shine upon Thy servant; save me in Thy lovingkindness."

• • •

Renee
Duchess of Ferrara

Renee, Duchess of Ferrara 1510–1575

In autumn of 1534, Francis I, king of France, ordered a crackdown on French Protestants, the Huguenots. Agents of the king arrested and tortured Huguenot ministers, and church courts declared them heretics. Francis ordered them burned at the stake as a grand show.

On January, 21, 1535, Francis I, wearing robes of purple velvet, and his wife, Queen Claudia, glittering with precious jewels, led a great procession on horseback through Paris. The royalty of France and other dignitaries followed on foot, carrying lighted candles. The churchmen held aloft sacred relics, including items claimed to be Christ's crown of thorns and Moses' stone tables of the Ten Commandments. After the procession, they feasted at a great banquet and then watched the burning of six Huguenots.

Huguenot leaders fled the country to Germany, Switzerland, Navarre, and Ferrara, a small duchy in northern Italy. They escaped to Ferrara for the shelter and hospitality of Renee, duchess of Ferrara. Renee's deceased father was King Louis XII of France, and her sister, Claudia, reigned as queen of France. Renee's marriage in 1528 to Ercole Este, duke of Ferrara, was not a marriage of love but a political arrangement. The tiny duchy of Ferrara, in order to preserve its independence, needed to maintain friendly relations with France, the German empire, and the pope. King Francis I, eager to strengthen France's hand in northern Italy, arranged for his sister-in-law, Renee, to marry the duke of Ferrara. But strong religious differences separated the duke and Renee.

Duke Ercole defended the teachings of the Roman

Catholic Church. Renee followed the Protestant Reformers and supported Huguenot preachers. Renee's parents died
when she was a little girl, and she was raised by a govern-
ess, Madame de Soubise, who came to her from England
with a hidden copy of Wyclif's Bible in her luggage. She
opened Renee's eyes to the Word of God. As a teenager,
Renee devoured all the writings of the French Reformers
and later brought Madame de Soubise to Ferrara as a member
of her royal court. They prayed, worshipped, and studied
the Scriptures together, listening to Protestant preachers
Renee brought to her court.

As the persecution in France grew, many Huguenots
fled to Renee's court in Ferrara, and among them were
Clemont Marot, preacher and translator of the Psalms into
French verse, and John Calvin, author of the *Institutes of
the Christian Religion.* Renee's activities infuriated her husband. He threw Madame de Soubise out of the royal court
and forbade Renee to travel outside of Ferrara. He inter-
cepted her mail and removed Protestants from her court.

After church leaders ordered the arrest of Calvin and
Marot, Renee aided their escape. When the pope summoned
the Italian preacher, Orchino, to appear before the Inquisition in Rome, Renee helped him to flee from Italy to
Geneva, where he worked with Calvin. Renee regularly sent
money to the Protestant refugees in Geneva. She brought
an Italian scholar, Antonio Bruccioli, to her court and supported his work translating the Bible into Italian.

Jesuit priests in Ferrara sent word to the pope, report-
ing that the duchess ate meat during Lent, refused to
attend mass, and erected a private chapel in the castle without
a crucifix or images of the saints. The pope sent a repre-
sentative to interrogate Renee. She refused to see him.

"My confidence is in God and none other," she told her
husband. The duke brought the Inquisition to Ferrara and
threw many of his Protestant subjects in jail. Renee
asked him to release them. "I beg you very humbly," she
wrote him, "to free the prisoners you have sent to the

inquisitors. Remember the grief of the poor fathers, mothers, and little children of those you have imprisoned." The duke ignored her requests.

When the popular preacher, Fanino Fanini, fell into the duke's hands, Renee pleaded with tears for his release. Fanini preached to huge crowds using Bruccioli's Italian translation of the Bible. When he traveled through Ferrara, Duke Ercole's men seized him and cast him into prison. Many people gathered outside the barred window of his cell to hear Fanini preach the Word of God. To break up the crowds, jailers moved him to an inner cell. Renee often visited him in prison, bringing him food and fresh clothing. She fired off letters to church leaders and the king of France on his behalf. The pope demanded that Duke Ercole burn Fanini at once and purge his duchy of all Protestants. He complained of Renee's interference on Fanini's behalf.

"My wife often acts without our knowledge and against our will," the duke wrote the pope. "As a Christian and Catholic prince, I intend to give Fanini the punishment he deserves."

When word came to the prison that Fanini would soon be executed, a fellow prisoner asked him, "What will become of your children?"

"They have the best of guardians," Fanini answered.

His cell-mate looked puzzled and asked, "And who is their guardian?"

"Our Lord Jesus Christ," Fanini answered with a smile. Under orders from the duke, guards dragged Fanini from his cell to the place of execution. A wooden crucifix was thrust in his hand. "Do I need this bit of wood to remind me of my Savior?" Fanini said. "Christ reigns and is engraved on my heart." The duke's men strangled Fanini and threw his lifeless body into the Po River.

Duke Ercole launched an all-out effort to rid his wife of her heresy, enlisting the help of the king of France. The French king sent several inquisitors at once to Ferrara. For three months, they daily preached to Renee and grilled her on her beliefs and actions on behalf of the Protestants. Renee told them that she was neither a Lutheran nor a Calvinist but simply a Christian. Her defiance forced the duke's hand. He shut up Renee in solitary confinement in the castle and placed a guard outside her door. Her daughters were forbidden to see her and were sent to a convent. The inquisitor threatened her with life imprisonment and even death if she did not recant.

Finally, exhausted and in tears, Renee agreed to confess her sins to a priest and attend mass. Her trial ended and the duke restored some of her privileges, but he burned all her books and surrounded her with spies. He told her that he did not believe the sincerity of her confession but pretended publicly to believe her to spare the duchy the scandal of heresy. Her son, Alphonso, said he believed his mother deserved to be burned at the stake as a heretic. For the remaining five years of their marriage, Renee and the duke remained unreconciled until his death in 1559.

Outwardly Renee conformed, but secretly she kept up her correspondence with Protestant leaders and sent money to aid Protestant exiles in France and Switzerland. At the death of his father, Alphonso became duke. He detested Protestants more than his father had.

"I would rather live with the plague," he said while visiting the French court, "then live with Huguenots." Shortly after being crowned, he issued an ultimatum to his mother—either she give up her Protestant faith completely or be banished from Ferrara forever. Rather than abandon her faith, Renee left the country where she had reigned as duchess for thirty-two years and returned to France. "My Son," she wrote in a note as she departed, "I could not say to you what was in my heart for fear of being overwhelmed with tears."

Renee found France on the brink of civil war. The Parliament of Paris declared the death penalty for anyone worshipping as a Protestant. Soldiers and mobs massacred Huguenots in twenty French cities. Enraged Huguenots took up arms, broke into churches, smashed images, and shattered windows. In some places, monks and priests were killed. In one city, two hundred people died when a Huguenot mob sacked the cathedral. Renee spoke out against violence.

"We are to render good for evil," she urged the Huguenots. "Hate and Christianity are incompatible. We must seek peace with all." Upon returning to France, Renee took possession of her inheritance, the castle of Montargis. As troubles escalated, she expanded the moat, reinforced the walls, installed cannons, and welcomed hundreds of Catholic and Protestant refugees fleeing the bloodshed. She set up a chapel in the castle for Protestant worship and encouraged the preaching of the good news of Jesus throughout the city. Renee forbade violence from either side and sent her soldiers to stop pillaging and murder whether committed by Catholics or Huguenots.

Battles raged across France and Catholic forces invaded Montargis. A commander ordered her to surrender her castle, and when she refused he set up cannon and threatened to open fire.

Renee told the commander, "Consider well what you are planning to do. There is no one in this kingdom who commands me except the king himself. If you come I will throw myself into the breach and see whether you will have the audacity to kill the daughter of a king." The commander backed down and withdrew his forces from the city. The castle and the refugees were saved. Renee's protection and hospitality became known throughout France. Huguenots called her castle "The Hotel of the Lord."

John Calvin rejoiced in her work and wrote Renee saying, "I know that you have been like a nursing mother to those poor, persecuted brothers and sisters who did not know where to go. God has done you a great honor in allowing you to carry His banner."

While Renee was in Paris in 1572, the king ordered the massacre of Huguenots on St. Bartholomew's Day. Blood ran in the streets and thousands were slaughtered. Renee could hear shouts and screams. For a week, she and her ladies remained behind a locked door and an armed guard. She hastily returned to Montargis and threw open the gates of her castle to hundreds of Huguenots fleeing for their lives.

For the next two years, she endured sickness and pain and did what she could to preserve life. She died among her Christian friends but was separated from her children, who rejected her religious beliefs. The king of France forbade her body to be laid to rest in St. Denis, where French kings and queens and their children were buried. Renee's body was placed in a simple wooden casket and buried without ceremony within her castle walls.

In her will, she left a long statement of her faith in Jesus Christ and concluded with a note to her children: "I pray that my children will read and listen to the Word of God in which they will find comfort and the true guide to eternal life."

• • •

COVENANTER COMMUNION

Post-Reformation

Great Courage and Great Awakening

Persecution and blessing abounded in the seventeenth and eighteenth centuries. Enemies of the truth labored to stamp out religious freedom, and the Holy Spirit awakened countless people to faith in Jesus Christ.

- Gustavus Adolphus
  Warrior King

- Richard Cameron
  Lion of the Covenant

- The Two Margarets
  The Solway Martyrs

- John Bunyan
  Happy Pilgrim

- Jonathan Edwards
  Great Awakening Theologian

- George Whitefield
  Great Awakening Preacher

- John Wesley
  The World His Perish

- John Newton
  Slave Trader Saved by Grace

Gustavus Adolphus
Warrior King

Gustavus Adolphus 1594–1632

In the 1620s Ferdinand, the Roman Catholic emperor of Germany and king of Bohemia, determined to wipe out the Protestant faith. He declared, "I would rather be cut in pieces than allow the Church of Rome to be despised." He crushed the Protestants of Bohemia, killing tens of thousands of people and scattering the rest to the winds. "I would rather rule a country ruined than a country damned," he said. After overrunning the free cities of central Germany, the imperial army pressed further north. The king of Denmark moved to stop them, but the imperial army routed the Danish army and occupied the country, closing churches and seizing property. The work of the Reformation on the continent of Europe seemed to hang by a thread.

Then Gustavus Adolphus determined to enter the battle. Gustavus was a devout Christian and king of Sweden who had been agonizing over the Protestant losses in Europe and was sickened by the reports of the cruelty of the emperor's soldiers. On May 20, 1630, in the great hall of the Diet in Stockholm, King Gustavus, tall, muscular, and with bright blue eyes and golden hair, stood before the representatives of the government with his four-year-old daughter, Christine, in his arms. Although just thirty-five years old, he had already achieved great things for Sweden by winning many victories on the battlefield and ruling justly at home.

"Now I am about to begin a most important struggle," he told them with solemn voice. "Emperor Ferdinand has forced me to resort to arms. He has insulted us and persecuted our friends, our religious brethren who sigh for deliverance. With the help of God, they will not have sighed in vain." Faces throughout the great hall grew long and creased with concern as they contemplated the terrible risks that awaited their king and army.

"I know the dangers," he said. "This is why before leaving the country, I commend you, body and soul, to Almighty God, that He may protect you and unite us all together in heaven. Yes, dear people of Sweden, I commend you to the protection of God and bid you farewell, perhaps forever." As the king finished his speech, all broke down in tears. "Now let us pray," Gustavus called out to be heard above the sobbing. Everyone stood with heads bowed. "Our God, be kind and merciful to us. Grant success to the work of our hands. May the work of our hands glorify You."

High winds and stormy seas battered the Swedish troop ships attempting to cross the Baltic. After five weeks, all the king's men set foot on German soil. Gustavus knelt in the sand and led them in prayer: "My Lord and my God, You who rule the winds and the seas, how can I praise and thank You for the protection You granted during the dangerous voyage? I give You thanks from the depths of my heart. You know, O Lord, I haven't come for my own glory, but to help Your oppressed church. Protect us and bring victory in this sacred work." Gustavus stood up and saw tears in the eyes of his men. "Weep not," he told them, strapping his sword to his side, "but rather pray to God with all your heart. To pray often is almost to conquer."

Gustavus launched an all-out offensive. Though usually outnumbered, the Swedish army won victory after victory, putting the enemy to flight and freeing the oppressed. But soon the imperial army struck back with terrible vengeance, attacking helpless German cities far from the Swedish army.

When they captured Magdeburg, the Imperial commander, Tilly, ordered a mass execution. He had ministers dragged into the streets, doused with oil, and set on fire. He ordered a church full of women and children to be nailed shut from the outside and then burned it to the ground.

The entire city was put to the torch. Laughing soldiers tossed children into the flames for sport. Of the city's 34,000 people, nearly 30,000 were massacred.

King Gustavus wept because he was unable to reach Magdeburg in time to rescue them. The Magdeburg massacre awoke the German Protestants from their slumber and thousands rushed to fight alongside the Swedes. On September 6, 1631, Gustavus and his men and an army of German Protestants found Tilly's imperial troops on the hilly fields outside the village of Breitenfeld. Gustavus's men formed battle lines with the Swedes on one side and their German allies on the other. The singing of psalms could be heard from one end of the line to the other.

Gustavus, in full armor and mounted on his stallion, said to his men, "I count on the justice of our cause more even than our arms and our allies; for we fight for the glory of God and the true evangelical faith. The God of all goodness, who has miraculously brought us across seas and rivers, through fortresses and enemies, will strengthen us to conquer. This is why we will attack with courage. God is with us. May these words be our rallying cry, and with the help of the Almighty, victory will be ours." Tilly's battle-hardened and undefeated army controlled the high ground with cannons loaded and aimed. The heavily armed imperial infantry and cavalry were grouped in massive lines and ready to attack.

Gustavus rode to the center of his line, removed his hat, and prayed in a loud voice, "Good God, You hold in Your hand victory and defeat. Turn your merciful face to us, Your servants. We have come far, we have left our peaceful homes, to fight in this country for liberty and for Your gospel. Glorify your holy name in granting us victory." Then he ordered the attack. Deafening cannon fire roared across the field. As thousands of soldiers raced over the dry and newly plowed fields, thick clouds of dust were kicked up, making it difficult to see. Seven times Tilly's men attacked the center of the Swedish line, and seven times they were thrown back. Then they turned and struck at the German Protestants' line, separating it from the Swedes. Most of the Germans fled in panic. Gustavus's men now faced the imperial forces alone.

Tilly directed all the might of his army against the Swedes. Gustavus rode quickly to his left and regrouped his forces, riding up and down the line, encouraging his men to bravery. After repelling the first attack, Gustavus led his men on an assault of the high ground; they captured the cannons and then fired on the enemy with their own guns. The imperial troops ran from the battlefield in confusion.

Removing his helmet and falling to his knees, Gustavus joyfully thanked God for the great victory. The triumph at Breitenfeld liberated most of the German Protestants. Gustavus, no longer threatened by any army of the emperor, moved quickly across Germany. The German Protestants formed a league of protection under his direction. For a year, Gustavus won more victories and strengthened the Protestants' hold.

In the meantime, Emperor Ferdinand regrouped the imperial army and sent it to crush Gustavus Adolphus. The two armies squared off for battle outside the town of Lutzen on the morning of November 6, 1632. After Gustavus arranged his army for combat, they sang Martin Luther's song of Christian warfare, "A Mighty Fortress is Our God" and "Fear Not, O Little Flock, the Foe":

> Fear not, O little flock, the foe
> Who madly seeks your overthrow;
> Dread not his rage and power:
> What though your courage sometimes faints,
> His seeming triumph o'er God's saints
> Lasts but a little hour.

The whole army knelt and turned to God once more in prayer. Then Gustavus mounted his horse and rode through the ranks telling his men: "Prepare to show yourselves the brave soldiers you are. Hold firm, stand by each other, and fight valiantly for your faith, your country, and your king. May God preserve you all." A thick fog blanketed the field, delaying Gustavus from beginning the attack. But when the fog began to lift around eleven o'clock, he cried out, "Now in the name of God, onward! Jesus, make us fight for the glory of Your holy name."

Waving his sword high above his head, he shouted, "Forward!" and led the charge. Fierce fighting raged on all sides. Then Gustavus rallied his men for a daring counterattack. "Follow me, my brave boys," he cried and galloped his horse toward the enemy. In the confusion of battle and the returning fog, Gustavus became separated from his men. A musket ball shattered his left arm. He fell to the ground bleeding. Imperial soldiers ran forward.

"Who are you?" they demanded.

"I am the King of Sweden," Gustavus answered, "and this day I seal with my blood the liberty and the religion of the German nation!" They opened fire, killing him instantly. When the Swedish army learned of the death of their king, their blood boiled for vengeance. With courage and fury, they pressed the attack on all fronts, broke through the enemy's lines, and defeated the imperial army. Ten thousand men died in the battle, and the war dragged on for many more years, but Gustavus had lived long enough to ensure the survival of strong and free Protestant lands in Germany. The Reformation in Europe was saved.

• • •

Richard Cameron
Lion of the Covenant

Richard Cameron 1644–1680

On a late afternoon in 1680 in the Central Lowlands of Scotland, two armed groups faced one another across a marshy field. One side, far larger and better equipped, were dragoons, the soldiers of King Charles II, who had been tracking their enemy for months. On the other side of the field stood a small band of men, fewer than sixty in number, poorly armed and not professional soldiers but farmers and tradesmen, most with no horse to ride into battle. Their leader was not a military commander but a minister. They were Covenanters led by Richard Cameron, the Lion of the Covenant.

The Covenanters were brave Scots who would not give up their religious liberty to the king of England. King Charles tried to pressure the Christians of Scotland to worship in ways contrary to their church, but the Covenanters declared, "Christ alone is the Head of the church." As one Covenanter preacher told the king, "Sir, there are two Kings and two Kingdoms in Scotland; there is you, the head of this commonwealth, and there is Christ Jesus the King and His kingdom, the church. In Christ's kingdom, you are not a lord, nor a head, but a member."

Richard Cameron had never dreamed he would lead troops into battle against the king. He had lived the quiet life of a school teacher until he went out to the countryside to hear a field preacher at a conventicle, which was an illegal worship service conducted by a minister thrown out of his church for disobeying the king's orders. There Richard Cameron had heard about Jesus and had become a believer.

Not long after, Cameron became a lay preacher, urging others to turn to Christ for the forgiveness of their sins. But the king's men were jailing, torturing, and sometimes killing preachers, so Cameron and hundreds of others fled across the sea to Holland. There he studied the Bible intensely and was ordained a minister. But Cameron was determined to return even if it meant certain death. Before he left Holland, a Scottish minister placed his hand on Cameron's head and cried out, "Behold, here is the head of a faithful minister and servant of Jesus Christ, who shall lose his head for his Master's interest, and it shall be set up before the sun and moon in the view of the world."

After returning secretly to Scotland, Cameron preached in the hills, marshes, and fields. Seeing the terrible cruelties of the king's soldiers, Richard Cameron, his brother, Michael, and some other brave men joined together to fight the oppressors of Scotland. Though poorly armed and trained, they vowed to defend the innocent men, women, and children of Scotland. "Be not discouraged at the fewness of your number," Cameron told his followers, "for when Christ comes to raise up His own work in Scotland, He will not lack men enough to work for Him."

Refusing to hide their intentions, they rode boldly into the town square of Sanquhar on June 22, 1680, sang a psalm, said a prayer, and read a declaration: "We disown Charles Stuart, who has been reigning, or rather tyrannizing, on the throne of Britain for many years. He has no right to the crown of Scotland, for he has lied and broken his covenant both to God and His church. We, being under the standard of our Lord Jesus Christ, Captain of Salvation, do declare a war with the tyrant and all his men, as enemies of our Lord Jesus Christ."

King Charles ordered a large reward for the capture of Richard Cameron, dead or alive. Although hunted throughout the land, no one told the soldiers Cameron's whereabouts. Even on the run, he continued to preach and lead services. Finally, the king's soldiers caught up with Richard

Cameron and his men. Before the battle began, Cameron bowed his head, raised his voice, and led his men in prayer one last time, asking the Lord to protect the lives of those who were not yet ready to die. "Spare the green and take the ripe," he prayed.

He turned to his faithful brother, "Come Michael," he said, "let us fight it out to the last; for this is the day that I have longed for, to die fighting against our Lord's enemies, and this is the day that we shall get the crown."

He strengthened his friends saying: "Be encouraged all of you to fight it out valiantly, for all of you who fall this day I see heaven's gates cast wide open to receive them." Together, they sang a final song of praise to God and then the dragoons attacked, their horses' hoofbeats thundering across the field, their halberds and swords flashing. Though greatly outnumbered, the Covenanters fought bravely. But when the battle was ended, Richard and Michael Cameron and several of their men lay dead.

The king's men cut off Richard's head and hands and brought them as trophies to the Council at Edinburgh. As they entered the city, a soldier hoisted Cameron's head high on the tip of his lance shouting, "Here is the head of a traitor, a rebel." The council ordered that Cameron's head and hands be set high in a prominent place in Edinburgh as a warning to anyone who dared resist the king. Before the head and hands were set in place, the king's men performed a final act of cruelty. Cameron's father was in prison for supporting the cause of the Covenanters. Soldiers went to his cell and dropped the hands and head into his lap.

"Do you know them?" they asked.

"I know them, I know them," he said, kissing the head and hands. "They are my son's, my own dear son's." Overcome with grief, he broke down and wept. "It is the Lord," he said through his tears. "Good is the will of the Lord, who cannot wrong me nor mine, but has made goodness and mercy to follow us all our days."

Even Richard Cameron's enemies admired his faith and

courage and that of his father and brother. One who saw his head mounted in Edinburgh said, "There are the head and hands of a man who lived praying and preaching and died praying and fighting."

Eight more years of bitter persecution awaited the Covenanters before the Glorious Revolution swept away King Charles II and the Stuart family from the throne forever. Even though thousands more were killed for the faith, the life and death of Richard Cameron shone as one of the brightest lights for Christ during those dark days of persecution.

• • •

The Two Margarets
The Solway Martyrs

Margaret MacLachlan 1622–1685
Margaret Wilson 1667–1685

The year 1685 is known in Scotland as "the killing times." Soldiers of King Charles II of England hunted down thousands of men, women, and children and killed them in the cruelest ways imaginable. Why? What terrible wrong had they committed? How had they so greatly offended the king? This was their crime: they loved Jesus Christ, believed that He alone was the head of His church, and sought to worship Him as the Bible directed them to. These brave Scots were called Covenanters.

Two Covenanters, Margaret MacLachlan and Margaret Wilson, were among those put to death during "the killing times." Margaret MacLachlan, a poor, grey-haired widow known by her neighbors as a generous and devout Christian, lived humbly in a small cottage. Officers of the king warned her that she must forsake her Covenanter minister and worship God only in the way that the king ordered. Although threatened and harassed, she would not violate her conscience. One day as she knelt worshipping the Lord, soldiers burst in and hauled her off to jail. There she endured cold and hunger until the date of her trial.

Eighteen-year-old Margaret Wilson and her thirteen-year-old sister, Agnes, refused to submit to the king's rules for worship, avoiding the king's men by living in the mountain forests and the marshes with other Covenanters. Their family and friends were ordered not to visit them nor give them food, clothes, or shelter. On a cold winter day, the two sisters, lonely, wet, and hungry, sneaked into town to visit some friends. While enjoying a hot meal and warm fire, they were discovered and arrested. Margaret Wilson and her sister were thrown in prison and locked up in the "Thieves Hole," the darkest and dankest cell, which was reserved for the worst criminals. With many sighs and tears, they waited two months for their trial.

On April 13, 1685, the two slight and fair teenage girls and Margaret MacLachlan stood before the court. The judge peered down at them and gave them one more opportunity for freedom.

"Will you swear the oath recognizing the king as head over the church?" he asked.

"No," they answered quietly.

"Then this court finds you guilty of treason," the judge said, "for denying the king's sovereignty in the church and attending unlawful worship services and meetings in the countryside." They stood silently.

"Kneel before the court as I pronounce the sentences upon you," ordered the judge. When they refused to kneel, guards seized them and roughly forced them to their knees.

"Margaret MacLachlan, Margaret Wilson, and Agnes Wilson, you are guilty of treason against His Majesty's government," the judge declared, "and are hereby sentenced to death. You shall be tied to posts fixed in the sand within the tideland, and there to stand until the tidewater overflow you and drown you."

Mr. Wilson, the father of the girls, approached the bench and in a trembling voice pleaded with the judge to show mercy to his daughters. Because of Agnes's young age, the judge agreed to release her if her father paid a fine of one hundred pounds sterling. Mr. Wilson paid the large fine for Agnes, and then he leapt on his horse and galloped off to Edinburgh to appeal a higher court to overturn Margaret's death sentence.

A small company of soldiers marched the two condemned Margarets out of prison and to a deep channel leading to the Solway, an inlet of the Irish Sea. They drove two long wooden poles deep into the sand of the tidelands, tying the older woman to the stake furthest from shore and strapping young Margaret to the pole closest to the bank. She would be able to watch Mrs. MacLachlan die first. They wanted Margaret Wilson to watch the horrible death of the old woman first in hopes that she would break down and recant. Many friends of the women gathered on the banks praying that the Margarets' lives might be spared.

The older Margaret said nothing as the cold seawater rose around her. She struggled to lift her head above the waves and gasped for air. One of the executioners turned to the young Margaret and sneered, "What do you think of her now?"

"I see Christ wrestling there," she answered. "Do you think we are the sufferers? No, it is Christ in us." Soon the waters covered the lifeless body of Margaret MacLachlan. As the rising tide swirled higher around young Margaret, she began to sing a song from Psalm 25:

> My sins and faults of youth
> Do thou, O Lord, forget:
> After thy mercy think on me,
> And for thy goodness great.
> God good and upright is:
> The way he'll sinners show;
> The meek in judgment he will guide
> And make his path to know.

Her tormentors left her hands free when they tied her to the stake and permitted her to hold a Bible. She turned to Romans Chapter 8 and read aloud: "I consider that our present sufferings are not worth comparing with the glory that will be revealed in us." Young Margaret read through to the end of the chapter: "For I am convinced that neither death nor life, neither angels nor demons, neither the present nor the future, nor any powers, neither height nor depth, nor anything else in all creation, will be able to separate us from the love of God that is in Christ Jesus our

Lord." Shortly after, the waters had risen to her neck. Soldiers waded out, loosened the ropes, and lifted her up.

"Pray for the king," they shouted, "for he is supreme over all persons in the church."

"I pray for the salvation of all men," Margaret answered. "I wish no one to be condemned." They pushed her head under the water, then yanked her up again. "Pray for the king! Swear the oath," they demanded.

"Dear Margaret," called out someone in the crowd, "say, God save the King." Her face pale and lips blue, Margaret caught her breath and prayed, "Lord, give the king repentance, forgiveness, and salvation, if it be Thy holy will."

"She has said it! She has said it!" several bystanders shouted. "Release her."

The chief officer was furious. "Let the dog go to hell! We do not want such prayers. Swear the oath," he cried.

"No! No!," she answered. "No sinful oaths for me. I am one of Christ's children. Let me go."

"Take another drink," a soldier sneered, thrusting his halberd on her shoulder and plunging her under the water for the last time. There she died for her love for Christ and her desire to follow His Word.

• • •

John Bunyan
Happy Pilgrim

John Bunyan 1628–1688

"As I walked through the wilderness of this world, I lighted on a certain place where there was a den, and I laid me down in that place to sleep; and, as I slept, I dreamed a dream. I dreamed, and behold, I saw a man clothed with rags, standing in a certain place, with his face from his own house, a book in his hand, and a great burden on his back. I looked, and saw him open the book, and read therein; and, as he read, he wept and trembled; and not being able to contain, he brake out with a lamentable cry, saying, 'What shall I do?'"

Thus begins John Bunyan's, *Pilgrim's Progress*, one of the most widely read and dearly loved books ever written. The story of Christian traveling to the Celestial City is the story of Bunyan's own coming to faith in Jesus Christ. This is his story.

One day as John Bunyan, a traveling tinker, leaned against a shop window cursing loudly, a poor woman wagged her finger in his face saying, "You are the most ungodly fellow for swearing that I have ever heard, you will spoil all the youth of the town if they come into your company." Her remark pierced him like a knife. Bunyan turned away tongue-tied and ashamed. The shame did not vanish quickly but remained, leaving him weak-kneed and depressed. "O that I might be a little child again," he said to himself, "and that my father might teach me to speak without this wicked way of swearing."

Bunyan vowed to become a new man. He stopped his cursing and began reading the Bible and talking about religion. Proud of his reformed life he said, "I please God as well as any man in England." Then one sunny day while walking down a lane in Bedford, Bunyan came upon some women sitting on a porch taking a short break from their labors. He overheard them talking about God. "I drew near to hear what they said," Bunyan wrote later, "for I was now a brisk talker also myself in the matters of religion, but now, I heard but I understood not; for they were far above me, out of my reach; for their talk was about a new birth, the work of God in their hearts. They spoke as if joy did make them speak; they spoke with such pleasantness of scripture language and with such appearance of grace in all they said that they were to me as if they had found a new world."

Bunyan left, his chest pounding, the pride in his religion evaporated. He couldn't get the talk of those women out of his mind. Their faith and joy stood in stark contrast to his fears and doubts. He felt as if he was shivering in the snow while the poor women of Bedford basked in pleasant sunbeams.

Time and again, Bunyan returned to speak with those women of Bedford. "You need to talk with our pastor," they told him. So they walked him across town and introduced him to their pastor, John Gifford. Gifford, a stout old man and a veteran of the English Civil War, warmly took his hand and invited him in. Bunyan poured out his heart to Gifford. The old pastor prayed with him and began to teach him from the Bible about Jesus Christ. That was the first of many long talks between them.

Some time later while worshipping at Gifford's church, the Lord touched John Bunyan's heart. "These words did suddenly break in upon me," he said later of that day. "'My grace is sufficient for you, My grace is sufficient for you, My grace is sufficient for you,' three times together; and O, I thought that every word was a mighty word unto me. And then this verse from John 6:37, 'Whoever comes to me I will never drive away.' I saw it was not my good frame of heart that made my righteousness better, nor yet my bad frame that made my righteousness worse; for my righteousness was Jesus Christ himself, the same yesterday, today, and forever."

Bunyan returned home as if walking on air. "I thought I could have spoken of His love and mercy even to the very crows that sat upon the plowed lands before me," he said. Before long the Bedford congregation elected Bunyan an officer of the church and sent him out as a traveling preacher to the neighboring villages. He continued to earn his living as a tinker but spent much of his time preaching.

At this same time, King Charles II pushed through laws forcing everyone, regardless of conscience, to worship as the Church of England directed. The king did not recognize the Non-Conformist preachers, those outside the Church of England like Bunyan, as true ministers of the Lord. On November 12, 1660, Bunyan rode out to preach at a country farmhouse, nestled in a field of elm trees. Upon entering the cottage, the people did not greet him with their usual joy but with anxious looks and warnings of danger. For word had leaked out that a justice of the peace had issued a warrant for Bunyan's arrest should he attempt to preach. Members of the congregation urged him not to go ahead with the meeting.

"Brother," one man said to Bunyan, "do you think it wise to proceed with the meeting? Perhaps we should call it off for another day."

"No, by no means," Bunyan said firmly. "I will not be stopped; neither will I have the meeting dismissed for this. Come, be of good cheer, and let us not be afraid. Our cause is good, we need not be ashamed; to preach God's Word is so good a work that we shall be well rewarded if we suffer for it." People filled the farmhouse for the service and Bunyan began with prayer. With Bible in hand, he was about to begin his sermon when in burst the constable and his men. Waving the arrest warrant, the constable ordered his men to seize Bunyan.

As they led him away he called to the people, "It is a mercy of God to suffer for doing good. Better by far to be the persecuted than the persecutors."

The next day, Bunyan stood before a judge who said, "Why do you go to such meetings and preach? You are a tinker, why don't you follow your trade? It is unlawful for you to carry on religious services as you do."

"I do follow my calling and preach the Word, too," Bunyan answered. "I look upon it as my duty to do them both as I have the opportunity."

"Mr. Bunyan, I intend to send you to jail unless you promise to stop preaching and calling the people together."

"I shall not stop speaking the Word of God," Bunyan answered. "I shall continue to counsel, comfort, and teach the people that desire it. I think that this is a work which has no harm in it. It is worthy of commendation not blame."

"Do you not love your wife and children?" asked the judge.

"Indeed I do, very dearly," Bunyan said, his heart breaking at the thought of leaving his wife and four children, "but in comparison with Jesus Christ I do not love them at all."

"Away to prison with him." the judge ordered.

Bunyan's home was now a cold and lonely cell. Being dragged from his wife and children, Bunyan said, "felt as if my flesh was pulled from my bones." Often tempted to give up preaching and return home, Bunyan resisted and clung to the promise of Jeremiah 49:11. "Leave your orphans, I will protect their lives. Your widows, too, can trust in me." He made leather boot laces to help support his family and wrote eleven books, including the story of his coming to faith in Christ, *Grace Abounding to the Chief of Sinners*. When permitted, Bunyan preached to as many members of the Bedford church as could crowd into the jail.

After twelve years, the laws against Non-Conformist preaching were relaxed and Bunyan was released. He threw himself into the work of preaching, writing, and organizing new churches. But after three years, the king revoked the license to preach granted to Bunyan and other

Non-Conformist ministers. John Bunyan refused to stop preaching and was thrown in jail for another six months. During that time he wrote *Pilgrim's Progress*, an allegory of the joys, sorrows, trials, and triumphs of the Christian life.

At the age of fifty-nine, Bunyan was struck down by a high fever. From his deathbed he encouraged his friends with short, insightful sayings; one of his last sayings was about prayer: "When you pray, better to let your heart be without words than your words without a heart." Perhaps John Bunyan's entry into heaven was like his description in *Pilgrim's Progress* of Christian and Hopeful at the gates of the Celestial City: "As they entered they were transfigured, and they had raiment put on them that shone like gold. All the bells in the city rang again for joy, and it was said unto them, 'Enter into the joy of your Lord.'"

Who would true valour see, let him come hither;
One here will constant be, come wind, come weather;
There's no discouragement shall make him once relent
His first avowed intent to be a pilgrim.

• • •

Jonathan Edwards
Great Awakening Theologian

Jonathan Edwards 1703–1758

It was midnight, and a second-story window flew open. A man stuck his head out and shouted, "Don't you fools know what hour it is? Go home and get to bed!"

"Good evening to you, too, sir," shouted the leader of a band of young men and women. "Why don't you come out and join us in our frolic?" A roar of laughter broke out from the group as they passed around a bottle of rum.

"You young people are getting out of hand," the man called. "You need the fear of God put in you."

"If Pastor Edwards can't do it then you certainly aren't going to," the leader answered. "Come on, old man, it's Friday night. You can have your fun on the sabbath, we'll have ours tonight." Off they trooped laughing and singing to the tavern. It was nearly sunrise before any of them staggered home to bed.

The summer of 1733 in Northampton, Massachusetts, brought a great deal of carousing and drunkenness among the young people who lived for their "frolics" and "nightwalks." Parents and church elders were concerned and none more so than Jonathan Edwards, the twenty-nine-year-old pastor of the Northampton Church.

Jonathan Edwards longed for the Northampton youth to know what he had experienced at the age of sixteen when he read in I Timothy: "Now to the king, eternal, immortal, invisible the only wise God, be honor and glory forever and ever. Amen." Suddenly a sweet delight in God had filled his heart. "As I read the words," he said, "there came into my soul a sense of the glory of God. I thought how happy I should be to enjoy God and be carried up to Him in heaven."

For six years Edwards had served the Northampton Church. It was frustrating work because many hearts were hardened, and the teenagers and young adults seemed so far from God. Edwards knew true believers had to be born again with a living faith and a new heart. Then early in 1734, as he preached a series of sermons on faith, the young adults began paying close attention and staying after church to discuss the sermons.

One day a young woman, one of the most rebellious girls in the town, knocked at his door. Pleasantly surprised, Edwards welcomed her into his study.

"Oh, pastor," she said, "for the last several days the weight of my sin has crushed me. Just when I thought I was without hope, the Lord warmed my heart and lifted me up." As they talked, it became clear to Edwards that Christ had touched her.

"I believe," he told her, "that God has given you a new heart." Immediately her life changed. Her selfishness turned to love. She never missed a worship service or prayer meeting. The news of her conversion, Edwards said, "was like a flash of lightning upon the hearts of young people all over the town."

Young men and women, some of them the most notorious sinners in Northampton, rushed to speak with her. Those who used to make fun of Pastor Edwards and disturb the services now hung on every word of the sermon. Soon people of all ages throughout the town, overwhelmed by their sin, cried out to Christ for forgiveness. No one spoke of anything but the things of God.

Nightly in the town, neighbors gathered for prayer and Bible reading. Edwards said, "It was never so full of love nor joy. It was a time of joy in families because of the Lord's salvation. Parents rejoiced over their children as new born, and husbands over wives, and wives over husbands." In the space of six months over three hundred people found forgiveness in Jesus Christ. The revival spread to several other towns in Massachusetts and Connecticut. It was the dawning of the Great Awakening.

But many people in New England stood firmly against the revival. Some ministers condemned it from their pulpits. Critics complained that Jonathan Edwards was stirring up emotions. "This is not a true work of God," they said. Supportive ministers in England and America, including Isaac Watts, the famous hymn writer, urged Edwards to write a report on the revival. He did and in 1737, *A Faithful Narrative of the Surprising Work of God* was read eagerly on both sides of the Atlantic, inspiring George Whitefield, John Wesley, and many others.

After a time, the fire of the revival cooled down, but when George Whitefield, the English preacher, arrived in October of 1740, the flames leaped up and spread throughout the American colonies. Tens of thousands, broken in spirit and weeping, turned to Christ through his preaching.

Not long after Whitefield arrived in America, Edwards sent him a letter: "In your journey through New England," he wrote, "would you be willing to visit Northampton? You have the blessing of heaven with you wherever you go, and I have a great desire, if it be the will of God, that same blessing may come down on this town. Please come and do me the favor of staying in my home."

Whitefield accepted and enjoyed his visit immensely. He was so impressed by the love between Jonathan Edwards and his wife, Sarah, that it kindled in him the desire to be married. Whitefield wrote in his journal about the Edwards, "A sweeter couple I have never seen." The Northampton church overflowed with people who flocked to hear the famous Whitefield. He preached Christ with such force and passion that at the close of the message everyone was in tears, including Edwards. The awakening rekindled and continued for nearly two years.

During the revival, Edwards often preached in other New England churches. On Sunday morning, July 8, 1741, he stood in the pulpit of the church in Enfield, Connecticut. Enfield had been strangely passed over during the many months of revival. All eyes fixed on Jonathan Edwards as he climbed the stairs to the pulpit. His six-foot-one-inch body seemed to tower over the congregation. "Hear the Word of the Lord," he said and then read Deuteronomy 32:35, "It is mine to avenge, in due time their foot will slip." Placing his leather Bible down, he picked up his sermon notes in his left hand and began. "Here the Lord warns us that sudden destruction can fall upon the wicked," he said. "There is nothing that keeps wicked men at any one moment out of hell but the mere pleasure of God. O sinner, consider the fearful danger you are in. You have offended God. His hand alone keeps you from falling into the fire of hell. This is true of everyone of you in this congregation that are outside of Christ."

As he preached, men and women sighed and wept, bowed down with their sin. Some cried out questions such as, "I am going to hell! O what shall I do to be saved?"

Edwards quieted them and continued. "You have now an extraordinary opportunity," he said, "a day wherein Christ has thrown the door of mercy wide open and stands calling to poor sinners. Many are flocking to Him. Their hearts are filled with love for Him who has loved them and washed them in His blood. Let everyone that is out of Christ now awake and fly from the wrath to come."

At the close of the service, many were melted to tears and some quaked with fear. Edwards stayed a long time talking and praying with the troubled souls. Many left with their hearts comforted, believing in Christ. The sermon, entitled "Sinners in the Hands of an Angry God" was used by God to transform Enfield. Because of it's powerful effect, it became the most famous sermon ever preached in America.

Throughout the years, Jonathan Edwards served his congregation, raised a large family, and wrote books. Pastors and laymen in America and Europe admired his books on theology, but trouble was brewing in Northampton. There were men and women who did not like him or his strong sermons.

In 1749 a problem erupted over the Lord's Supper. For many years the church at Northampton had permitted people to take the bread and wine even if they did not have a personal faith in Jesus Christ. Edwards came to believe that communion was only meant for those who openly declared a saving faith in Jesus. When Edwards took steps to change the church's policy towards the Lord's Supper, his enemies accused him of being judgmental and divisive. They started spreading lies about him. Finally, the congregation voted to remove him. For twenty-three years he had served the church as a devoted minister; now the note in the Northampton Church Record Book read simply, "June 22, 1750—The Reverend Jonathan Edwards was dismissed."

In his farewell sermon he did not criticize or lay blame but gently urged them to live for the Lord. In closing he said calmly: "Finally, brethren, farewell. Be perfect, of one mind, live in peace, and the God of love and peace shall be with you. May God bless you with a faithful pastor and let me be remembered in your prayers. Never forget our future solemn meeting on that great day of the Lord." Many returned home that Sunday morning grieving, wishing they had not voted their pastor away.

Edwards became a missionary to the Housatonic Indians at Stockbridge, a tiny settlement on the edge of the Massachusetts wilderness. For seven years he worked among the Indians and also wrote several books. Later, the College of New Jersey (later Princeton) called him to be president, but he died of smallpox just two months after arriving there. On his deathbed, he turned to his daughter, Lucy, and said, "And as for my children, you are now to be left fatherless, which I hope will cause you all to seek a Father who will never fail you."

His doctor wrote Mrs. Edwards that her husband had faced death with a "calm, cheerful resignation and patient submission to the Divine will. For him, death had certainly lost its sting." Although Edwards suffered terrible pain and swelling in the throat which prevented swallowing, he endured it with peace and joy. After sending messages of love to his family and friends he looked around the room and said, "Now where is Jesus of Nazareth, my true and never-failing friend?"

• • •

George Whitefield
Great Awakening Preacher

George Whitefield 1714–1770

Late in the winter of 1734, a college tutor led a man carrying a black bag to a small, third-story room.

"His body is wasting away to nothing, Doctor," the tutor said. Quietly opening the door, he whispered, "I am afraid that he's gone quite mad." There, laboring for breath, lay George Whitefield, a twenty-one-year-old Oxford student, his skin ghostly pale, one hand discolored by a large black spot of frostbite, his eyes sunken and blood-shot, his thin body drenched in sweat.

"Young man," the doctor said, "your health is ruined, it looks like you haven't eaten in weeks. How did you get like this?" With trembling voice, Whitefield explained how he had sought to save his soul through self-denial. He was encouraged in this by the Holy Club, an Oxford religious society led by John and Charles Wesley, whose members observed a strict regimen of prayer and fasting. Whitefield soon surpassed his friends in self-denial. Wearing tattered clothes, he spent several hours each morning before sunrise outdoors in prayer, often in freezing temperatures. He survived on a small daily ration of coarse bread and sage tea. Mocking students called him a "madman" and threw dirt clods at him. The master of the college threatened to expel him. Even members of the Holy Club told Whitefield he had gone too far. Through it all, the guilt of his sin remained; he felt no closer to God.

"This morning," Whitefield told the doctor, "I had grown so weak that I was scarcely able to crawl up the stairs to my room."

"Mr. Whitefield," the doctor ordered firmly, "I am

confining you to bed. You will die if your body doesn't get proper nourishment and rest." For weeks, he lay in bed trying to regain his strength, depressed and doubting if his sins could ever be forgiven. But then he came across a little book called *The Life of God in the Soul of Man.* It turned his ideas about God and forgiveness upside down, for Whitefield believed that men earned God's favor through good works. "God showed me," he said, "that I must be born again or be damned! I learned that a man may go to church, say his prayers, receive the sacrament, and yet not be a Christian." With book in hand, Whitefield fell to his knees and prayed, "Lord if I am not a Christian, or if I am not a real one, show me what Christianity is that I might not be condemned at last!"

Not many days later, realizing that he could do nothing to earn salvation and that only God's mercy could save him, he trusted Christ for forgiveness. "Joy unspeakable filled my soul when the weight of my sin fell off, and the pardoning love of God broke upon my troubled soul," Whitefield said. "My joys were like a spring tide and overflowed the banks. I felt that Christ lived in me and I in Him."

Studying the Bible became his passion and delight. "I began to read the Holy Scriptures upon my knees," he said, "and praying over every line and word. This was meat and drink indeed to my soul. I got more true knowledge from reading the Book of God in one month than I could have ever acquired from all the writings of men." As his health returned, he dedicated several hours each day to visiting prisoners, the poor, and the elderly. In simple words, he told them of God's love to sinners. Many believed in Jesus Christ. When Whitefield completed his college degree, he became a minister in the Church of England.

From the beginning, the Lord remarkably blessed his work. Churches which had stood nearly empty for decades overflowed with people wherever he preached in England. At times more people were turned away than could find a place. "It was wonderful," Whitefield said, "to see how the people hung upon the rails of the organ loft, climbed upon the leads of the church, and made the church itself so hot with their breath that the steam would fall from the pillars like drops of rain. Often, it was with great difficulty that I managed to reach the pulpit through the crowds."

Thousands turned to Jesus Christ for the forgiveness of their sins. From sunrise till midnight, anxious seekers lined up to speak with him. His printed sermons sold out as soon as they rolled off the presses. Bible studies and prayer groups sprang up in the towns and cities where he preached. Nothing like it had ever been seen in England. Not everyone, however, rejoiced in Whitefield's ministry. Church leaders, jealous of his popularity with the people, called him a rabble-rouser. Pastors complained that church members couldn't find seats when Whitefield preached and that the large crowds were hard on the pews. Many ministers closed their churches to him.

Finding it increasingly difficult to find churches open to him, Whitefield decided to preach outdoors in the open air. This was a bold idea, for church leaders considered it improper, even sinful, believing that field preaching would stir up the crowds and lead to wild, unruly behavior. By preaching outdoors, Whitefield ran the risk of confrontation with the rulers of the Church of England, but he was determined to preach the gospel no matter what the consequences.

He first preached in the open air at Kingswood, a large coal mining district near Bristol. Whitefield had wanted to preach there ever since he had been told, "No need to go to America to find heathens; there are heathens enough at Kingswood." Kingswood was home to thousands of colliers, the men, women, and children who worked the dark and dangerous mines. They lived in ignorance and poverty. Strangers avoided Kingswood, a place of violence, fearing for their lives. No church or school had ever been built there. English society cared nothing for the colliers. But Whitefield thought otherwise. "My heart aches," he said, "for the poor colliers; they are like sheep without a shepherd."

On a bitterly cold Saturday in February, he entered the narrow lanes of Kingswood. The colliers gaped wide-eyed to find a well-dressed, educated minister in their midst. "Good day," Whitefield said, extending his hand to a collier. The man, covered from head to toe with coal dust, hesitantly raised his arm and shook Whitefield's hand, blackening his palm and fingers with a thin layer of coal dust. Whitefield smiled saying, "At two o'clock today, I will be preaching on the hill at Rose Green, and I would be honored to see you among the congregation."

He passed the word on the street, knocked on doors, and stood at the entrance to the mines, inviting all to come. At the appointed hour over two hundred colliers waited before the grassy mound where Whitefield took his stand. His words formed clouds of gray condensation in the chill air as he began to preach. "Friends," he said, "the Lord stood on a hillside long ago among a crowd like this. And Jesus taught them saying: 'Blessed are the poor in spirit for theirs is the kingdom of heaven'" (Matt. 5:3).

His message melted the hearts of many. For the first time, they realized Christ loved them and they sensed that Whitefield had a genuine love for them, too. Whitefield left rejoicing, promising to return in a few days. "Blessed be God," he said, "I believe I was never more acceptable to my Master than when I was standing to teach those hearers in the open field. Some may criticize me, but if I try to please men I would not be a servant of Christ."

On Wednesday afternoon, he stood again on the hill in Kingswood, this time bathed in brilliant sunshine. Nearly two thousand colliers had gathered, waiting in total silence. "I tell you the truth," Whitefield proclaimed, his strong voice easily heard by all, "no one can see the kingdom of God unless he is born again." For an hour he preached the love of Christ and the wonders of His death on the cross. "And after all this," he said, "do you think the Lord will turn away any poor sinner who comes to Him? No! Away with such dishonorable thoughts—leave your sins He came to die for and hear Him say, 'Though your sins be like scarlet they shall be like wool; though they be red like crimson, they shall be whiter than snow.'"

By the end of the sermon, hundreds of colliers were weeping, their coal-blackened cheeks streaked white by their tears. Over the next several weeks, tens of thousands came to hear Whitefield preach at Kingswood. Many believed in Jesus Christ, and the power of God wonderfully transformed the community. Drunkenness, gambling, and violence nearly disappeared. Prayer meetings began in every neighborhood. A school was started.

Whitefield preached outdoors throughout Britain and America, sparking a great revival of faith in Christ. He encouraged other ministers to field preach, including his old friends Charles and John Wesley, who also pointed thousands of hearers to Jesus Christ. Before his death at the age of fifty-five, Whitefield preached over eighteen thousand sermons to millions of hearers across England, Scotland, Wales, and America. No wonder George Whitefield has been called the greatest evangelist since the apostle Paul.

• • •

John Wesley
The World His Parish

John Wesley 1703–1791

In December of 1737, having failed miserably as a missionary in Georgia, John Wesley stood on the deck of a ship sailing from the Carolina coast to England. "I went to America," he said, "to convert the Indians, but oh! who shall convert me? Who will deliver me from this evil heart of unbelief?" For many years, Wesley had tried to win God's favor through self-denial and observance of religious rules. At Oxford University, he and his brother, Charles, formed a religious group known as the Holy Club. Although the members of the Holy Club studied the Bible, prayed, fasted, gave money to the poor, and cared for the sick, their strict discipline and good works did not bring them peace with God.

John and Charles Wesley sailed to the wilderness of the American colonies to preach, but John Wesley wondered if he himself knew God. On board ship, he met some Moravian missionaries. The Moravians were German Christians who understood that no man can save himself by his own good works.

Seeing a faith in the Moravians that he did not see in himself, Wesley asked one of them, "Do you have any advice for me as to how I should serve God in America?"

"My Brother," the Moravian answered in a thick German accent, "I must first ask you one or two questions. Does the Spirit of God bear witness with your spirit that you are a child of God?" Wesley looked long into the Moravian's eyes but said nothing. "Do you know Jesus Christ?" the man asked.

"I know He is the Savior of the world," John Wesley answered.

"True," the Moravian said with a nod, "but do you know He has saved *you*?"

"I hope he has died to save me," Wesley answered weakly.

"But do you know it for yourself?" the Moravian asked.

Wesley paused for a moment and then said hesitantly, "I do," but he feared that his answer was untrue.

After two discouraging years in America, John Wesley decided to return to England. But during that difficult time, he came to understand the true condition of his heart before God. As he sailed home, he wrote in his journal: "This, then, I have learned in the ends of the earth—that my whole heart is evil. There is nothing in me that can please God. My only hope is that if I seek I shall find Christ, and be found in Him, not having my own righteousness, but the righteousness of God which comes by faith."

His brother, Charles, met him in London, having left America several months earlier. John and Charles sought out Peter Boehler, a Moravian minister visiting London. Boehler asked Charles, "Do you hope to be saved?"

"Yes," Charles answered.

"For what reason do you hope it?" he asked.

"Because," Charles said, "I have used my best efforts to serve God."

Boehler shook his head. John began talking about good works as a way to God; but Boehler interrupted him, "My Brother! My Brother! Those ideas of yours must be purged away!"

"Should I stop preaching?" John asked him. "How can I preach to others when I do not have faith myself?"

"By no means," Boehler answered.

"But what can I preach?" John asked.

Boehler said, "Preach faith *till* you have it; and then *because* you have it, you *will* preach faith." A few weeks later, Charles came to a living faith in Jesus after reading Martin Luther's commentary on Galatians.

"I now found myself at peace with God," he said. "I saw that by faith alone I stood." Three days later, John Wesley attended a Bible study at a Moravian meeting house.

"In the evening," John said, "I went very unwillingly to a meeting in Aldersgate Street, where one was reading from Luther's introduction to Paul's letter to the Romans. About a quarter hour before nine, while he was describing the change which God works in the heart through faith in Christ, I felt my heart strangely warmed. I felt I did trust in Christ, Christ alone for salvation. An assurance was given me, that he had taken away *my* sins, even *mine*, and saved *me* from the law of sin and death." John Wesley and his Moravian friends ran to tell Charles Wesley. Bursting into his room, John declared, "I believe!" They all rejoiced, prayed, and sang a hymn which Charles had written a few days earlier.

John and Charles preached with new power, but the ministers of London, disliking their enthusiasm and their message, closed their churches to them. So they preached in meeting houses, prisons, and hospitals, inviting all to come by faith to Jesus Christ. At this same time, their friend, George Whitefield, was preaching to huge crowds in the open air. Whitefield urged John Wesley to preach outside where he would not be restricted by church leaders. Whitefield, who was leaving for America, wanted Wesley to take over his preaching work at Kingswood. Wesley agreed and came to watch Whitefield preach there. "At first," Wesley said, "I could scarce reconcile myself to this strange way of preaching in the fields, for all my life, till very lately, I should have thought the saving of souls almost a sin if it had not been done in a church."

The next day, Whitefield left and Wesley preached in the open air. He stood nervously on a little hill in a brick yard and preached to three thousand people. Many of them turned to Jesus for the forgiveness of their sins. "As soon as he got up on the stand," one man said of Wesley, "he stroked back his hair and turned his face towards where I stood, and I thought he fixed his eyes on me. When he spoke, I thought his whole message was aimed at me. When he finished I said, 'This man can tell the secrets of my heart.'"

Wesley traveled throughout England, speaking to larger and larger audiences. Wesley described their reaction in his journal: "Many of those that heard began to call upon God with strong cries and tears. Some sank down, and there remained no strength in them." Town leaders feared the large crowds, and church leaders disliked the emphasis on personal faith in Jesus Christ.

Once when Wesley was preaching near the city of Bath, a prominent man stopped him and asked, "By whose authority do you do this?"

"By the authority of Jesus Christ," Wesley answered.

"This meeting is against the law," the man said, his face reddening.

"Sir," Wesley said, "unlawful meetings are ones which call for rebellion, but this is not such."

"I say it is," the man shouted, "and besides, your preaching frightens people out of their wits. I desire to know what these people came here for?"

"Sir," said an old woman stepping from the crowd, "You take care of your body; we take care of our souls; we came here for food for our souls." The man stood silent, staring at the ground. Wesley went on preaching.

Often the crowds were difficult and violent. "As soon as we went out," Wesley said of one place, "we were saluted, as usual, with jeers and a few stones and pieces of dirt." Once when he was walking through Bristol to preach, a mob rose up against him. "All the street, upwards and downwards, was filled with people, shouting, cursing, and swearing at us," Wesley said, "and ready to swallow the ground with fierceness and rage." As the mob prepared to attack Wesley, the mayor called out the constable, who restored order. Later some of the rioters went to hear him preach and believed in Jesus Christ.

Even many of Wesley's friends disapproved of his open

air preaching. One said to him, "How can you justify going into the parishes of other ministers to preach? How is it that you gathered Christians who are none of your charge to sing psalms, and pray, and hear the Scriptures explained?"

"I look upon the whole world as my parish," Wesley told him. "I think that it is good and right to declare to all who are willing to hear the good news of salvation."

Wesley concentrated his efforts on the cities where most of the people lived in poverty and ignorance. As people turned to Christ, Wesley raised money to build meetinghouses, orphanages, and schools. But John Wesley did not stay in one spot for long; he travelled from place to place on horseback preaching to the crowds. Soon he realized that in order for the new believers to grow in their faith, they needed regular teaching and encouragement. Preaching, without pastoral care and teaching, Wesley said, was like "weaving a rope of sand." So Wesley trained leaders to disciple the new converts, teaching them to read the Bible, pray, and serve others. Those who followed Wesley's methods came to be called Methodists. The Methodist groups in an area were organized into a circuit under the care of horseback riding, traveling preachers called circuit riders.

During his fifty years of ministry, John Wesley rode over 250,000 miles and preached more than 40,000 sermons. Charles Wesley, a faithful preacher too, is best known as a hymn writer. He wrote 7000 hymns, among them, "Hark the Herald Angels Sing" and "Christ the Lord is Risen Today."

Even at the age of eighty-eight, John Wesley kept working. "I am now an old man," he said, "decayed from head to foot. However, blessed be God, I do not slack my labour. I can preach and write still." As John Wesley lay dying, he said to his friends in a clear voice: "The best of all is—God with us!"

• • •

John Newton
Slave Trader Saved by Grace

John Newton 1725–1807

A terrible storm whipped the frigid waters of the North Atlantic into a frenzy. Eighty-mile-an-hour winds and thirty foot swells battered the English merchant ship, *Greyhound*, to the brink of sinking. With sails and masts destroyed, water rushed over the deck with each cresting wave, washing several men overboard. Sailors toiled desperately at the pumps to plug the leaks.

John Newton, a drenched and shivering twenty-two-year-old seaman, tied to the helm, did his utmost to keep the ship on a steady course. The fear of death drove him to examine his life. Memories of his rebellion against God filled him with despair; for he had mocked and cursed God for years. "I am sinking," he said to himself, "under the weight of all my sins into the ocean and into eternity."

John Newton's life began with great happiness and promise. His father, a sea captain, was often away, but his mother showered him with love. A devout Christian, she filled John's young mind with Bible stories, Scripture verses, and the songs and hymns of Isaac Watts. "When you grow up," she often told him, "you will be a faithful minister of God."

Then when Newton was seven years old, his mother died, depriving him of her spiritual nurture. Shortly thereafter, his father remarried. Newton's stepmother showed little interest in him or the Lord. The Christian light in the home vanished. John Newton, often left to himself, took up with the worst characters in the neighborhood, replacing the faith of his mother with the cursing and lying of his friends. Newton hated life at home and school, so he begged his father to take him to sea. At age eleven, John Newton began work as a cabin boy on his father's ship and adapted quickly to life on the sea and the sinful ways of the sailors. After a few years, he left his father's ship and worked on other vessels, finally ending up on a slave-trading ship.

Giving no thought to the poor African men, women, and children whose lives were destroyed through the slave trade, Newton shackled them in irons and packed them like sardines below decks, where many died of filth and disease before reaching the shores of the New World. He saw them as the other sailors did—just another form of cargo, like sugarcane or beeswax.

Over the years, Newton became an able seaman and a crude trouble maker. Despising those in authority over him, Newton composed vulgar songs which ridiculed the captain and the ship. Crew members filled the air with these wicked songs. "I not only sinned with a high hand myself," Newton later admitted, "but I made it my practice to tempt others upon every occasion."

Captains hated him. On several occasions his behavior led to a public flogging. Newton's back was bared and his hands and feet tied to a wooden grate. A dozen or more lashes tore the flesh from his back until he collapsed unconscious. At one point, in order to flee from a particularly cruel captain, Newton jumped ship in Africa. He went to work for a slave trader who ended up enslaving him. When not working, Newton was locked up and survived on a small ration of rice and raw fish. He feared that his life would end as a miserable slave on the African coast.

Newton's father, worried about his son, asked ship captains leaving England to look for him. The *Greyhound*, trading along the West African coast, met up with Newton. "Your father is concerned for your welfare," the captain told him. "You're welcome to join us and return to England." Newton came aboard and began the journey northward, but not far from home they hit high winds and heavy seas.

And so Newton found himself strapped to the helm of the near-sinking *Greyhound* and felt as broken as the storm-tossed ship. But then he found his thoughts turning to Christ for the first time in years. "Christ died for sinners, but could He forgive my sins which are so many and so terrible?" he wondered. "I rejected the truth of God taught to me by my mother; could He forgive that?"

When his watch at the helm ended and the storm subsided a bit, he found a New Testament and began reading. Luke 11:13 inspired him to put his life in the Lord's hands: "If you then, though you are evil, know how to give good gifts to your children, how much more will your Father in heaven give the Holy Spirit to those who ask Him."

"If this book is true," Newton said to himself, "the promise in this passage is true likewise. He has promised here to give the Spirit to those who ask. I must therefore pray, and if it is of God, He will make good His word." With tears, he prayed for forgiveness and a new life. The ship managed to stay afloat and John Newton touched land again a changed man. He attended church immediately, received the Lord's Supper, and vowed to serve God. Newton studied the Bible in earnest and read the best Christian books he could find, and he developed close friendships with George Whitefield and other Christian leaders.

It wasn't long before Newton, with the encouragement of his friends, felt the call of God to enter the ministry. He passed the ordination exams of the Church of England and began to pastor in Olney, a poor town north of London. "The Lord has sent me here," he said, "not to acquire the character of a ready speaker but to win souls for Christ."

His loving care, prayers, and bedside visits won the hearts of the people of Olney. He started a midweek prayer meeting and Sunday evening gatherings in his home. Although he and his wife were childless, Newton loved children. "I want to talk to them and explain the Scriptures to them in their own little way," he said. So he began a children's meeting. The children delighted in his exciting stories and the model ships he made out of paper. Soon more than two hundred children gathered around him each week to learn the things of God.

Putting his talent for poetry to work, Newton composed hymns, hundreds of them. At times, he wrote a new hymn for each weekly prayer meeting. "Amazing Grace," "Glorious Things of Thee are Spoken," and "How Sweet the Name of Jesus Sounds in a Believer's Ear" are the best loved.

He wrote the story of his coming to faith in Christ, which became a best seller in England and America. Newton worked tirelessly to stop slavery in the British Empire, writing pamphlets and testifying before Parliament and inspiring English statesmen like William Wilberforce to use their power to stop the slave trade. As his fame and influence grew, he never lost sight that he was a sinner saved by grace. On his deathbed he said to a friend, "My memory is nearly gone; but I remember two things: that I am a great sinner, and that Christ is a great Savior." He wrote the words that later appeared on his gravestone:

> John Newton
> Once an infidel and libertine,
> a servant of slaves in Africa,
> was by the rich mercy of our Lord and Saviour
> Jesus Christ, preserved, restored, pardoned,
> and appointed to preach the faith
> He had long labored to destroy.

At the age of eighty-two, John Newton died. His remarkably changed life and his hymns of praise live on as a testimony to Christ's amazing grace.

> Amazing grace! How sweet the sound!
> That saved a wretch like me!
> I once was lost, but now am found;
> Was blind, but now I see.

• • •

LIVINGSTONE LION ATTACK

Modern Missions

The Gospel to the Ends of the Earth

In the eighteenth and nineteenth centuries, Christians in Britain and America, impassioned by God's call to proclaim the good news of Jesus Christ to every nation, sent pioneering missionaries to the remotest ends of the earth.

- David Brainerd
  Preacher to the
  North American Indians

- William Carey
  Father of Modern Missions

- David Livingstone
  Missionary Explorer

- John Paton
  Witness to the Cannibals

- Hudson Taylor
  Founder of the China Inland Mission

- Amy Carmichael
  Mother to Outcast Children

David Brainerd
Preacher to the North American Indians

David Brainerd 1718–1747

In the black of night, a horse and rider made their way slowly along the bank of the Susquehannah River. It was spring in 1745, and David Brainerd, a twenty-seven-year-old missionary, was preaching to the Indians living in scattered villages along the river. He traveled through drenching rains and bitter winds. With little rest, sleeping outside on the ground, he had driven himself to exhaustion. A burning fever shook his body, his head and stomach were racked with pain, and a deep rumbling cough brought up blood. "If I don't find shelter soon," he thought, "I'll die in this wilderness."

For two years he lived among the Indians. Despite his preaching, his prayers, and countless acts of kindness, they remained stuck in idol worship, drunkenness, violence, and superstition. Now it appeared that his work would end with an early death. He pressed his horse forward with the last of his strength and prayed, "Lord, I'm ready to die and be with Christ, but I long to live to see the salvation of the Indians."

Just then he noticed through the trees a wooden shack. He slid off the saddle and stumbled to the door. The Indian trader who lived there brought Brainerd in, fed him, and put him to bed. After several days of rest, the fever disappeared. His strength returned and he made the long ride back to his home in the Pennsylvania frontier among the Delaware Indians.

When safely back in his little hut, he slipped away to a quiet place in the woods for his nightly prayers. "Bless You, Heavenly Father," he said, kneeling in the moist moss and bark, "for You have kept me safe through hundreds of miles of riding, and my health is greatly restored." Then he cried out to God for the Indians. "Oh, Lord, bow the heavens and come down and do some marvelous work among them."

A short time later, Brainerd and his Indian interpreter rode eighty miles to the southeast, deep into the New Jersey woods, to tell the good news of Jesus to an Indian tribe living near a place called Crossweeksung. Arriving there, he found only a few women and children, for that tribe lived in small settlements scattered over many miles. Through his Indian interpreter, he preached to them, and to Brainerd's surprise, they did not mock or argue but listened attentively. At the close of the sermon he said, "I wish to visit you again tomorrow." Immediately, the women set out in all directions.

"Where are you going?" Brainerd called to them.

"To tell our friends to come and hear the words of God," they answered. He preached daily, and each time the number of hearers grew; no one raised an objection; they hung on every word. Brainerd had never seen Indians so receptive to the message of Jesus Christ.

After twelve days, as Brainerd prepared to return home to the Delaware tribe, two Indian women came to him sobbing, "I wish God would change my heart," one said.

"I want to find Christ," cried the other. Then an old man, a chief, approached Brainerd with tears in his eyes saying, "What will become of my poor soul?"

Brainerd promised to return quickly, God willing. As he rode northward he prayed, "Father, only You can open the ears and draw the hearts of these poor pagans to You. Change them with Your saving grace."

One month later, he returned to Crossweeksung and found a great stirring of the Spirit of God. The Indians, anxious to find peace with God, had forsaken their pagan feasts, and they wouldn't take a bite of food until Brainerd asked a blessing. When he preached on the verse: "This is love: not that we loved God, but that He loved us and sent

His Son as a sacrifice for our sins," scarcely an eye was dry. That evening, they crowded around Brainerd.

"What must we do to be saved?" Men and women, boys and girls wept over the badness of their hearts and cried out, "Guttummaukalummeh! Guttummaukalummeh!" which means, "Have mercy on me! Have mercy on me!" Many trusted in Christ for forgiveness. With joy they took their friends by the hand saying:

"Come and give up your heart to Christ. He is good. Oh, come and enjoy Him."

"It was," Brainerd said of the movement of God among the Indians, "like a mighty rushing wind bore down upon us." Soon nearly all the Indians in the area believed, offering heartfelt worship to God. "I have often times thought," Brainerd wrote, "that they would cheerfully attend worship twenty-four hours straight if they could. I don't know of any group of Christians where there seems to be so much of the presence of God and brotherly love so abounds."

David Brainerd journeyed home, asking the Lord in prayer to pour out His grace upon the hard hearted Delawares, as He had upon the Indians of Crossweeksung. One Indian man who lived near the forks of the Delaware River, not far from Brainerd's hut, was particularly difficult. He was a powwow, an Indian priest of magic and spirit worship. He led the people away from Brainerd's teaching. Although a drunkard and a murderer, the people were awed by the Indian priest's chanting, rattle shaking, and dancing. "Hear me," he cried, "for the power of the spirits live in me."

At times Brainerd hoped God would slay the powwow; for he seemed to snuff out any interest among the Indians for Jesus Christ like water poured on the first sparks of a fire. But when Brainerd returned home from Crossweeksung, the powwow listened to his preaching with sighs and tears.

"I feel the Word of God in my heart, where once the devils lived," he told Brainerd. Before long, he trusted in

Jesus Christ. His boasting and anger turned to humility and kindness.

"If God can wash my sins away," he told others, "He can forgive you too." He became Brainerd's close friend and traveled with him when he preached to neighboring tribes. Once on a cold, February morning, as Brainerd preached to an Indian band near the river, an old man, a powwow, rose up.

"Stop speaking your lies," he shouted, waving his arms. "Get out of here or I'll cast a spell of doom on you and all your friends!"

Before Brainerd could answer, his Indian friend walked over, stood face to face with the old man, and said, "We are not afraid of your magic. Go ahead, cast your spell; you have no power to hurt us. Not long ago, I was a powwow, and I hated the preacher's words too. But then I felt the Word of God in my heart and the devil's power within me vanished. I was filled with peace and love." Stretching out his hand to the old man he said, "The Word of God will change you too once you feel it in your heart."

That night Brainerd wrote about his friend in his diary: "May God have the glory for the amazing change He has made in him. What was said of Paul is now true of him, 'He preaches the faith he once tried to destroy.'"

Over the next year and a half, the revival spread to other tribes. Brainerd spent twenty hours a week in the saddle, riding thousands of miles, preaching, teaching, and baptizing Indians. All the while he suffered from constant sickness, coughing, and terrible headaches. When Brainerd became so weak he couldn't preach, he rode to New England hoping medical attention and a change in climate would strengthen him.

Some days as he traveled he felt a little better, but by the time he reached Northampton, Massachusetts, and the home of Jonathan Edwards, his body gave out. Edwards and his family cared for Brainerd for several months as he lay near death. Their time together, Brainerd wrote, "seemed like a little piece of heaven." And he was a great encouragement to Edwards. "I found him," Edwards said, "a deeply spiritual man whose prayers flowed from the fullness of his heart."

Through the years of his ministry, Brainerd kept a diary wherein he expressed his doubts, struggles, and joys. He never intended for it to be read by others. But as he lay dying, his friends urged him to allow it to be published as a testimony to God's grace. After much prodding, he agreed. "But only," he said, "if it is placed in the hands of Jonathan Edwards to decide what parts would most glorify the Lord."

Not long before his death, Brainerd said, "I am almost in eternity. I long to be there. All my desire is to glorify God in heaven." He died early in the morning on October 9, 1747. He was just twenty-nine years old. Jonathan Edwards edited the diary and saw to its publication in 1749. *The Life and Diary of David Brainerd* was read widely in America and Europe. Through the years, many missionaries, including William Carey and David Livingstone, were inspired to serve the Lord by David Brainerd's example. It continues to challenge Christians to follow the Lord wholeheartedly to this day.

• • •

William Carey
Father of Modern Missions

William Carey 1761–1834

In 1787, a poor shoemaker labored in the workroom of his cottage at the far end of the English village of Moulton. His rough, stained hands skillfully shaped the leather. William Carey was not making a pair of shoes but stitching a South Sea island onto a large leather globe which depicted the lands of the world in different colored leathers, each remarkably accurate in size and location.

A hand-painted paper map covered one whole wall of the workroom. On it Carey had labeled each nation of the world with its population and its condition before God, whether Christian, Muslim, or pagan. As he showed the globe and map to all who came to his workshop, he wept openly for the millions of people without the knowledge of Jesus Christ, saying as he pointed to nation after nation, "And these are pagans, and these are pagans, and these are pagans. . ."

In addition to being a shoemaker, he served the Baptist church of Moulton as their preacher. He pointed the people to Christ and traveled tirelessly preaching in the surrounding villages. A friend criticized him for neglecting his shoe-making business for all the preaching. "Neglecting my business!" Carey replied. "My business, Sir, is to extend the kingdom of Christ. I only make and mend shoes to help pay expenses."

Many of Carey's hearers believed in the Lord, but he often found his thoughts drawn away to the lost souls of other lands living without the good news of Jesus Christ. At the age of twenty-two, Carey read *Captain Cook's Voyages*. Cook, an English explorer who sailed the world charting sea routes and claiming territories for the British Crown, wrote about the people of the lands he discovered. Carey couldn't put the book down.

Reading about the sin and misery of the peoples of the world without Christ fueled his desire to be a missionary, and afterward he never finished a prayer without asking God to save the heathen, even though the churches of that day did not see the need for spreading Christ's message to foreign lands. He also read about John Eliot and David Brainerd, preachers to the North American Indians, who became his heroes in the faith and in the cause of world missions.

Carey's church belonged to the Northampton Baptist Association, and the ministers of the association gathered together each year for encouragement and prayer. At the first meeting which Carey attended, the chairman asked him to suggest a topic for discussion.

"Let us consider," Carey said, standing in front of the group, "whether the command given to the apostles to teach all nations was not binding on all succeeding ministers to the end of the world."

"Young man, sit down, sit down!" an older minister said gruffly. "You're an enthusiast. When God pleases to convert the heathen, He'll do it without consulting you or me." Refusing to abandon the idea, Carey pressed the need with the ministers individually for sending out missionaries.

"We mostly regarded it," one minister said later, "as a wild impractical scheme and gave him no encouragement. Yet he would not give it up but talked with us one by one till he made an impression."

At the ministers' meeting in 1791, Carey tried again, presenting an eighty-seven page paper entitled: *An Enquiry Into the Obligation of Christians to Use Means for the Conversion of the Heathen*. In it, he argued persuasively for world missions. "We ought to be keen to get everywhere for Christ, till all closed doors are opened," he wrote. "British traders press into the East Indies, Persia, China, and Greenland. Cursed slave traders dare deep into Africa. Should we

Christians be less resolved and adventurous than these?"

At the association's next meeting, Carey delivered the opening sermon. With great passion, he exhorted the ministers from the Bible to begin a mission society and challenged them with an unforgettable phrase: "Expect great things from God; attempt great things for God." Though deeply moved, the ministers doubts and fears returned, and they refused to take the step. Greatly distressed, Carey grabbed Andrew Fuller, an influential minister, by the arm and cried, "Is there nothing again going to be done, sir?"

Mr. Fuller, cut to the quick, took the floor and passionately urged the men to reconsider. Filled with zeal and fresh courage, the ministers voted to form a mission society. In less than one year the society sent to India their first two missionaries, John Thomas and William Carey. "It is the folly of a madman," Carey's father said when he learned of his son's plans. But Carey was convinced. "I am perfectly sure that it is the will of heaven that I must go," he said.

After a five month sea voyage, Carey, his wife, children, and John Thomas arrived in Calcutta, India. Carey's heart went out to the Hindu multitudes trapped in a rigid caste (class) system in which they blindly accepted that their lives were determined by fate. A better life awaited them in the future, they believed, through the reincarnation of the soul. They bowed down to idols representing thousands of petty, quarreling gods. Carey saw men throw themselves upon spikes, tearing their flesh and bones, and others were hoisted high in the air from hooks embedded in their backs and swung about—all to appease the gods. They paid homage each morning to the Ganges River, and some childless women promised to sacrifice a child to the sacred river if it would grant them children. Countless babies were thrown into the river to drown or be eaten by crocodiles in fulfillment of these vows.

One evening Carey witnessed with his own eyes, Sati, widow-burning, a widespread practice throughout India. He came upon a number of people gathered at the river side.

"Why are you here?" Carey asked.

"To burn the body of a deadman and his wife," they answered.

He saw the widow robed in white standing beside a large pile of wood on which lay the body of her dead husband. Carey argued with all his might that they were committing murder by burning the woman to death.

But they pushed him away saying, "It is a great act of holiness. If you do not want to see it, leave."

"I will stay and see the murder," Carey said, defiantly standing his ground, "and I will bear witness of it before the judgment seat of God." As the woman calmly mounted the pile, Carey called out, "Don't throw your life away; no evil will come to you if you refuse to be burned."

Ignoring his pleas, she lay down beside her dead husband. A high mound of dry leaves was heaped over them. Bamboo poles pressed the leaves down and prevented the woman from moving. As they ignited the pile, the people yelled out a shout of joy to Shiva, the god of destruction. If the woman screamed it could not have been heard over the noise of the crowd. Trembling, Carey left, sickened with horror at the scene.

Carey labored at the difficult task of learning Bengali, the language of the people in that region of India, but before long he knew enough to preach a simple sermon. In many villages the people rejoiced in his preaching, but they lacked the courage to obey. "It is in our hearts to follow your teaching," they said, "but we cannot do it for that would break caste. The Brahmins must embrace the faith first."

The Brahmins, the highest caste and spiritual guides of the land, were the most difficult to reach with the Christian message. At times they hired thugs to mock and hiss Carey's preaching and throw stones. Often Carey returned home with his head and face bloodied and bruised. He studied the sacred writings of the Hindus and surprised the Brahmins with his knowledge of their religion. Each day, Carey presented the sufferings and death of Christ on the cross for sinners, and yet for over six years no one came to believe in Jesus Christ.

Since first arriving in India, Carey asked God to send missionaries to proclaim the good news of Jesus Christ. "India needs ten thousand ministers of the gospel," he wrote back home to the Mission Society. "Ought not every church to turn it's attention to the raising up of missionaries and sending them abroad?"

In his sixth year, two fine English missionaries, Joshua Marshman and William Ward, joined him in the work. The three men worked as one and took as their motto Carey's phrase: "Expect great things from God; attempt great things for God." Together they organized a mission compound at Serampore, a city under Dutch rule, which was a short distance from Calcutta. Not long after Marshman and Ward arrived, a Hindu man, a carpenter, named Krishna Pal turned to Christ. Krishna told his wife and sister-in-law and a friend, and they also believed. "Christ has removed our sins," Krishna said, "He is all to us. From now on a Brahmin's curse or blessing is nothing."

Krishna and the others broke caste by eating with the missionaries. Furious, his neighbors taunted, threatened, and beat him. One night when they surrounded his house and dragged him away, Carey found Krishna's wife terrified and crying in the road. With tears in his eyes he calmed her saying, "Faithfulness to Christ has brought you this trouble. He'll treasure your tears in His bottle and will never forsake you."

The mob planned to murder Krishna Pal and his family that night, but the Dutch governor heard of the plot and protected them. Krishna proclaimed the good news of Jesus to his neighbors, and many put their trust in Jesus Christ, but members of the higher castes scoffed. "What great thing is it if a carpenter or laborer breaks caste?" they said. "Have any Brahmins believed?"

But within a few months a Brahmin followed Christ and broke caste by associating with Krishna and the missionaries. When the Brahmin told his high caste friends about his new faith in Jesus, they cursed him and threw dung at him. "Insults," he said, "are sweet to me for Christ." Hindus who turned to Christ endured ridicule, threats, and violence. One man was thrown out of his village with his mouth, eyes, ears, and nose stuffed with mud. Several were kidnapped, and at least one was murdered. But still the numbers of new believers grew. "Eighteen months ago," Carey wrote in a letter, "we would have been overjoyed to have seen one Hindu eat with us; now it is sometimes difficult to find room for all who come."

Carey put most of his time into Bible translation so the people could read God's Word for themselves. He stayed up late, rose early, and often skipped meals as he worked. One of his Indian translation helpers asked, "What kind of body has Mr. Carey? I cannot understand him. He never seems hungry nor tired and never leaves a thing until it's finished." Carey, with Indian helpers, translated the whole Bible into six languages, and the New Testament into more than thirty. When Carey was asked how he learned so many languages he answered, "None knew what they could do till they tried. I can plod and persevere. That is my only genius. The God who can do for and through a poor shoemaker all He has done for and through me can bless and use anyone."

William Carey's missionary zeal inspired many different Christian groups to send out missionaries. Within a few years of his departure for India, the Church of England, the Church of Scotland, and the Methodists formed foreign mission boards, and the London Missionary Society and several American missionary societies were created. One church historian wrote, "The light which William Carey had kindled spread from hill to hill like beacon fires till every Christian church in turn recognized the signal and responded to the call." This is why he is called the "Father of Modern Missions."

As Carey lay dying at the age of seventy-two, a friend visited him and recounted all the accomplishments of Carey's missionary life. In a feeble voice Carey corrected him. "You have been speaking about William Carey; when I am gone, say nothing about William Carey. Speak about William Carey's Savior."

• • •

David Livingstone
Missionary Explorer

David Livingstone 1813–1873

In February of 1844, the Bakhatla tribe in southern Africa faced a vexing problem. For some time, lions had been leaping into their cattle pens and destroying cows and sheep. Believing that the lions were bewitched, they told David Livingstone, a thirty-year-old Christian missionary living among them, "We have been given into the power of the lions by the neighboring tribe." Although the Bakhatlas knew that if one lion in a group is killed the others will leave the area, their fear of evil spirits in the lions made them unwilling to kill one to protect their herds.

"Take courage," Livingstone said to them, "I will help you get rid of these beasts." The men agreed, and they set out, Livingstone with his gun, the natives armed with spears. They found the lions on a small, tree-covered hill. Forming a circle around the lions, the natives slowly went up the hill. But when the lions bolted, the men separated and did not throw their weapons. Livingstone held his fire for fear of hitting one of the men. As they walked back to the village, Livingstone noticed one of the lions crouching behind a bush about thirty yards away. Leveling his shotgun, he aimed and fired both barrels.

"He is shot! He is shot!" the tribesmen yelled, jumping and raising their arms. "Let's go see it." As they ran to the spot, Livingstone spied the wounded lion's tail sticking up from behind the bush.

"Stop," he called, "wait till I reload my gun." While ramming the bullets down the barrel, he heard a shout, turned his head, and saw the bleeding lion springing upon him. Livingstone and the lion tumbled into the tall grass together.

It bit into his arm, shaking him like a dog shakes a rat. When some of the natives tried to spear the lion, it left Livingstone and bit one man in the leg and another in the shoulder before it suddenly dropped dead from the bullet wounds.

The bite crushed Livingstone's upper arm to splinters. For many days, he lay near death from loss of blood and fever. Several months passed before he regained his strength. Later he was asked, "What were you thinking about when the lion had you in its jaws?" With a twinkle in his eyes, the missionary answered, "I was wondering what part of me he would eat first." Although able to joke about the attack, Livingstone suffered terrible pains for a long time and was never again able to lift his left arm above his shoulder.

Despite the dangers and hardships, Livingstone loved his life and work in Africa. As a young man, he was inspired by the lives of pioneer missionaries William Carey and Henry Martyn. Livingstone studied medicine and the Bible because he wanted to heal the bodies and souls of those who did not know Jesus Christ. "God had an only Son," Livingstone said, "and He was a missionary and a physician. In this service I hope to live, in it I wish to die." While studying in London, he met Dr. Robert Moffatt, a missionary to South Africa.

"Do you think I could be of help in Africa?" Livingstone asked him.

"Yes," Moffatt answered, "if you will push on to the vast unoccupied district to the north, where on a clear morning I have seen the smoke of a thousand villages, and no missionary has ever been."

When David Livingstone arrived in southern Africa, the missionaries there urged him to stay near the established mission stations, but Livingstone said, "All my desires tend forward to the north. Beyond us, where no missionary has gone, all is dark." So he traveled deep into the interior of Africa. When he came to the Bakwain tribe, he found the people and their chief, Sechele, eager to hear his message.

"The Son of God came down from heaven to die for us," he told them. "All who put their trust in Jesus Christ will live with Him in heaven. But a day of judgment is coming," David warned them, "and all who die unforgiven will be lost forever."

"It is the custom of our nation," Chief Sechele said, "when any new idea is brought before us to ask questions about it. May I ask you questions about your religion?"

"Please do," Livingstone said.

"You have told us of a coming day of judgment. Did your forefathers know of a future judgment?" Sechele asked.

"Yes, they did," Livingstone answered. "The Scriptures tell us that God will sit on a great white throne judging all men. Those who do not know Jesus Christ will be cast into hell for all eternity."

"You startle me," Sechele said, his face drawn and his hands trembling. "These words make all my bones shake; I have no more strength in me. But my forefathers were living at the same time yours were, and how is it that they did not send them word about these terrible things sooner? They all passed away into darkness without knowing where they were going." Livingstone felt heartsick that Christians had not come to these people earlier.

"I am sorry that it has taken so long," Livingstone said, "but one day the whole world will know the good news of Jesus."

Sechele, raising his arm and pointing north to the great Kalahari desert, said, "You never can cross that country to the tribes beyond." Sechele's words lit a fire in Livingstone's heart, and from that moment he planned to cross the Kalahari and lead the northern tribes to Christ. Livingstone brought Christians from the southern tribes and trained them as native teachers to go out to the northern tribes with the message of Jesus. His work angered the Boers, descendants of Dutch settlers, who had recently settled in the area and considered the black natives their subjects. Some of the Boers forced the natives to work without pay.

When Livingstone first met their leader, the Boer commander told him, "You must teach the blacks that they are not our equals." Other Boers said, "You are wasting your time, you might as well teach the baboons as the Africans."

"Well then," Livingstone said to them, "let's do a test to see who can read the best—you or my native helpers." The Boers refused the test.

After months of preparation, Livingstone thought the time was right to cross the Kalahari desert and contact the distant northern tribes. Two Englishmen, hunting in the area, decided to join him, and with some native guides, they set out across the Kalahari.

A chief on the edge of the desert sent Livingstone a message. "Where are you going? You will be killed by the sun and thirst, and then all the white men will blame me for not saving you." Livingstone sent the chief a gift and told him, "Don't worry, the white men will blame our deaths on our own stupidity."

For weeks they trekked north through the blazing heat of the Kalahari. At times they trudged two and three days without water, near death from thirst, until they found a spring or watering hole. At last they reached a broad and deep river and followed it for three hundred miles to the shores of a huge lake called by the natives "Ngami." When word reached England that David Livingstone had crossed the Kalahari desert and discovered Lake Ngami, the Royal Geographical Society and the queen of England honored him.

His trip across the Kalahari was the first of many journeys. He spent less time preaching and more time exploring. He led an expedition to explore the Zambezi River, which he called "God's highway into the interior," and he became the first white man to see Victoria Falls. Livingstone's book about his discoveries, describing his adventures and the land and people of Africa, made him famous throughout the world. He could have returned to England a national hero and a wealthy man. "I still prefer poverty and mission service to riches and ease," he said. "It's my choice."

The most difficult thing Livingstone faced in his travels was not lack of water or attack from wild animals but seeing the horrors of the slave trade. "It is impossible to overstate the evils of the slave trade," he said. "The sights I have seen are so sickening that I always strive to drive them from my memory. But the slavery scenes come back unbidden and make me start up at the dead of night, horrified by their vividness." He prayed, "O Almighty God, help, help! and leave not these wretched people to the slave dealer and Satan."

Some people in England, critical of David Livingstone, said it was wrong for a missionary to spend most of his time on exploration, but Livingstone disagreed. "My goals," he said, "are to help end the slave trade and to bring the Bible, God's Word from heaven, to people living in darkness." He believed that by opening up pathways into the interior of Africa, he was preparing the way for other missionaries to follow. He hoped that the African slave trade would end when the world learned of its horrors and the African interior was opened up for travel and honest trade.

Wherever Livingstone went, he tried to free captives of the slave trade. On his Zambesi expedition, he ran into a large group of natives being led away through the bush to the slave market. "We saw a long line of men, women and children," Livingstone wrote, "come wending their way around the hill and into the valley. The black slave drivers, armed with muskets marched jauntily in the front, middle, and rear of the line. But the instant they caught a glimpse of us, they darted off like mad into the forest, leaving the slaves behind. They ran so fast that we caught but a glimpse of their red caps and the soles of their feet. We got busy cutting the women and children loose. It was more difficult to cut the men free, as each had his neck fastened in the fork of a stick, six feet long, with an iron bar across his throat. One by one the men were sawn out. The freed captives made a fire with the slave sticks and cooked a meal for themselves and their children. Freedom seemed to them too good to be true."

Livingstone explored for the rest of his life, enduring fevers, torrential rains, animal attacks, threatening tribes, and countless other hardships. Once when asked how he could make such sacrifices, Livingstone answered, "I never made a sacrifice. We ought not to talk of sacrifice when we remember the great sacrifice which Christ made when He left His Father's throne on high to give Himself for us."

A few weeks before he died at the age of sixty, he wrote in his journal: "Nothing earthly will make me give up my work in despair. I encourage myself in the Lord and go forward." He died while at prayer. His native helpers found him kneeling motionless at his bedside, his head buried in his hands. After his death, hundreds of missionaries followed his trail into central and southern Africa, and many Africans turned to Christ.

• • •

John Paton
Witness to the Cannibals

John Paton 1824–1907

The war chief of the cannibals—Miaki—flushed with rage, his dark face streaked with red and black paint, whipped his men into a frenzy.

"Missi and the worship of Jehovah have brought great troubles to our land," he shouted. "Who will join me to fight Missi and the friends of the worship?" The tribesmen, feathers twisted in the long locks of their hair, jumped, yelled, and shook their spears.

"Before the sun goes down," he said, "let's cook his body and give it to every village on the island." As the warriors rushed off through the bush to kill Missi, their blood- curdling shrieks echoed across the island.

"Missi" was the natives' name for John Paton, a Scottish missionary to Tanna, a part of the South Pacific island chain called the New Hebrides (Vanautu). John Paton watched, listened, and prayed from his perch high up in a spreading chestnut tree where he hid from the tribesmen.

For three years John Paton had proclaimed the good news of Jesus Christ to the people of Tanna, but the aggressive, war-loving Tannese did not receive it with joy. They clung to their stone idols, superstitions, and rituals, worshipping out of fear alone. An endless cycle of warfare, murder, and revenge cast a dark cloud over the island. The strong abandoned the weak and elderly to die. Husbands took many wives and treated them as slaves. Wife-beating and wife-killing were common place. They honored liars, thieves, and back-stabbers as strong men. And the greatest thrill in their life came in killing and eating an enemy.

Early on, Paton took a strong stand against the beating

and killing of women, although missionaries on nearby islands warned him that to do so would mean certain death. Once when he was pleading for an end to the mistreatment of women, a chief said to him, "If we did not beat our women, they would never work; they would not fear and obey us. But when we have beaten, and killed, and feasted on two or three, the rest are all very quiet and good for a long time to come!"

John Paton had lost count of the number of times the Tannese had tried to kill him. Once two warriors burst into his home intending to crack his skull open with their war clubs, but Paton's dogs leapt in their faces and saved his life. Another time a cannibal ambushed him, throwing three spears, but they all missed. Often he talked his way out of sure death. One day, hearing a strange bleating from his goats, Paton rushed to investigate and found himself surrounded by a band of armed men ready to strike. Paton spoke kindly and firmly to them. "If you kill me, the Lord Jehovah will punish you for this terrible sin. I love you and want only your good. If you kill me, you kill your best friend." Then he began to pray aloud for them and for all the people of Tanna. By the time he finished his prayer, the men had left.

A group of Miaki's warriors once surrounded his home intending to murder him, when suddenly word came that an English warship was sailing into the harbor. The tribesmen fled in terror. "I believe," Paton said, "that the same Hand that restrained the lions from touching Daniel held back these savages from hurting me."

But death did come to Paton's home on Tanna. Six months after John and his wife arrived, she gave birth to their firstborn son but within a few weeks both mother and child died from fever. He laid them to rest in a mounded grave covered with crushed white coral. Though overwhelmed by loneliness and sorrow and urged by friends to leave the island altogether, he remained on Tanna, believing that God wanted him there.

Now from his hideout in the chestnut tree, with the warriors seeking to kill him, Paton realized that the time had come to leave. Taking his Bible, a few Tannese translation pages, and a blanket, he fled across the island. In time, an English ship arrived, and John Paton left Tanna. After several years of traveling the world recruiting new missionaries and raising money for the New Hebrides Mission, Paton remarried and returned to the field, but not to Tanna, for it remained too dangerous. Instead he went to the cannibals on Aniwa, the nearest island to Tanna. Despite the threatening and cold response of the Aniwas, Paton cared for the sick, mastered their language, and told them about Jesus Christ. Slowly interest grew and a number of the Aniwas believed in the Lord. Then came an event that led to the conversion of nearly everyone on the island.

Aniwa is a flat coral island with scarce rainfall. Often during the year the people got sick from lack of clean drinking water. Praying for success, John Paton decided to dig a well, though he feared that the water, if he found any, would be undrinkable salt water.

One morning Paton said to a gray-haired and wrinkled-skinned chief, "I am going to sink a deep well down into the earth, to see if our God will send us fresh water up from below."

Looking at Paton with wide eyes, the chief said, "Rain comes only from above. How could you expect our island to send up showers of rain from below?"

"Fresh water," Paton told him, "does come springing up from the earth in my land at home, and I hope to see it here also."

"O Missi," the chief said sorrowfully, "your head is going wrong, or you would not talk wild like that!"

The next day, Paton chose a spot near the mission house. With pick and shovel, hammer and crowbar, he began the difficult job of digging through the dirt and coral, making slow progress under the burning tropical sun. The old chief made his men take turns watching Paton.

"Poor Missi!" he said, "that's the way with all who go mad. There's no driving a notion out of their heads. Watch and make sure he doesn't try to kill himself." Day after day Paton toiled in the hole, blistering his hands and straining his muscles. He rigged a crude pulley with a rope and bucket to remove the dirt as the hole deepened.

All the while the chief implored him, "Give up this madness. No rain will be found by going downwards on Aniwa. If you do reach water, you will drop into the sea and the sharks will eat you." When the hole reached a depth of thirty feet, the soil felt damp. Paton rejoiced, but he feared that the water would be saltwater. That evening in the village, taking a great risk yet trusting in God's goodness, he told the tribesmen, "Come to the well tomorrow, I hope and believe that Jehovah God will send you rain water up through the earth."

At daybreak, the chief and his men gathered around the well as Paton climbed in and dug down another two feet. Water rushed up and filled the bottom of the hole. He scooped up a handful, tasted it, and fell to his knees in praise to the Lord. It was fresh water. He filled a jug, brought it up to the waiting tribesmen, and handed it to the old chief. Cautiously the chief dipped in his finger and then took a few drops into his mouth. With a beaming face he shouted, "Rain! Yes, it is rain! But how did you get it?"

"Jehovah, my God," Paton said, "gave it out of His own earth in answer to our labors and prayers. Go and see it springing up for yourselves." One by one each man peered down the well overcome with the wonder of "Jehovah's rain".

"Missi," the old chief exclaimed, "wonderful, wonderful is the work of your Jehovah God! No god of Aniwa ever helped us in this way. The world is turned upside down since Jehovah came to Aniwa! Missi, will you drink it all, or shall we also have some?"

"You and all your people," Paton answered, smiling broadly, "may come and drink and carry away as much as you wish. I believe there will always be plenty for us all, and the more of it we use the fresher it will be. That is the way with many of our Jehovah's best gifts to men, and for it we praise His name!"

"Missi," the old chief whispered, taking Paton by the arm and pulling him aside, "I think I can help you next Sabbath. Will you let me preach a sermon on the well?" Paton agreed and word spread throughout the island that Chief Namakei was to be the missionary on Sunday. A great crowd assembled in eager expectation. All was quiet as the old chief rose to speak. His voice quaked with emotion, and he swung his tomahawk to emphasize his words.

"Friends, people of Aniwa, listen to my words," he said. "Since Missi came here he has spoken many strange things we could not understand. We thought they were lies. He said that Jehovah God loves us and has sent His Son Jesus to die for us and bring us to heaven. He said Jehovah God can send us rain up from the earth. We laughed at him but now we believe him. For by the power of Jehovah, Missi has brought forth rain from the ground. If Jehovah God has sent us rain from earth, why should he not also send us His Son from heaven? So I, your chief, do now firmly believe that when I die, I shall see the invisible Jehovah God with my soul, as Missi tells me, not less surely than I have seen the rain from the earth below. I, Namakei, stand up for Jehovah!"

That very day the old chief and many of his people rounded up their idols, burned them, and came to Paton, eager to learn about God. In the following years, most of the people of Aniwa believed in Jesus Christ. Paton translated the Bible into their language and taught them to read. John Paton never returned as a missionary to Tanna, but he lived to see others restart the work there, and he rejoiced to hear that some on that dark island had turned to the Lord. Several of Paton's children, grandchildren, and great-grandchildren followed him in serving Christ in the South Pacific islands.

• • •

Hudson Taylor
Founder of the China Inland Mission

Hudson Taylor 1832–1905

A large crowd surrounded Hudson Taylor, eager to hear his message. This was unusual because the Chinese had shown little interest in hearing about Jesus Christ since Taylor's arrival in Shanghai eighteen months earlier in March of 1854. Taylor's sandy-colored hair and English clothing made him look very different from his hearers. He wore a double-breasted, English overcoat, complete with rows of buttons on the front and back. The Chinese men shaved their heads bald, leaving a long pony tail in the back which they tied with a silk cord. The people listened attentively, but one man standing in front appeared to hang on every word.

Thrilled by the man's interest, Taylor turned to him at the conclusion of the message and asked, "Well, honorable Sir, what do you think about what you have heard?"

"Yes, yes," the man answered, bowing from the waist, "what you say is doubtless very true. But honorable Foreign Teacher, may I ask you one question?" A broad smile swept across Taylor's face. This was why he had come to China.

"Please ask your question," he said.

"I have been pondering all the while you have been preaching," the man said. "But the subject is no clearer to my mind. The honorable garment you are wearing, Foreign Teacher, has upon one edge of it a number of round objects that look like buttons, and on the opposite edge, certain slits in the material probably intended for button holes?"

"Yes, that is so," Taylor said. His heart dropped and his shoulders drooped when he realized that the man's interest was in his coat and not in Jesus Christ.

"The purpose of that strange device I can understand," the man continued. "It must be to attach the honorable garment in cold or windy weather. But, Foreign Teacher, this is what I cannot understand. What can be the meaning of those buttons in the middle of the honorable back?"

"Why, yes," the people joined in, "what about the buttons in the middle of the honorable back!" Hudson Taylor could not give them a good reason for the three useless, decorative buttons on the back of his coat. As the crowd slipped away, the words—"in the middle of the honorable back"—rang in his ears. It was clear, his English clothing hindered his message.

Not long before, while he sat cross-legged, eating a bowl of duck eggs and fried rice with chopsticks, several Chinese men looked on.

"Look how well he uses chopsticks," one man said.

"Honorable Teacher," another added, "if you shaved your head and wore our style clothes, you would be just like us." Taylor decided to make himself look Chinese. A barber shaved his head, leaving a small pigtail in the back which Taylor dyed black. When he put on his new satin robe and shoes, he looked Chinese from top to bottom.

The next day, when he went out to preach, the change in the people was remarkable. They received him as an honored guest, not as a strange, outsider and concentrated on his words instead of his wardrobe. Although the Chinese welcomed his new appearance, he met stiff opposition from the Englishmen in the International Settlement in Shanghai who laughed at and shunned him. "He is hurting British prestige in the eyes of the natives," they said. Other missionaries, disgusted by his appearance, thought he had lost his mind. But Taylor stood his ground saying, "We should seek to make them Christians, not Englishmen."

Later, when he proposed marriage to a young English woman from the International Settlement, her guardian refused to let her consider it. "He is not a gentleman," her guardian told her. "He is a ranter. And . . . and he wears Chinese clothes." Although the criticism of his countrymen stung, he sensed the Lord's smile and pressed on. "I must wait on God and trust in Him," he wrote his parents, "and all will be well."

Hudson Taylor worked long hours preaching, caring for the sick, helping the poor, and seeking new ways to bring the good news of Jesus deeper into China. But the strain of his workload broke his health, forcing him to return to England to regain his strength. Back home in his little study in London hung a large wall map of China. Every day as he looked at it, he found his eyes drawn away from the coastal cities to the vast regions of inland China where millions lived without any knowledge of Jesus Christ, for missionaries were forbidden outside of a few coastal cities. Overwhelmed by the great needs of the inland Chinese, Hudson visited the leaders of all the mission societies in England. "You must open up inland China for the gospel," he urged them. But they turned him away. "We don't have enough missionaries," one told him, "and it is too expensive. Besides, with a civil war raging in China, we wouldn't expand into the interior even if we had the money and men."

Taylor refused to give up. Traveling the country, he implored people in prayer meetings and chapel services saying, "The Chinese Empire is 104 times larger than England. More than four hundred million live in that great land and only a few thousand know Jesus Christ. And in all the inland provinces there is not a single missionary. A million people a month are dying without God."

At a large gathering of English and Scottish church leaders, he told a story which powerfully moved his audience.

"Once when I was sailing on a Chinese ship," Taylor told them, "a young Chinese man fell overboard in shallow, muddy water. I leapt overboard in the hope of finding him. Unsuccessful, I looked around in agonizing suspense and saw close to me a fishing boat with a dragnet furnished with hooks, which I knew would bring him up.

'Come and drag this spot quickly; a man is drowning here,'
I called.

'It is not convenient,' they said.

'Don't talk of convenience! A man is drowning I tell
you!'

'We are busy fishing and cannot come.'

'Never mind your fishing,' I said, 'I will give you more
money than many a day's fishing will bring; only come now.'

'How much money will you give us?' they asked.

'We cannot stay to discuss that now! Come, or it will
be too late. I will give you five dollars.'

'We won't do it for that,' replied the men. 'Give us twenty
dollars and we will drag for him.'

'I don't have that much money; but do come quickly
and I will give you all I have!'

'How much is that?' they asked.

'I don't know exactly, about fourteen dollars.'

'At last, the boat was paddled slowly over and the net
let down. In less than a minute, the body of the missing
man was brought up. The fishermen angrily demanded their
money while I worked to get him breathing again. But all
was in vain. His life was gone.'"

Although no one in the audience spoke, Taylor could
see in their strained faces a righteous anger over the cold
indifference of the fishermen. Then Taylor continued,

"We condemn those heathen fishermen. We say they
were guilty of the man's death because they could have saved
him and did not. But what of the millions whom we leave
to perish eternally? What of the plain command, 'Go ye
into all the world and preach the gospel to every creature?'"

After the service, many rushed forward to pledge financial support. Soon seven men and women joined Hudson
Taylor and his wife, Maria, and the China Inland Mission
was born. The China Inland Mission, unlike any other mission agency, maintained its headquarters in China. It required all missionaries to dress and wear their hair in Chinese style and forbade them to ask churches or individuals

directly for money. "I felt it best just to leave ourselves open to receive gifts of money as God might lay on the hearts of his children to send," Taylor said. Whenever one of their number worried about money, he told them, "God is sufficient for God's work."

Upon returning to China in 1866, the Taylor family and three other missionaries went to Yangchow where not a single foreigner lived. Not long after they arrived, city leaders posted handbills throughout the city warning, "Beware of Foreigners!" They spread lies, saying the missionaries kidnapped and ate Chinese children. One official called Taylor into his office and told him, "I know perfectly well what you plan to do. You want to deceive our hearts and then seize the whole land for yourselves." Then one night, enraged by a rumor that the missionaries had kidnapped twenty-four Chinese babies, a thousand rioters, carrying torches, surrounded the mission house. They threw bricks at the windows and screamed, "Foreign devils!"

Taylor realized that their only hope for survival was to get troops from the city magistrate to break up the mob. He offered a short prayer and ran for help with another man. "The foreign devils are fleeing," someone shouted, spotting the two missionaries running away. With a pack of angry men close on their heels, pelting them with rocks, Taylor and his friend barely got to city hall and collapsed inside, bloodied and panting. "Save life, save life!" they called. The magistrate kept them waiting for nearly an hour while the noise from the rioters echoed across the city.

"Ah, Mr. Taylor," the magistrate said with a sly smile, "Tell me, what did you really do with those babies?"

"Your Excellency," Taylor said with a bow, "we are living in your city legally, we have done nothing wrong, and you are responsible for maintaining law and order. You will be held accountable for any loss of life." Reluctantly, the magistrate agreed to send his men, but Taylor feared it was too late. When they returned with armed guards they found the mission house partially burned, with smashed furniture and burned books strewn around the courtyard. Thieves had stolen most of their possessions. There was no sign of life.

In the midst of the riot, Maria, the children, and the other missionaries had jumped from a second-story window and hid in a well-house and then slipped into a back room of a neighbor's home. That is where Taylor found them, injured but alive. Later that night, after the armed guards left, looters came to steal the rest of their property.

Hudson Taylor went out to the courtyard, stood on a broken chair, and said, "We came from far away to do you good. If we meant you evil, would we have come unarmed? Or with our women and children? Without cause, you have stolen our property and tried to burn down our house. And now you come back in your greed for plunder to do us more mischief. But we did not raise a stick against you or throw one stone. If you hurt us we will not retaliate. But our God, in whom we trust, is able to protect us and punish you if you offend against Him." They left shamefaced.

The next day, the commander of the city guards told them to leave Yangchow. "My men cannot keep down the people," he said. "I will send you away under escort by boats. When we have repaired the house, we will invite you to return." For the three months the missionaries were away, they prayed for a softening of hearts in Yangchow. Upon their return, they found the people ready to hear about Jesus Christ. Those who had tried to kill them now sat at their feet to learn from them. Soon many in the city trusted in Jesus for the forgiveness of their sins. Meanwhile, Taylor made plans to send more missionaries further inland.

In the years that followed, the China Inland Mission sent men and women to every province in China. Before Hudson Taylor died at the age of seventy-two, there were over a thousand China Inland missionaries in the land. The Lord drew hundreds of thousands of Chinese to Himself through their efforts.

• • •

Amy Carmichael
Mother to Outcast Children

Amy Carmichael 1867–1951

Amy Carmichael's mother taught her to ask anything of God, for He promises to hear and answer. So three-year-old Amy knelt at her bedside and fervently prayed: "Dear Lord please make my brown eyes blue. Amen." With those words she slipped into bed and fell asleep, confident that she would awake with dazzling blue eyes. In the morning Amy rushed to the mirror only to discover that her eyes were as brown as ever. As a wave of disappointment rolled over her, she suddenly realized that "no" is as much an answer as "yes." She had learned a valuable lesson. The Lord does answer prayer, but often the answer is no.

Mr. and Mrs. Carmichael raised their four sons and three daughters with strict discipline and a sober yet joyful view of the world. Clearly laying down the rules for behavior, they punished the children immediately for disobedience, and all punishments were to be received with a polite, "Thank you, Father," or "Thank you, Mother." A ringing bell called the family to devotions. Amy's father read the Scriptures and told the children stories about the martyrs—men and women who sacrificed everything to remain faithful to Christ.

A test of Amy's faith came with the sudden death of her father. Painful as it was, Amy did not respond with doubts and anger but channeled her sorrow into faithful service to others, especially helping to relieve her mother's burden by caring for her younger brothers and sisters.

An even greater turning point in Amy Carmichael's life came on a wet and windy Sunday morning. While walking home from church with her family, they met a poor old woman burdened with a heavy load. Taking pity on her, Amy and her brothers picked up the bundle and walked arm and arm with her. The respectable churchgoers frowned upon this. Although Amy and her brothers felt awkward and embarrassed, they plodded on with the old woman. Suddenly the words from First Corinthians flashed through the drizzle: "Gold, silver, costly stones, wood, hay, straw, his work will be shown for what it is, because the day will bring it to light. It will be revealed with fire, and the fire will test the quality of each man's work. If what he has built survives."

Later Amy wrote, "the blinding flash had come and gone; the ordinary was all about us. We went on. I said nothing to anyone, but I knew something had happened that had changed life's values. Nothing could ever matter again but the things that were eternal." Amy's heart went out to the neighborhood children for whom she organized a weekly program of Bible study, song, and prayer. The poor young women of the town, shunned and neglected by most church members, were loved by Amy. Eyebrows raised whenever Amy trooped into church with several of the young women from the "wrong side of town."

Besides those in her own community that needed Christ, Amy prayed for the countless millions in Asia living under the dark cloud of idolatry and superstition. She felt as if the hand of God was pulling her into the foreign mission field, but what about her widowed mother? Could she leave her? Amy wrote her mother a long letter explaining her desire to serve Christ in Asia.

"Dearest Amy," her mother answered, "God has lent you to me all these years. . . . When He asks you now to go away from within my reach, can I say no? No, no Amy, He is yours; you are His to take where He pleases and to use you as He pleases." With tears of joy, Amy thanked God for her mother's reply and shortly thereafter, in 1895, she left her homeland for South India. The poverty and teeming masses overwhelmed her senses with strange sights, sounds, and smells. The people's slavish devotion to idols, offering incense, flowers, and food to images of wood and metal; their lack of compassion for the poor, and the rigid caste system threw an oppressive spiritual darkness over the land.

The caste system is the foundation of Hinduism. Everyone is born into a caste, a place in society, and there one stays. It dictates who you can marry, what you can do and where you can live. As Carmichael learned more of this way of life, the cruelty of it broke her heart.

Once when visiting the shack of a poor family, Carmichael saw a small boy suffering from the agonies of a painful eye disease. He couldn't sleep, he cried constantly, and he rubbed his puffy, red eyes. Two months later, she returned and found the boy had withered away to near death, still crying with his eyes inflamed. Carmichael pleaded, "Please, take him to the hospital-they can help him there."

"Oh no," his father answered firmly, "we could never do that. Going to the hospital is against our caste."

"Then he is to suffer till he is blind or dead?" Carmichael asked.

"What can we do?" they said, shrugging their shoulders. "Can we destroy our caste?" Amy Carmichael prayed, and then left the house weeping. She couldn't stop thinking about the needless suffering of the little boy. The caste system made it very difficult for an Indian man or woman, boy or girl to become a Christian. To do so would be to break caste. Those who turned to Christ were often threatened with murder, and some were killed. One man whose daughter was considering becoming a Christian said, "She shall burn to ashes first!"

Danger surrounded the missionaries too. Once when a girl received Christ as her Savior and fled to the mission compound, her family burned the mission school to the ground. Threats were common. In a letter home Carmichael wrote, "Pray that we who are His sworn soldiers abroad may throw our kid gloves to the winds and *fight*!" Carmichael hoped to spend her days traveling about telling people about Jesus or holding evangelistic meetings, but then a seven-year-old girl named Pearleyes arrived.

Pearleyes had been sent by her mother to a Hindu temple as a "servant of the gods," a virtual slave to the temple masters. Wanting no part of the wicked world of the temple, Pearleyes escaped home, begging her mother not to return her. Her mother, afraid to displease the gods, dragged the little girl back to the temple. But Pearleyes refused to stay. Though closely watched, she escaped again and found her way to Carmichael's mission compound at Dohnavur, pleading to stay. The young girl explained the terrible wickedness that went on in the temple. "Pearleyes," Carmichael said, wrapping her arms around her, "you have a home with us."

And so began Carmichael's work rescuing children bound for the temples. Before long, she was playing mother to scores of children.

"Children tie the mother's feet," is an old Indian proverb. Carmichael found it to be true. At first, frustrated with changing diapers, wiping noses, fixing large meals, and rocking sick little ones to sleep, Carmichael asked, "Could it be right to turn from so much that might be of profit (evangelistic tours, convention meetings for Christians, and so on) and become just a nursemaid?"

But then Amy was powerfully struck by the image of Christ wrapping himself in a towel and stooping to wash the disciples' feet. The Savior did not view humble service as small or unimportant. So Amy Carmichael willingly let her "feet be tied" for the love of Him whose feet were pierced. They called her "Amma" (mother) and she called them "Lotus Buds." They built a school and medical clinic as the number of children grew. Although Amy insisted on discipline and obedience, she sought to fill their lives with joy. "Children must have laughter round about them," Carmichael said. Carmichael belly-laughed with the children in jokes and games, and she filled the compound with song. She got on all fours in the dirt, teaching them how to plant seeds in the flower garden, by working their little hands to prepare the soil, set the seed, and then water it. In the warm climate of southern India, brilliant colored flowers brightened the compound year-round.

For fifty years, Carmichael raised children for the Lord, and she wrote books. She wrote about the children and the joys and sorrows of the Christian life. More than a dozen of her books are still in print and continue to inspire believers to follow in the steps of Jesus Christ. Amy Carmichael died at the age of eighty-three. She was buried on the grounds where she had worked all those years. According to her wishes, no gravestone marks the spot. The Dohnavur Fellowship lives on, doing the work that Carmichael began—providing a Christian home for children in great need.

• • •

SPURGEON PREACHING

Recent Times

Standing for Christ

For the last 150 years the unbelief of the modern world has assailed the church, but God raised up bright and bold men and women to stand for Christ and the trustworthiness of Scripture.

- Charles Spurgeon
  Prince of Preachers

- Chinese Christians
  In the Boxer Rebellion

- Abraham Kuyper
  Theologian and Statesman

- J. Gresham Machen
  Valiant for Truth

- C. S. Lewis
  Chronicler of Narnia

- Richard Wurmbrand
  Tortured for Christ

Charles Spurgeon
Prince of Preachers

Charles Spurgeon 1834–1892

It was 1843 in Stambourne, England, and the door to the pastor's study hung slightly ajar. Nine-year-old Charles Spurgeon pressed his eye to the narrow crack and saw his beloved grandfather, head in hand, sighing deeply. With knitted brow, Pastor Spurgeon sat grieving over Thomas Roads, a backsliding member of his church, who recently turned his back on the church and spent all his time drinking to excess in the local pub.

Seeing his grandfather, his hero, so forlorn drove a stake in Charles' heart. When he thought of Mr. Roads, his chest tightened and his temples throbbed. He made up his mind to do something about it. Bursting into the study he declared, "I'll kill old Roads, that I will!"

"Hush, hush! my dear," said his grandfather, who was quite shocked by the outburst, "you mustn't talk so; if you do anything wrong, you know, you'll get taken up by the police."

"I shall not do anything bad, Grandpa, but I'll kill him though, that I will."

Charles marched out of the house and straight down the dusty lane to the pub. Peering through a grimy window into the smoke-filled room, he spotted Mr. Roads leaning back in his chair laughing heartily. Charles threw open the door, boldly approached Roads, pointed his finger at him, and said, "What are you doing here sitting with the ungodly . . . and you a member of the church and breaking your pastor's heart. I'm ashamed of you! I wouldn't break my pastor's heart, I'm sure."

Charles turned on his heels and rushed out the door.

Arriving back at his grandparents' home he announced, "I've killed old Roads; he'll never grieve my dear grandpa anymore."

Pastor Spurgeon's face turned ashen white, drawing Charles to his side he asked, "My dear child, what have you done? Where have you been?"

"I haven't been doing any harm, grandpa, I've been about the Lord's work, that's all."

Charles rushed outside to play, leaving his grandfather worried and perplexed about what he had done. A short time later, Mr. Roads knocked at Pastor Spurgeon's front door. With downcast eyes he said, "I'm very sorry indeed, my dear pastor, to have caused you such grief and trouble. It was very wrong, I know; but I always loved you and wouldn't have done it if I'd only thought."

Pastor Spurgeon threw his arms around Roads and assured him of his love and forgiveness. Then Mr. Roads told him what Charles had done.

"To think an old man like me should be took to task, and reproved by a bit of a child like that! Well, I did feel angry at what the boy said, but I knew it was all true, and I was guilty; so I put down my pipe, and did not touch my beer, but hurried away to a lonely spot and cast myself down before the Lord, confessing my sin and begging for forgiveness. I believe the Lord in mercy pardoned me; and now I have come to ask you to forgive me, and I'll never grieve you anymore, my dear pastor." The repentance proved true and long-lasting. Mr. Roads abandoned his sinful ways and remained ever after an earnest Christian, faithful at worship and prayer.

Yet despite being raised in a Christian home and church where the good news of Christ was clearly taught, Charles Spurgeon had not been given a new heart by the Spirit. "The light was there," Spurgeon wrote later, "but I was blind." When Charles Spurgeon was fifteen years old, his lost state before God and the guilt of his sin weighed heavily upon him. One Sunday morning in the midst of a snowstorm, he popped into a little Methodist chapel, brushed off the snow from his coat and boots, and sat down with the few other worshippers. But the minister never showed up. At last a very thin man, an unschooled tradesman, stepped to the pulpit and read a line from the Bible: "'Look unto me, and be ye saved, all the ends of the earth.' My dear friends," the man said, "this is a very simple text indeed. It says 'Look unto Me.' Many of ye are lookin' to yourselves, but its no use lookin' there. You'll never find any comfort in yourselves." After speaking for a few minutes, he looked at Spurgeon and said, "Young man, you look very miserable and you always will be miserable—miserable in life and in death—if you don't obey my text; but if you obey now, this moment, you will be saved." Right then, Spurgeon looked to Jesus, and God made him a new man. He joined a Baptist church and before long was preaching, but how he began to preach, at the age of sixteen, was surprising.

One Saturday morning, Mr. Vinter, the director of an association which sent lay preachers into the rural villages, sought out Charles Spurgeon and asked, "Would you be willing to go over to Teversham on Sunday evening? A young man is to preach there who is not used to leading services and would be glad of company." Later Spurgeon admired the ingenuity of Mr. Vinter's request, for the young man that he intended to preach was Spurgeon himself. When Sunday afternoon arrived, he began to walk to Teversham with the young man that he had been asked to assist. They enjoyed some pleasant conversation until Spurgeon said, "I hope you will feel the presence of God tonight while preaching."

The man stopped abruptly and said, "I've never preached in my life, I couldn't possibly do it. You are to preach. I was asked to come along and support you." Spurgeon stood for a moment unable to speak.

Then wide eyed he pleaded, "I'm no minister, I've never preached either and furthermore I'm completely unprepared."

"But Mr. Spurgeon, I'm here to help with any other part of the service, but if you do not preach this evening there will be no sermon."

With head bowed, Spurgeon resigned himself to do his best. "Lord," he prayed, "help me to tell these poor cottagers of the sweetness and love of Jesus." In Teversham, they entered the low-pitched room of a thatched cottage where a few humble families had gathered for worship. The butterflies in his stomach disappeared as Charles proclaimed a simple message of Christ's love. The cottagers, surprised by his passionate and eloquent words, listened with rapt attention and many eyes brimmed with tears.

"Bless your dear heart, how old are you?" one old woman asked at the close of the service.

"Never mind my age," Spurgeon answered, "think of the Lord Jesus and His preciousness." They called him the "boy preacher" and begged him to come again. Soon he was preaching every evening throughout the countryside in barns, farmhouses, and meeting rooms. Large numbers of people believed in Jesus Christ and news of the "boy preacher" spread quickly from village to village.

"How do you do it?" someone asked Spurgeon.

"I speak in plain simple English that a child could comprehend," Spurgeon said, "and with all the earnestness of which I am capable." In 1851, when Charles Spurgeon was just seventeen and with no university or seminary training, the church in the village of Waterbeach called him to be their pastor. The church's forty members worshipped in a small chapel which once housed a pigeon coop. Poverty, drunkenness, and crime reigned in Waterbeach. Until God, as Spurgeon put it, "turned the whole place upside down."

Shortly after Spurgeon began to preach there, the little chapel was crammed. Dirty vagabonds and stiff-necked criminals who came to taunt the "boy preacher" left in a flood of tears. "Where there had been robberies and villainies of every kind," Spurgeon said, "all around the neighborhood there were none, because the men who used to do the mischief were themselves in the house of God, rejoicing to hear of Jesus crucified." Joyful songs of praises echoed down each narrow lane where before only shouting and cursing was heard.

It was not long before Spurgeon came to the attention of the churches in London. Although he dearly loved his congregation in Waterbeach, he accepted a call to New Park Street Chapel in London, for he longed to reach the millions of lost souls who lived in that great city. The New Park Street Chapel could seat 1,200 people, but fewer than 200 attended. Within a few weeks of Spurgeon's arrival, people jammed the sanctuary. Eager listeners crowded outside the open windows to hear the sermon. The church officers decided to build a huge, new sanctuary and while it was being constructed, they rented Surrey Gardens Music Hall, where over 10,000 people squeezed shoulder to shoulder to hear Spurgeon preach each Sunday. Countless people, from wealthy nobles to street beggars, turned to Christ.

Once when he was scheduled to speak in one of the largest auditoriums in London, he went the day before to the auditorium to find the best location for the pulpit. In order to test how well his voice could be heard, he cried out in a loud voice, "Behold the lamb of God who takes away the sins of the world!" High in one of the galleries, a workman heard the words and they pierced his soul. Overwhelmed with the guilt of his sin, he dropped his tools, ran home, and soon found forgiveness and new life in Jesus Christ.

Charles Spurgeon remained the pastor of his congregation until his death at the age of fifty-seven. He wielded the sword of his biblical preaching and writing against liberal ministers who rejected the inerrancy of the Bible, made light of sin, and denied Christ's bodily resurrection. "Yet these enemies of the faith," Spurgeon said, "expect us to call them brethren and maintain an alliance with them!"

Many urged him to avoid controversy and just preach the gospel, but Spurgeon felt compelled to defend the Christian faith and the Word of God. "Controversy," Spurgeon said, "is never a very happy thing for the child of God—he would rather be in communion with his Lord than be engaged in defending the faith or in attacking error. But the soldier of Christ must follow his Master's commands."

Over the years, he became the most well-known Christian speaker in the world, preaching to tens of thousands of people each week. He wrote commentaries and devotional books which sold millions of copies. Not since the days of Whitefield and Wesley had God so blessed the preaching of an English minister. His printed sermons and books continue to draw people to Jesus Christ to this day.

• • •

Chinese Christians
In the Boxer Rebellion

Boxer Rebellion 1900–1901

The twentieth century began with terrible persecution in China. Secret society members known as Boxers, hateful of foreigners and Christians, organized across the land. "Christian devils trouble our country," they declared. In 1900, they struck out, determined to kill every foreign missionary and Chinese Christian in the land. Bands of armed men tore down churches, burned houses, and murdered thousands of Christians. Many Chinese Christians risked their lives to protect the missionaries and faced death with faith and courage.

Late in May of 1900, Pastor Meng was attending a church conference in Peking when word came that the Boxers were destroying the railway between Peking and his hometown. Meng decided to return home at once. Friends, concerned for his safety, urged him to stay.

"The missionaries and the church members will need me," he told them. He returned home and despite the danger continued preaching to his congregation and in the street chapel.

A gentleman asked Pastor Meng, "Why don't you hide away for a time?"

"I am the shepherd of the flock," Meng answered. "Can I leave them?" Another man told him to leave the foreign missionaries, for as a Chinese man, he could easily find a safe place until the troubles passed.

"The missionaries have stayed by us," Meng said, "and I shall stay and live or die with them." By the end of June, Boxers controlled the city, and everyone knew that those living in the mission compound were doomed die. The

Chinese Christians in the compound still had time to escape, but the three foreign missionaries could not slip away unnoticed.

Pastor Meng pulled aside his son and said, "Ti-to, I have arranged for a friend to hide you from the Boxers. I cannot forsake my missionary friends and the Christians who have no one else to depend upon, but I want you left to take up the work after I am gone."

"Father," his son said with tears in his eyes, "I want to stay here with you; I am not afraid to die."

"No," his father answered, "if we are all killed, who will be left to preach Jesus to these poor people?" In the dead of night, Ti-to climbed over the high wall of the mission compound and fled to safety. The next day, when Pastor Meng preached in the city chapel, Boxers burst in, stabbed him in the head, and dragged him to a pagan temple. They demanded that he renounce his faith and reveal the whereabouts of Christians in the city. Although they scorched his shoulders with burning candles and tore one of his arms out of joint, he told them nothing. When it was clear he would not cooperate, the Boxers drew their knives and killed him.

Ti-to went on to study at a Christian academy and prepare for the ministry. Later, he returned to his hometown and discovered that nearly all of his family were murdered by the Boxers. "I am not sad or lonely," he said. "How could I have thought a few months ago during the terror that I would so soon be with our Christian friends; that I would have a chance to study; that I could go to church every Sunday with hundreds of God's people who had escaped from the Boxers? God has been very good to me."

•

Mrs. Kao and her daughter, Jessica, a recent graduate of a missionary school in Peking, were bright and beautiful women of God. Mrs. Kao spent her days telling women about Jesus Christ. She visited medical clinics and homes, passing out Christian literature and Bibles and sharing her faith in Christ. One day when her husband was away, Boxers banged angrily at the gate of the cluster of houses where she lived. "Kill! Kill!" the Boxers screamed as they kicked in the gate.

"Where are the Kaos?" they shouted. Trembling women and children cowered in the corner of the yard. Mrs. Kao stepped calmly from her door and said,

"We are the Kaos. These other families are not Christians. Please permit my daughter and I to put on our long coats and then we will go with you."

"Take and bind them!" the Boxer leader ordered.

"We are women," Mrs. Kao said gently, "why bind us? We are believers in the Lord; if we promise not to run, we surely will not do it."

"Bind them tightly lest they escape," the leader bellowed, glaring at Mrs. Kao. They tied their thumbs together tightly behind their backs and pushed the women from their home. At the gateway, Mrs. Kao turned to her terrified neighbors in the courtyard and said, "Sisters, I have been the cause of great fear coming to you today. Farewell. If I am permitted to see you again, I shall rejoice; if not, I hope that we may meet in heaven. I should be so glad if you all believed in Jesus." The Boxers shoved them into the dusty street and led them through an angry mob.

"Aha!" one man shouted. "See the followers of the foreign devils whom the Boxers have captured! They'll soon be done for."

"Isn't that Mrs. Kao, the woman preacher?" Someone called.

"Yes, and that pretty girl must be her daughter, the one who has been studying for years with the foreign devils in Peking," another answered.

It was impossible for Mrs. Kao to walk quickly, for her feet had been crippled by tight binding as a child. "Hurry up!" the Boxers yelled, hitting their backs with the flat edge of their swords.

"My mother's feet are small," Jessica protested, "it isn't easy for her to walk. Don't hurry her so." The Boxers pushed them forward roughly to the courtyard of a pagan temple where they were made to stand in the scorching sun.

Mrs. Kao looked into Jessica's eyes and asked, "Are you afraid?"

"Mother," she answered, "Jesus is with us, there isn't anything to fear."

"Let's pray together," Mrs. Kao told Jessica. With their hands tied behind their backs, surrounded by a jeering crowd, they knelt in the dust and prayed. When they arose, Mrs. Kao smiled; she turned to her daughter and said, "Jessica, I see Jesus has come; do you see him?"

"Mother," she answered, "I believe that Jesus is always with those who love Him." They separated mother from daughter and hustled Mrs. Kao through a trial, sentencing her to death.

After guards marched her to the place of execution, Mrs. Kao said to the Boxer leader, "I am only a condemned criminal, but I ask of you one favor. Please give me a little time to pray to my Heavenly Father." He granted her a moment and she knelt and prayed, "Father, forgive them; they don't understand what they are doing." An executioner beheaded her on the spot. Jessica, spared from the sword, died from disease a few months later. She told her father on her deathbed, "Father, now I am going before you to see my mother's face. The one important thing is that you should hold fast to the holy truth of God, and go, as I am going, to the heavenly home."

•

During the Boxer Rebellion, Shansi was known as the martyr province. The Shansi governor spared no effort in murdering Christians. One day soldiers drove about sixty missionaries and their children like cattle into the courtyard of the governor's mansion. The governor ran his eyes over the missionaries and ordered the death sentence. Then a thirteen-year-old, golden-haired girl, a daughter of a missionary, walked forward and stood before the governor.

"Why are you planning to kill us?" she asked in a loud voice easily heard by all. "Haven't our doctors come from far-off lands to give their lives for your people? Many with hopeless diseases have been healed. Health and happiness have been brought into thousands of your homes because of what our doctors have done. Is it because of this good that has been done that you are going to kill us?" The governor hung his head and said nothing. "Our missionaries," she continued, "have come from foreign lands and have preached Jesus to drug addicts and gamblers, and Jesus has saved them and given them power to live rightly and to love and obey their parents. Is it then, perhaps, for this good that has been done that we are to be killed?" Red-faced and writhing, the governor signaled to a soldier, who snatched the girl by the hair and cut off her head with one swift blow of his sword. In minutes, all the Christian men, women and children in the courtyard were slaughtered.

A Chinese scholar who was in the governor's courtyard that day was amazed by the fearlessness and calm of the Christians facing death. "I saw fifty-nine men, women, and children killed that afternoon," the scholar told a missionary a few years later. "Even in the very moment of death every face seemed to hold a smile of peace. Is it any wonder, therefore, that such marvelous courage should have led me to search your Scriptures and compelled me to believe that the Bible is truly the Word of God?" He turned to the missionary, his eyes a flood of tears, and said, "I am convinced that there can be no salvation for us sinners except through the Redeemer, Jesus Christ."

After troops from Europe and America crushed the Boxers, they forced the Chinese government to pay restitution to Christians who made claims for property lost in the rebellion. Surviving missionaries and Chinese Christians came out of hiding and returned home. They faced a great challenge in forgiving their enemies—those who had killed their loved ones and destroyed their houses. One Christian young man, Mr. Chen, a preacher like his father, returned to his hometown to find that his father and mother and two of his sisters had been killed and the family home burned down.

"What payment do you want for your loss?" an official asked him.

"I do not want payment," he answered, "but I would like to go and preach the gospel to the people who murdered my parents." He went and told the murderers about the love and forgiveness of Jesus Christ.

•

In the city of Shinminfu, the Boxers killed many Christians. Nearly every Christian family lost a father or mother or child during the rebellion. In the hope that one day they could seek revenge, Christian survivors wrote a list of 250 names of people in the area who participated in the killing. A few years later, a revival of faith swept through Shinminfu. In a church meeting, one young man stood up and said, "In 1900, the Boxers came to my house and killed my father. All along I have felt that I should grow up and avenge that wrong. But during these last days, the Holy Spirit has made me so miserable that I haven't been able to eat or sleep or do anything. I know He is urging me to forgive the murderers for Jesus' sake."

The next day, the list of 250 murderers was brought to the front of the church. They tore it into bits and stomped it under foot. "Praise God," one man said, "He gave me the grace to forgive the murderer of my father." In the years following the Boxer Rebellion, thousands of Christian missionaries rushed to China to replace the hundreds who had died. The Chinese turned to Christ in vast numbers and flourishing churches sprang up in every province. The old saying proved true in China: "The blood of the martyrs is the seed of the church."

• • •

Abraham Kuyper
Theologian and Statesman

Abraham Kuyper 1837–1920

"And so, gentlemen," the professor concluded, "in light of all I have learned in recent years through a modern study of the Bible, I can no longer accept as historical fact that Jesus' body rose from the dead."

The Dutch theological students crowding the lecture hall jumped to their feet, applauding loudly. One of those clapping with enthusiasm was Abraham Kuyper, a twenty-one-year-old training for the ministry. Although raised by his parents to believe that the Scripture is the inerrant Word of God, Kuyper was won over to a liberal view of the Bible soon after beginning his studies at Leiden University in 1858. The liberals denied the miracles and the deity of Christ, rejecting everything in the Bible which could not be proven by modern science.

Within four years Kuyper earned a doctorate of divinity, got married, and accepted a call to pastor a country church in the village of Beesd. "In this church, pastor," a member told him when he first arrived, "you will find a few malcontents. They are peculiar, critical people who make life miserable for every minister. But since they are of the lower economic and social classes, you'll do well, as former ministers did, to pay no attention to them."

But unwilling to ignore any of his parishioners, Kuyper talked with several of the so called "malcontents," finding them devout people who took the Word of God seriously. One woman of very strong convictions was Pietronella Baltus. She scorned half-hearted sermons, and when the minister failed to preach the truth, she found her comfort in reading the Bible for herself as well as the great old books from the church's past.

Kuyper's preaching did not impress Pietronella. She despised his liberal ideas and feared that under his preaching the church would slide further from Scripture.

When Kuyper began visiting parishioners, Pietronella's neighbor said to her, "The minister is visiting the people in our neighborhood and will probably soon come to see you."

"I have nothing to do with that man," Pietronella answered sharply.

"But don't forget, Pietronella," her friend reminded her, "that our pastor too has an immortal soul and that he is also traveling to eternity." Realizing her friend was right, Pietronella welcomed Pastor Kuyper when he came to call. She talked with him for hours, sharing her living faith in Christ and her confident hope in heaven.

"Pastor," she said solemnly, looking him squarely in the eye, "you too must have that same faith and hope or you will be lost forever." Kuyper returned often to speak with Pietronella and the other ernest believers in the congregation. He listened, argued, and tried to find common ground on which they could agree but often left irritated by their unwillingness to compromise. They stubbornly insisted that the Bible must be believed completely or not at all and that God must be worshipped as the sovereign Lord over all things or not at all.

For some reason, he found himself drawn to them, and he noticed that his sermon preparation came easier after spending time with them. Before long he found himself at a crossroads. "I must either stand firmly against them," he said to himself, "or go all the way with them in believing the Bible and the sovereign grace of God." He soon embraced their ideas wholeheartedly. "Their unwavering persistence has been the blessing for my heart, the rise of the morning star in my life," he wrote later. "They brought me, in their simple language, to the adoration and exaltation of a God who works all things to do and to will, according to His good pleasure."

Kuyper found in the common words of these Dutch peasants the same truths which John Calvin, the reformer of Geneva, had written about over three hundred years earlier. Kuyper studied Calvin's books with a new understanding and appreciation. Calvin's watchword: "God absolutely sovereign," became Abraham Kuyper's too. A new spirit invigorated all he did. His sermons extolled the justice, holiness, and love of God. He faithfully visited his flock, read widely, taught weekly Bible classes, and wrote articles for newspapers and Christian journals, standing firmly for the Bible against the liberals. Often he worked till four o'clock in the morning until his wife urged him to sleep. The blessing of God accompanied his efforts as sinners turned to Jesus Christ and Christians sought lives of greater holiness and usefulness. Before long his preaching and writing were known throughout the Netherlands.

After a time, he accepted a call to minister in the city of Utrecht, and then in Amsterdam, the largest city in the land, where he challenged Christians to engage in politics in order to return Dutch society to its biblical roots. Some criticized him, saying ministers shouldn't meddle in the business of government. "Being afraid and shying away from politics," Kuyper said, "is not Christian and not ethical."

So in addition to preaching, teaching classes, and performing his pastoral duties, he served in the leadership of the Antirevolutionary Party, a Christian party for reform. In a famous speech, Kuyper inspired the Antirevolutionaries to action saying, "We are called to cling to the banner of the Cross, to go heroically into battle, not for personal honor or power, for high office or financial gain, but for Christ and His future, for the spiritual deliverance of our country, so that when Christ returns, there will be found on our soil, too, which once received the blood of the martyrs, a people that does not strive against Him but hails Him with a Hallelujah!"

At first the Antirevolutionary candidates were throttled at the polls, but Kuyper did not lose hope. "We are working for the future," he wrote, "we are not concerned with the seeming victory of the moment but with the final triumph. With us the question is not what influence we can exert now but what power we can exercise fifty years hence, not how few men we have today but how many will arise out of the younger generation who will be men of our principles. Yet we also know that the hour of victory will someday come."

Through Kuyper's writings and the work of the Antirevolutionary Party, the Dutch people woke up to the need for change. After years of persistence, Kuyper was elected to the Parliament, and later when the Antirevolutionary Party controlled Parliament, Kuyper became the Prime Minister of the country. Seeking to shine Christ's light into every area, he said, "In all of human life there is not a square inch of which Christ, who alone is sovereign, does not declare, 'That is Mine.'" He worked to increase the freedom of choice in education from elementary schools to universities, believing that parents who sent their children to Christian or other nonstate schools should be reimbursed for the amount of money those schools were saving the state. His successful service as prime minister ended after four years.

Fed up with the theological liberals who controlled all the Dutch universities and seminaries, Kuyper spoke out, not mincing words on what he believed the liberals did. "They destroy the church's theology," he said, "they rob the church of her Bible and destroy her liberty in Christ." So Abraham Kuyper, with the help of like-minded men and women, founded the Free University. It was called Free because it was not under the control of Parliament or the liberal state church. Since there had never been an independent university in Holland, critics said, "It won't last five years." Kuyper, who taught theology at the Free University, inspired the students from the start saying, "We desire to train men of granite and steel who, like the

Puritans of old, will stand steadfast and immovable; men who, like the old Covenanters, will if necessary fight the living devil in hand-to-hand combat; men who do not look forward to a place of ease and quiet but who dare to fight the battles of the Lord."

Although he lived to be eighty-three, Abraham Kuyper never retired, remaining active as a churchman, Antirevolutionary Party member, supporter of the flourishing Free University, and writer of weekly Bible meditations for the newspapers. Although he excelled as a minister, scholar, author, professor, statesman, husband, and father, Kuyper knew that only his standing with Christ ultimately mattered.

• • •

J. Gresham Machen
Valiant for Truth

J. Gresham Machen 1881–1937

A great battle raged in the early decades of the twentieth century in the churches of the United States. Theological liberals were those who denied many of the truths of the Bible, such as the miracles and resurrection of Christ. They spread their influence by having taken over more and more seminaries and pulpits. Opposing them were those who held to the infallibility of Scripture and the historic truths of Christianity. Princeton Seminary was the best known seminary of the Presbyterian Church in the United States of America, and had stood for Biblical Christianity when many seminaries throughout America embraced liberalism. Princeton's professors were among the strongest defenders of traditional Christian faith. Most notable in this group was J. Gresham Machen.

Though by the 1920s most denominations had embraced theological liberalism, the Presbyterian Church in the USA, led by the men of Princeton, had resisted it. Then on Sunday, May 22, 1922, Harry Fosdick stood in the pulpit of First Presbyterian Church of New York and preached a sermon called, "Shall the Fundamentalists Win?" Fosdick called it deplorable that the fundamentalists demanded that all churchmen must hold to the historic doctrines of Christianity. "Our modern minds cannot use many of the Bible's teachings about Jesus," he said. "Christianity must be changed to fit into the modern, scientific age." The sermon was read widely throughout the country.

Machen rose to defend the Christian faith, traveling away from home nearly every weekend to speak at Bible conferences, lecture at colleges, or preach in churches, warning

Christians against drifting away from Scripture. He wrote a book called *Christianity and Liberalism*, in which he showed that liberalism is not Christian at all but a separate religion altogether. Machen pointed out that Christianity had always been centered on Christ's work on the cross. Believers are saved from their sins because Christ paid the penalty for those sins on the cross. But liberals cared very little about sin and viewed Christianity as a set of ideas to live by. Machen said, "Christianity depends not upon a set of ideas, but upon an event—the life, death, and resurrection of Jesus Christ."

Machen's strong arguments in *Christianity and Liberalism* opened the eyes of many Christians to the true nature of liberalism and encouraged them to stand up for the faith. But liberalism had already spread rapidly. Even the new president of Princeton wanted to change the seminary to make it more agreeable to the liberals. For several years, the president worked to convince church leaders that Machen and the other professors were wrong and that Princeton would be better if it were more open to liberal views of the Bible. Step-by-step efforts were made to weaken the biblical stand of the Presbyterian Church and Princeton Seminary. During that time, Machen made many enemies by insisting that the church hold fast to Scripture and by speaking out against the liberals. One Princeton Seminary professor called Machen "unkind, suspicious, and bitter." Sharp personal attacks on his character became common. But Machen fought on boldly for the truth.

The crisis came to a head in the spring of 1929 when more than eight hundred ministers and elders gathered in St. Paul, Minnesota for the annual General Assembly of the Presbyterian Church of the United States of America. The Assembly planned to vote on whether to allow Princeton Seminary to remain as it had been for over one hundred years or to reorganize it in favor of the liberals.

Machen asked that sufficient time be given to debate the issue before taking the vote. But only twenty-five minutes were allowed for discussion. Machen had five minutes to present his arguments. Standing before the Assembly in a dark suit and tie, Machen, with somber face, spoke in a strong voice. "We at Princeton Seminary have been proclaiming an unpopular gospel," he said. "Yet it is a gospel of which we are not ashamed. We have received our authority to preach this unpopular gospel not from any wisdom of our own but from the blessed pages of God's Word. But the world has been gradually drifting away from this gospel. Countless colleges and seminaries throughout the world which once stood for the gospel of the Bible do so no longer. Many are looking to Princeton Seminary for something to be said against modern unbelief and in favor of the full truthfulness of God's Word. If you destroy old Princeton today, there are many who will rejoice; for there are many who think the old gospel and the old Book are out of date. But if there are many who will rejoice, there are also those who will grieve."

Despite Machen's words, the Assembly voted to change Princeton Seminary. The liberals had won even at Princeton. The strong, biblical teaching of Princeton soon faded away. Although not wanting to leave his beloved Princeton, Machen and three other professors resigned and started Westminster Seminary in Philadelphia, determined to make it faithful to the Scripture in everything.

A few years later another great dispute involving Machen arose in the Presbyterian Church. The Board of Foreign Missions had sent out some missionaries who actually denied the fundamentals of the Christian faith. One woman, a missionary to China, wasn't sure if Jesus ever lived at all. "Preaching Christ," she said, "is of no value." Machen and others complained to the Board. "We must return to the power of the Word of God," Machen said. "May God raise up men and women who will go forth and not be ashamed to carry the gospel to the ends of the earth." Machen and his colleagues tried to bring a vote to the General Assembly which would require that all missionaries hold to the truths of the Bible, but they were prevented from doing so.

When the Board of Foreign Missions refused to preserve a true Christian message on the mission field, a number of elders and ministers organized the Independent Board of Foreign Missions with Machen as president. They sent out only Bible-believing Christians to tell the people of the world about Jesus Christ. The General Assembly ordered Machen and the others to abolish the Independent Board, warning them that if they did not do so, they would be considered lawbreakers and disloyal to the church. Machen wrote an eighty page reply to the General Assembly, clearly showing that the General Assembly's order violated the constitution of the church. "I cannot obey your order to end my connection with the Independent Board for Foreign Missions," Machen said, "for the order is contrary to the gospel of Christ and would involve substitution of a human authority for the authority of the Word of God."

Even though Gresham Machen was a godly minister and faithful to the Bible and the constitution of the Presbyterian Church, he was brought to trial before a church court. Newspapers around the country carried the story. The *New York Times* ran a front-page story under the headline: "Machen to be Tried as a Rebel." Machen based his whole defense on the fact that the General Assembly's order was illegal. But the church court refused to let him speak of it in the trial. In effect, they forbade Machen to defend himself. On March 29, 1936, the church court declared him guilty and stripped him of his ministerial credentials.

The injustice against Machen outraged many. One newspaper editor wrote: "The strangest of all church trials is that which has just convicted Professor Gresham Machen of disobedience to the Presbyterian Church. He is a man of great scholarship and unquestioned devoutness who for twenty years has warned that the church was turning toward liberalism and away from the gospel of the Bible."

"No church, in this day," one minister said, "can afford

to lose believers in the gospel like Gresham Machen." Together with a number of like-minded ministers and church members, Machen formed a new denomination, the Orthodox Presbyterian Church, a denomination committed to proclaiming all the truths of Scripture. But Machen did not live long enough to help direct and build the new denomination. A few months after it was begun, Machen traveled to North Dakota in the dead of winter on a preaching tour, where the temperature was twenty degrees below zero. Despite much pain and shortness of breath, he preached several times until he was rushed to the hospital with pneumonia. Doctors couldn't control the infection or fever and J. Gresham Machen died at the age of fifty-five. Among his last words were: "I'm so thankful for the active obedience of Christ. No hope without it."

• • •

C. S. Lewis
Chronicler of Narnia

C. S. "Jack" Lewis 1898–1963

Nearly a hundred years ago, two young boys were out for an afternoon walk. They were brothers and best friends. As they drew closer to home, they saw a brilliant rainbow which appeared to end in their own front yard. Jack said to his older brother, Warren, "Look! The rainbow ends right between the gate and the front door. Come on. Let's get a shovel and find the pot of gold."

The boys dug with all their might, creating a very large hole. At nightfall, tired and discouraged, they went inside with plans to dig deeper in the morning. Soon after, their father came home from the office and fell into the hole. His hat flew off, and his legal papers scattered across the yard. He went inside, his business suit covered with dirt. Quite naturally, he was upset. He thought the boys had set a trap for him. He loved his sons, but their vivid imaginations and adventurous spirits often tried his patience.

Jack and Warren Lewis lived with their parents in Belfast, Northern Ireland, in a large, three-story brick house with a view of the sea and the surrounding hills. The boys liked the long hallways and sunlit rooms, but what they liked best was the attic. The attic ran the full length of the house and echoed with the sounds of gurgling water pipes and the wind whistling through the roof tiles. They laid claim to one of the attic rooms where no one would disturb them. Their attic room was well stocked with paper, paints, chalk, and pencils. Here the boys drew pictures and wrote stories; and here they created an imaginary world. Though Jack was younger, he was clearly the most creative. Jack's real name was Clive, but when he was four-years-old he said, "My name is Jacksie." Ever after, his family and friends called him Jack.

Jack delighted in tales of knights in battle and stories of dressed animals like those in the books of Beatrix Potter. So he created Animal-Land. King Bunny reigned assisted by Sir Peter Mouse and Sir Ben, the frog, and many others. Not content to just describe and illustrate Animal-Land and its characters, Jack created an entire history, stretching back over a thousand years. Warren called his make-believe world India. He made detailed maps and charts of the land, including timetables of the coming and going of ships and trains. The boys put their two lands together and called it Boxen. Boxen grew and developed for many years. While Warren was away in England at boarding school, Jack wrote often to tell him of the latest happenings in Boxen. Once he wrote: "At present Boxen is *slightly convulsed*. The news has just reached her that King Bunny is a prisoner. The Prussians and Boxonians are at fearful odds against each other. General Quicksteppe is making plans for the rescue of King Bunny."

Mr. and Mrs. Lewis loved to read, and their home was crammed with books. To Jack's young eyes, there appeared to be books everywhere, endless books—"Books in the study, books in the drawing room, books in the cloakroom, books (two deep) in the great bookcase on the landing, books in the bedrooms, books piled shoulder high in the attic." Jack and Warren read many of them. Mrs. Lewis home-schooled Jack in French, Latin, and literature. But before his tenth birthday, his mother died of cancer. Much of the happiness and security in his life disappeared with her. Soon after her death, Jack's father sent him far away to an English boarding school. And so began many years of loneliness and difficulty, broken up by short periods of happy holidays at home with Warren and his father.

At age eighteen, Jack Lewis won a scholarship to Oxford, the oldest and most famous university in England. He excelled in his studies and eventually became an English instructor there. Through his school and college days, Lewis had become an atheist—someone who denies that God exists. Being a proud and self-sufficient man, he thought himself too sophisticated to believe in God. Besides, he saw God as an interferer, and he wanted to be left alone. As a respected teacher at Oxford, he looked forward to a life devoted to himself and doing as he pleased. But as he later wrote, "God, the great Angler, played His fish and I never dreamed that the hook was in my mouth."

His coming to Jesus Christ started slowly. Lewis began to realize that his favorite authors were Christians. They wrote about a life full of wonder and joy. Christianity, at least for some, was not merely a set of rules. Then he befriended some bright Oxford men who believed the Bible and who showed him there were strong historical facts to support Christianity. For several years, he read more about Christianity and continued to argue with his friends about their faith in Christ. Then one sunny morning it happened. Lewis, deep in thought, sat in the sidecar of his brother's motorcycle on the way to the zoo. "When we set out," Lewis wrote, "I did not believe that Jesus Christ was the Son of God, and when we reached the zoo I did."

Although Lewis continued to teach at Oxford, the work of his life changed dramatically. With Christian students, he formed the Socratic Club, which hosted Monday evening debates and discussions between Christians and non-Christians. As Lewis's wit and intellect became widely known, it became more difficult to find opponents of Christianity willing to speak. Students filled the chairs and spilled on to the floor in order to hear Lewis challenge the views of unbelievers.

Once a philosopher, a Relativist, ended his speech saying, "The world does not exist, England does not exist, Oxford does not exist, and I am confident that I do not exist."

When Lewis rose to reply he said, "How can I talk to a man who's not there." Using his gifts for thinking and writing clearly, he wrote books that showed how

Christianity alone makes sense of the world. "I believe in Christianity," he wrote, "as I believe the sun has risen; not only because I can see it, but because by it I see everything else." Many people who never would have opened the Bible or darkened the door of a church read his books and were drawn to Christ.

During the early, dark days of World War II, German warplanes bombed London, destroying homes and apartments and killing thousands. The British government wanted to move as many children as possible away from the danger of the city, and so a call went out to the English countryside for help. C.S. Lewis, like many of his countrymen, opened his home, an old, brick house near a pond, to the needy children. Since he was unmarried with no children of his own, he took in several boys and girls.

As Lewis got to know the children, he was surprised by how little they read and how dull their imaginations seemed to be. Remembering the books and make-believe world of his childhood, he knew how much they were missing. One day, one of the girls, busy exploring the house, grew curious about a large, old wardrobe in a spare room upstairs. "May I go inside of it?" she asked Lewis. He opened the door and let her poke around the heavy coats hanging inside. "I wonder if there is anything behind it," she said.

The girl left the room and rushed outside to play, but her question set his mind to work. He decided to write a story for the children to encourage their imaginations and point them to Jesus Christ. Lewis entitled the story *The Lion, the Witch and the Wardrobe*. It begins: "Once there were four children whose names were Peter, Susan, Edmund and Lucy. This story is about something that happened to them when they were sent away from London during the war because of air-raids. They were sent to the house of an old Professor who lived in the heart of the country."

The adventures begin when Lucy steps inside a bedroom wardrobe and finds that it leads into a magical world called Narnia. It is full of fauns, dwarves, and talking animals. A white witch has cast her evil spell over Narnia, making it "always winter and never Christmas." Aslan, the Lion and the true King of Narnia, breaks her spell by sacrificing his own life for the sake of others. Aslan rises from the dead, conquers the witch, and brings peace to the land. Lewis wanted children to see the connection between Aslan's victory and the triumph of Christ's death and resurrection. Following this first story, he wrote a series a books about Aslan's world called *The Chronicles of Narnia*.

In August of 1941, when Nazi Germany appeared invincible and fear about the future troubled the minds of English men and women, Lewis delivered a series of radio talks on the Christian faith. "I remember," one man said, "being at a pub filled with soldiers on one Wednesday evening. At a quarter to eight, the bartender turned the radio up to hear Lewis. 'You listen to this bloke,' he shouted, 'He's really worth listening to.' And the soldiers did listen attentively for the entire talk." With his rich voice and quick wit, he defended Christianity logically and convincingly, urging people to follow Jesus. "If you look to yourself," Lewis told his radio listeners, "you will find in the long run only hatred, loneliness, despair, rage, ruin, and decay. But look to Christ and you will find Him, and with Him everything else thrown in." One man, influenced by Lewis, said, "The war, the whole of life, everything tended to seem pointless. We needed a key to the meaning of the universe. Lewis provided just that. Better still, he gave us back our old, traditional Christian faith so that we could accept it with new confidence."

The chief chaplain of the Royal Air Force invited Lewis to talk to the servicemen. He traveled away every weekend for months speaking at RAF bases across the country, trying to persuade the airmen to believe in Christ. After the war, British Prime Minister Winston Churchill praised Lewis for all his efforts during the war. Lewis wrote many books and nearly all of them became best sellers. But Lewis was not a wealthy man because he gave away the money he made on his Christian books to ministries and charities. Although C. S. Lewis died in 1963, his books continue to show people the way to Jesus Christ. Nearly 50 million copies of his books are in print today in many different languages.

• • •

Richard Wurmbrand
Tortured for Christ

Richard Wurmbrand 1908–

In August 1944, one million Russian troops overran Romania and installed a communist government. Like the government of the Soviet Union, it was a brutal dictatorship, jailing and murdering tens of thousands of innocent people. Hoping to control and eventually wipe out Christianity, the communists confiscated church property and forbade ministers to work without licenses from the government. Soon after taking power, they convened a congress of all the Christian bodies in Romania. Four thousand priests, bishops, and ministers assembled in the great hall of the Parliament building before a huge portrait of Stalin, the Russian dictator. Under fear of imprisonment, torture and death, one Christian leader after another praised the new communist government, declaring that communism and Christianity had similar goals and could thrive together.

Sitting in the meeting were Richard Wurmbrand, a tall well-educated Lutheran pastor, and his wife, Sabina.

Sabina turned to her husband with flaming eyes and said, "Richard, stand up and wash away this shame from the face of Christ. They are spitting in His face."

Richard whispered to her, "If I do so, you lose your husband."

"I don't want to have a coward as a husband," Sabina replied.

So Richard arose and requested permission to speak. He walked to the rostrum, looked out over the sea of faces, and spoke into the microphone which broadcast the message live to the whole country. "It is our duty as ministers," Wurmbrand reminded the audience, "to glorify Christ.

Our loyalty is due first to Him and not to earthly powers." As Wurmbrand talked on, applause burst forth from every part of the hall. Many jumped to their feet cheering.

"Your right to speak has been withdrawn!" a red-faced Communist official shouted from the platform.

"My right to speak comes from God," Wurmbrand answered. Officials cut off the microphone, and the day's meeting ended in an uproar. Wurmbrand and Sabina knew that he would pay for his boldness, but they believed it was worth it.

Sometime later on a beautiful Sunday morning in 1948, as Wurmbrand walked to church, a black van roared along side him and screeched to a halt. Agents of the communist secret police leapt out, seized Wurmbrand, shoved him into the back seat, and sped away to jail. His wife and son, Mihai, did not know whether he was alive or dead. With harsh lights blinding him, interrogators grilled Wurmbrand for hours. "Write down the names of everyone you know, where you met them, and what your relations with them were," they demanded. Communist officials wanted to know who helped him print and distribute Bibles and host secret church meetings, but Wurmbrand refused to reveal anything about the activities of others.

And so the tortures began. Guards forced him to stand for hours in a narrow box with sharp, metal spikes projecting out of every wall. His feet swelled and his legs trembled, and when he collapsed the razor sharp spikes tore his flesh. The soles of his feet were beaten bloody. Torturers whipped, branded, and knifed him. "Why don't you give in?" they cried. "You're only flesh, and you'll break in the end."

Wurmbrand asked his tormentors, "Don't you have any pity in your hearts?"

"There is no God, no hereafter, and no punishment for evil. We can do as we wish," they answered.

"Christ was whipped and crucified," Wurmbrand reminded himself, "and it is my joy to share in His sufferings." When interrogation and torture failed, the

Communists tried brainwashing. Permitting the prisoners to barely survive on a small ration of dirty swill and bread crusts, they blared over loudspeakers the repeated message seventeen hours a day for months and years on end: "Communism is good. Christianity is stupid. Give it up. Communism is good. Christianity is stupid. Give it up," and "Christianity is dead. Nobody loves you now. Christianity is dead. Nobody loves you now." The brainwashing drove the prisoners to the brink of insanity, but Wurmbrand clung to his faith in Christ.

Once a top official brought Wurmbrand to a prison office and offered him freedom, a return to his family, a comfortable living, and the leadership of the Romanian Lutheran church.

"We need men like you," he told Wurmbrand. "If you are prepared to help us in the struggle against superstition, you can start a new life at once. What do you say?"

"I would like some time to think about it," Wurmbrand answered. He desperately missed his wife and son. The temptation to accept the official's offer overwhelmed him. Returning to his cell, he threw himself facedown, crying out to God for help, his tears wetting the concrete floor. The next day the official called for him again.

"I don't feel worthy to be a bishop;" Wurmbrand said, "I wasn't worthy to be a pastor, and even to be a simple Christian was too much for me. The first Christians went to their deaths saying simply—'I'm a Christian'—but I haven't done that; instead I considered your shameful offer. But I cannot accept it."

"You know, of course, what this will mean for your future?" The official asked.

"I have considered well and weighed every danger," Wurmbrand answered, "and I rejoice to suffer for what I am sure is the ultimate truth."

Later, Wurmbrand was tortured by a young, devoted communist named Lieutenant Grecu, who ordered him to write a confession of his crimes against the communist government. Wurmbrand admitted that he tapped Bible verses using Morse code to prisoners in adjoining cells, but he wrote, "I have never spoken against the Communists. I am a disciple of Christ, who has given us love for our enemies. I understand them and pray for their conversion so that they will become my brothers."

Grecu, swinging his torture club, picked up Wurmbrand's confession and began reading it, and as he did so his stern expression softened. He set aside his club, and his jaw dropped as a troubled look swept over his face. "Why do you say that you love me? I know this is one of your Christian commandments, but I don't believe anyone could keep it. I couldn't love someone who shut me up for years in prison, who starved and tortured me."

Wurmbrand smiled and answered, "It's not a matter of keeping a commandment. When I became a Christian it was as if I had been reborn, with a new character full of love." For two hours they discussed Christianity and communism. Under the pretext of interrogation, Grecu summoned Wurmbrand to his office nearly every day for two weeks to hear about the love and forgiveness of Christ.

"I was brought up an atheist and I will never be anything else," Grecu sighed. But Grecu listened carefully to Wurmbrand and began to study the Bible, and soon he put his trust in Jesus. The next day, the Communist lieutenant in his crisp uniform confessed his sins to Wurmbrand. From then on Grecu pretended to be a loyal Communist officer, but he secretly helped prisoners as best he could. Before long he was discovered and arrested. He, too, became a prisoner for Christ.

After eight and a half years Wurmbrand was suddenly released under a general amnesty. Guards pushed him out of the prison gates wearing a tattered, dirty shirt and a patchwork of rags for pants. He made his way to Bucharest and his own front door, uncertain if his wife and son were free or in jail, alive, or dead. Opening the door, he saw a tall young man who stared at him for a moment and then cried,

"Father!" His son, Mihai, was eighteen, and Wurmbrand had not seen him since he was nine-years-old. Sabina ran in from the kitchen, and they all embraced.

"I must tell you something," Wurmbrand said, holding back tears. "Don't think that I have come from misery to happiness. I've come from the joy of being with Christ in prison to the joy of being with Him in my family."

"Father," Mihai said, "You've gone through so much. I want to know what you have learned from your sufferings."

Wurmbrand wrapped his thin arms around his son saying, "Four things were always on my mind. First, there is a God. Second, Christ is our Savior. Third, there is eternal life. And finally, love is the best of ways." Mihai nodded and told his father that he had recently decided to become a pastor.

The authorities forbade Wurmbrand to preach or engage in any religious work. But he and Sabina threw themselves into helping the underground church. Wurmbrand preached to hidden groups of Christians huddled in basements, attics, and in the open fields. If someone questioned their gathering together and singing, they answered, "We are celebrating a birthday." Many small Christian families celebrated thirty or forty birthdays a year! Wurmbrand knew that his activities would eventually be discovered by the secret police. He prayed often, "God, if You know men in prison whom I can help, whose souls I can save, send me back and I'll bear it willingly."

After two years of freedom, the secret police burst into his home in the middle of the night and hauled Wurmbrand away for five more years of torture. But when Wurmbrand was released the second time, he went right to work again for the underground church. Christians from the free world helped by smuggling in Bibles, Christian books, and money for suffering Christian families. Wurmbrand wanted to remain in Romania, but the leaders of the underground church urged him to leave the country. "Be the voice of persecuted Christians to the free world," they told him.

Two Christian groups paid a $10,000 ransom to the communist government to bring Wurmbrand and his family out of Romania. The secret police told him before he left, "Go to the West and preach Christ as much as you like, but don't speak a word against us! If you do our agents will kidnap or kill you." Before leaving the country, Wurmbrand placed a flower on the grave of the Communist official who first had ordered his arrest and torture. "I hate the communist system, but I love the men," Wurmbrand said. "Communists can kill Christians, but they cannot kill their love toward even those who kill them."

Wurmbrand and Sabina came to America and founded *The Voice of the Martyrs*, a ministry to persecuted Christians throughout the world which sends Bibles, encouragement, and relief to the families of Christian martyrs and informs the world about atrocities committed against Christians. After the communist government in Romania collapsed in December of 1989, Wurmbrand and Sabina returned to their homeland, bringing the message of Jesus Christ to overflowing churches and national television. They began a Christian library and print shop to publish and circulate Christian books and Sunday school materials. The new government offered storage space to warehouse the books. It turned out to be a former prison cell where Wurmbrand was held for three years. "God chose this very place to vindicate his cause," Wurmbrand said, choking back tears as he returned to the cell to see it full of Christian books. "God could not have done it better," he beamed. Wurmbrand and Sabina proclaimed the forgiveness of Christ, urging Romanians to forgive the Communists and turn to God. His message was the same one he had written over twenty years before, "Love your persecutors. Love their souls, and try to win them for Christ."

• • •

Thanks to Voice of the Martyrs and Living Sacrifice Books for permission to use source material in this chapter.

• • •

And they sang a new song, saying: "You are worthy to take the scroll, And to open its seals; For You were slain, And have redeemed us to God by Your blood out of every tribe and tongue and people and nation, And have made us kings and priests to our God; And we shall reign on the earth" (Rev. 5:9–10).

When He opened the fifth seal, I saw under the altar the souls of those who had been slain for the word of God and for the testimony which they held. And they cried with a loud voice, saying, "How long, O Lord, holy and true, until You judge and avenge our blood on those who dwell on the earth?" Then a white robe was given to each of them; and it was said to them that they should rest a little while longer, until both the number of their fellow servants and their brethren, who would be killed as they were, was completed (Rev. 6:9–11).

Then I, John, saw the holy city, New Jerusalem, coming down out of heaven from God, prepared as a bride adorned for her husband. And I heard a loud voice from heaven saying, "Behold, the tabernacle of God is with men, and He will dwell with them, and they shall be His people. God Himself will be with them and be their God. And God will wipe away every tear from their eyes; there shall be no more death, nor sorrow, nor crying. There shall be no more pain, for the former things have passed away" (Rev. 21:2–4).

Then one of the seven angels who had the seven bowls filled with the seven last plagues came to me and talked with me, saying, "Come, I will show you the bride, the Lamb's wife." And he carried me away in the Spirit to a great and high mountain, and showed me the great city, the holy Jerusalem, descending out of heaven from God, having the glory of God. Her light was like a most precious stone, like a jasper stone, clear as crystal (Rev. 21: 9–11).

• • •

Further Reading
for Parents, Teachers, and Older Children:

General Histories

Dowley, Tim, *Eerdman's Handbook to the History of Christianity*, (Grand Rapids, MI: Eerdmans, 1977)

Foxe, John and Chadwick, H., *The New Foxe's Book of Martyrs*, (North Brunswick, NJ: Bridge/Logos, 1997)

Houghton, S.M., *Sketches In Church History*, (Edinburgh: Banner of Truth, 1980)

Schaff, Philip, *History of the Christian Church*, (Grand Rapids, MI: Eerdmans, 1995)

Early Church

Augustine, *Confessions of St. Augustine*, (Oxford, England: Oxford University Press, 1992)

Bede, *A History of the English Church and People*, (New York, NY: Dorset Press, 1985)

Brown, Peter, *Augustine of Hippo*, (Berkeley, CA: University of California Press, 1969)

Elliott, T.G., *The Christianity of Constantine the Great*, (Scranton, PA: University of Scranton Press, 1996)

Eusebius, *The History of the Church from Christ to Constantine*, (New York, NY: Dorset Press, 1984)

Middle Ages

Abbott, Jacob, *Alfred the Great*, (New York, NY: A.L. Fowle, 1906)

Bonaventure, *The Life of St. Francis*, (Rockford, IL: Tan Books, 1988)

Daniel-Rops, Henri, *Bernard of Clairvaux*, (New York, NY: Hawthorn Books, 1964)

Eadmer, *Life of St. Anselm*, (Oxford, England: Clarendon Press, 1979)

Einhard and Notker, *Two Lives of Charlemagne*, (London, England: Penguin Books, 1969)

Monk of Whitby, *The Earliest Life of Gregory the Great*, (Cambridge, England: Cambridge Univ. Press, 1985)

Wylie, J.A., *History of the Waldenses,* (Washington, D.C.: Review & Herald, 1889)

Reformation

d'Aubigne, J.H.M., *The Reformation in England,* (Edinburgh, Scotland: Banner of Truth, 1971)

Bainton, Roland, *Here I Stand, A Life of Martin Luther,* (New York, NY: Abingdon Press, 1950)

Bainton, Roland, *Women of the Reformation in France and England,* (Minneapolis, MN: Augsburg Pub., 1973)

Barton, F. Whitfield, *Calvin and the Duchess,* (Louisville, KY: Westminster/John Knox Press, 1989)

Edwards, Brian, *God's Outlaw,* (Darlington, England: Evangelical Press, 1996)

Knox, John, *The History of the Reformation in Scotland,* (Edinburgh, Scotland: Banner of Truth, 1994)

Post-Reformation

Bunyan, John, *Grace Abounding to the Chief of Sinners,* (Springdale, PA: Whitaker House, 1993)

Dallimore, Arnold, *George Whitefield,* (Westchester, IL: Cornerstone Books, 1981)

Edwards, Brian, *Through Many Dangers: The Story of John Newton* (Darlington, England: Evangelical Press, 1994)

Fletcher, C.R., *Gustavus Adolphus and the Struggle of Protestantism for Existence,* (New York: Putnam's Sons, 1890)

Howie, John, *The Scots Worthies,* (Edinburgh, Scotland: Banner of Truth, 1995)

Murray, Ian, *Jonathan Edwards, A New Biography,* (Edinburgh, Scotland: Banner of Truth, 1987)

Purves, Jock, *Fair Sunshine: Character Studies of the Scottish Covenanters,* (Edinburgh, Scotland: Banner of Truth, 1997)

Wesley, John, *The Works of John Wesley,* (New York, NY: Abingdon Press, 1988)

Whitefield, George, *Whitefield's Journals,* (Edinburgh, Scotland: Banner of Truth, 1965)

Modern Missions

Brainerd, David, *Life and Diary of David Brainerd,* (Grand Rapids, MI: Baker Book House, 1995)

Elliot, Elizabeth, *A Chance To Die: The Life and Legacy of Amy Carmichael,* (Grand Rapids, MI: Revell, 1987)

Paton, John, *John Paton: Missionary to the New Hebrides,* (Edinburgh, Scotland: Banner of Truth, 1965)

Seaver, George, *David Livingstone: His Life and Letters,* (New York, NY: Harper Brothers, 1957)

Taylor, Dr. & Mrs. Howard, *Hudson Taylor and the China Inland Mission,* (London, England: C.I.M. Publishing, 1955)

Recent Times

Headland, Isaac, *Chinese Heroes in the Boxer Uprising* (Chicago, IL: Missionary Campaign Library, 1902)

Sayer, George, *Jack: C.S. Lewis and His Times,* (San Francisco, CA: Harper and Row, 1988)

Spurgeon, Charles; *C.H. Spurgeon Autobiography,* (Edinburgh, Scotland: Banner of Truth, 1973)

Stonehouse, Ned, *J. Gresham Machen: A Biographical Memoir,* (Edinburgh, Scotland: Banner of Truth, 1987)

VandenBerg, Frank, *Abraham Kuyper: A Biography,* (St. Catharines, Canada: Paideia Press, 1978)

Wurmbrand, Richard, *In the Face of Surrender: Over 200 Challenging and Inspiring Stories of Overcomers,* (North Brunswick, NJ: Bridge/Logos, 1998)

Wurmbrand, Richard, *Tortured For Christ,* (Bartlesville, OK: Living Sacrifice Books, 1998)